The Age of Entheogens
&
The Angels' Dictionary

The Age of Entheogens
&
The Angels' Dictionary

Jonathan Ott

NATURAL PRODUCTS CO.
KENNEWICK, WA
1995

Other books by Jonathan Ott:

HALLUCINOGENIC
PLANTS OF NORTH AMERICA
(Wingbow Press, Berkeley, 1976,1979)

TEONANÁCATL: HALLUCINOGENIC
MUSHROOMS OF NORTH AMERICA
Co-Edited with J. Bigwood
(Madrona Publishers, Seattle, 1978,1985)

THE CACAHUATL EATER: RUMINATIONS
OF AN UNABASHED CHOCOLATE ADDICT
(Natural Products Co., Vashon, WA, 1985)

PERSEPHONE'S QUEST: ENTHEOGENS
AND THE ORIGINS OF RELIGION
Co-Authored with R.G. Wasson,
S. Kramrisch and C.A.P. Ruck
(Yale University Press, New Haven, 1986,1992)

PHARMACOTHEON: ENTHEOGENIC
DRUGS, THEIR PLANT SOURCES AND HISTORY
(Natural Products Co., Kennewick, WA, 1993)

AYAHUASCA ANALOGUES: PANGÆAN ENTHEOGENS
(Natural Products Co., Kennewick, WA, 1994)

Design by Pablo Moya, typography by Jonathan Ott
Obverse/Softcover: *Anadenanthera in the Ancient Atacama*
by Donna Torres, oil-on-canvas, 1994; photographed by C. Manuel Torres
Verso/Softcover: *Psychoactive Plant Series: San Pedro*
by Donna Torres, oil-on-canvas, 1983; photographed by C. Manuel Torres
Mixtec vignettes from *Lienzo de Zacatepec* and *Codex Vindobonensis* by Martín Vinaver
Drawings of Remojadas figurine on page 10 and Xochipilli on page 62 by Tim Girvin

ISBN 0–9614234–6–3 (hardcover) $36.00
ISBN 0–9614234–7–1 (paperback) $18.00

Sales: Jonathan Ott Books / Post Office Box 1251 / Occidental, CA / USA 95465

TABLE OF CONTENTS

Dedicated to the great German
writer and pioneering psychonaut

ERNST JÜNGER

On the occasion of his 100th birthday

The Age of Entheogens,
The Pharmacratic Inquisition
&
The Entheogenic Reformation

Terra cotta figurine of female shaman with mushroom-shaped drum, *circa* 300 A.D. in Remojadas style from Tenenexpan, Veracruz, México. Pen-and-ink drawing by Tim Girvin, Olympia, WA, 1976.

Exordium

The Mexican Indian with his *teo-nanácatl* has no need for Transubstantiation because his mushroom speaks for itself. By comparison with the mushroom, the Element in the Christian agape seems pallid.

R. Gordon Wasson
Mushrooms Russia and History [1957]

The rediscovery by R. Gordon Wasson of the traditional shamanic use of entheogenic[1] mushrooms in southern México in 1955, and Wasson's publication in *Life* magazine two years later of a popular article describing his 'great adventure' partaking of the holy sacrament with Mazatec shaman María Sabina, engendered an astonishing revival of interest in shamanic inebriants [Wasson 1957; Wasson & Wasson 1957]. The entheogenic drug psilocybine, isolated from María Sabina's mushrooms by Albert Hofmann, together with LSD-25, a semi-synthetic mushroomic entheogen discovered serendipitously by Hofmann 12 years before Wasson lifted the veil of the Holy Mystery in México, went on to become key catalysts in an anachronistic international revival of archaic religion, which was destined to shake western society to its core [Horowitz 1991; Ott 1978]. The resulting 'counter-cultural' movement of the 'Psychedelic Sixties' marked an unprecedented departure from business as usual, setting the stage for a modern Entheogenic Reformation, which promises to evoke more radical and far-reaching changes in western religion than did its predecessor. Indeed, Martin Luther's 95 theses of October 1517 packed far less punch than did Gordon Wasson's *one* thesis 440 years later—for Wasson had peeled away the ossified accretion of many, many layers of symbol and dogma which enshrouded the core Mystery in impenetrable obfuscation; had laid bare before the eyes of an astonished world, in all its dazzling quotidian humility, *the holy sacrament itself*, a sacrament which "carried its own conviction" and did not limp along encumbered by faith in an absurd Doctrine of Transubstantiation; a sacrament *which obviated the necessity of faith itself*, allowing every communicant to attest to "the miracle he has experienced" [Ott 1990; Wasson 1961].

Although María Sabina's mushrooms and psilocybine were the original inciters of this remarkable phenomenon, LSD-25 was to emerge as a standard-bearer in the Entheogenic Reformation. For technical and economic reasons, LSD came to be

[11]

widely manufactured by the incipient underground chemical network jerry-built after the suspension of legal LSD manufacture in 1965 and the subsequent international proscription of this unique pharmacotheon. This strange drug could be manufactured for about a penny a dose, even with the grossly inflated prices for starting materials and reagents which prevailed under the black-market conditions.[2] In part owing to a vigorous propaganda campaign against LSD by the governments of the United States and other countries, the drug's popularity waned as the sixties gave way to the seventies [Ott 1993]. Furthermore, as one part of a 'back-to-nature' movement, itself in large measure another consequence of the Entheogenic Reformation, a hard-core of established entheogen *aficionados* became more interested in phytoentheogens than in purified products of the chemical industry, however countercultural, and LSD was wrongly stigmatized as a 'synthetic' (that is, artificial[3]) 'chemical.' This fact, combined with the introduction between 1976 and 1978 of reliable, low-technology methodology for small-scale cultivation of psilocybine-containing mushrooms [Harris 1976; Oss & Oeric 1976; Ott & Bigwood 1978] caused the focus of attention to shift back to psilocybine as the primary entheogen in countercultural circles [Ott 1993]. Thus psilocybian mushrooms, especially *Psilocybe cubensis* (Earle) Singer, became the entheogen of choice in the late seventies and early eighties, while LSD became ever more difficult to procure.

Toward the end of the 1980s, as a feature of the international ecological movement favoring tropical rainforest conservation, a movement which also had its roots in the Entheogenic Reformation, the continuing interest in visionary drugs began to focus ever more on *ayahuasca*, a pan-Amazonian entheogenic potion made from tropical rainforest plants [Ott 1994]. As the eighties became the nineties, *ayahuasca* was thrust ever more into the limelight as the new, modern, 'hip' entheogen of the *cognoscenti*. By 1980 the phenomenon of '*ayahuasca* tourism' began to appear [Ott 1993], much as 'mushroomic tourism' had followed Wasson's astonishing discoveries in México [Ott 1975,1976]. Few fragile surviving threads of preliterate spirituality in Amazonia, and the ephemeral 'pharmacratic peace' [Escohotado 1989] which had seen *ayahuasca* overlooked in the contemporary crusade against shamanic inebriants, were gravely jeopardized by the sudden arrival in Amazonia of perfervid contingents of cosmopolitan *ayahuasca* tourists [Ott 1994].

Contemporary ethnobotany of *ayahuasca* is complicated by the fact that this shamanic inebriant, more so than any other entheogen we know, had managed to find a place for itself in the modern world long before its recent rediscovery by the entheogenic counterculture. Mestizo *ayahuasqueros* had continued to use the Amazonian *amrta*[4] in urban areas of Perú and Colombia, even as their Indian forebears continued, in ever-decreasing measure, to commune with *Sacha Runa* (the 'jungle man') and other 'plant-spirits' in ever-diminishing islands of primary rainforest throughout Amazonia [Dobkin de Ríos 1972,1992; Lamb 1974; Luna 1984a,1984b, 1986,1991; Luna & Amaringo 1991]. Furthermore, the last six decades have seen the growth of a remarkable syncretic Neo-Christian religion with *ayahuasca* as the sacrament. Following humble beginnings in the state of Acre in Brasilian Amazonia, these contemporary religious groups communing with *santo daime* or *chá hoasca* (as *ayahuasca* is known to them) have grown into major international religious movements with thousands of members [Centro 1989; Henman 1986; Lowy 1987; MacRae 1992; Prance 1970]. Far from being an aberration or anachronism, these churches, together with the African Bwiti religion centered on the entheogenic sacrament *iboga* [Fernandez 1972,1982; Samorini 1993], and the North American Native American Church, employing the entheogenic cactus *péyotl* [La Barre 1938; Stewart 1987], rather represent the future of Christianity, stripped of its Doctrine of Transubstantiation by the Entheogenic Reformation, and with one or another *genuine* entheogen replacing the *placebo* sacrament!

These syncretic Christian churches on three continents constitute the religious manifestation of a great historical movement which is unfolding simultaneously in the overdeveloped world as this astonishing revival of interest in shamanism and especially in shamanic inebriants—what Terence McKenna aptly characterized as *The Archaic Revival* [McKenna 1991]. To be sure, shamanism is the pangæan[5] Ur-religion of our remote Eurasian ancestors, the "highest vehicle for the expression of man's religious yearnings" throughout the timeless millennia characterized by R. Gordon Wasson as the Age of Entheogens [Wasson 1980]. While the Bwitists of Africa, like the peyotlists of North America and the *Daimistas* and *Vegetalistas* of South America, are replacing the placebo sacrament with the real thing, albeit still within the confines of Christian liturgy, the entheogenic psychonauts of the industrialized world are going back to the source, not just of Christian symbols like the Eucharist and the Tree of Life/Knowledge of Good and Evil, but of Christianity itself and of every other religion... far, far back in our remote past, to shamanism and shamanic plant-teachers, which first instilled in our primordial forebears the awe, terror, fascination and mystery of a divine presence.

By the same token, the contemporary World War on Drugs is nothing more nor less than the modern manifestation of the millennial struggle between state power and individual freedom; between the *proselytizers* of purely symbolic simulacra of religion—propagandists of what Blake called "pale religious letchery"—and the *practitioners* of the real thing—for religion is an *experience*, not merely a "social activity with mild ethical rules" [Wasson 1961]. This War on Drugs originally started as a War on Religious Experiences, and it is nothing new—it dates back, in the Old World or Palæogæa, at least to the end of the fourth century of our era; and in the New World or Neogæa,[6] to the second decade of the sixteenth century, when Europeans began to sow a genocidal reign of terror throughout the vast reaches of the Americas. It is the Pharmacratic Inquisition, distinguished from outcroppings of brutal bigotry in other eras only by the choice of scapegoat [Szasz 1970,1974], and with a pseudoscientific veneer of rational civility which, however ingeniously constructed or vociferously defended, remains far too small and transparent to conceal the ignorant superstition and unrestrained cruelty which fuels it.

Shamanic ecstasy is the *real* 'Old Time Religion,' of which modern churches are but pallid evocations. Shamanic, visionary ecstasy, the *mysterium tremendum*, the *unio mystica*, the eternally delightful experience of the universe as energy, is a *sine qua non* of religion, *it is what religion is for!* There is no need for faith, it is the ecstatic experience itself that *gives* one faith in the intrinsic unity and integrity of the universe, in ourselves as integral parts of the whole; that reveals to us the sublime majesty of our universe, and the fluctuant, scintillant, alchemical miracle that is quotidian consciousness. Any religion that *requires* faith and gives none, that *defends against* religious experiences, that promulgates the bizarre superstition that humankind is in some way separate, divorced from the rest of creation, that heals not the gaping wound between Body and Soul, but would tear them asunder... is no religion at all [Ott 1994]!

We stand on the threshold of a new millennium which will determine whether our species continues to grow and prosper, or destroys itself in a cataclysmic biological and cultural Holocaust unprecedented in the last 65 million years of life on this planet. We suffer a crisis of faith in the modern world, we frightened somnambulists stumbling in a lethean, penumbral dream-world of materialistic delusion, and we desperately need the healing balm of shamanic ecstasy to salve the lesions of materialism. The Entheogenic Reformation is our brightest hope for overcoming the evil and hypocritical, sixteen-hundred-year-old crusade to excise religious experience from human memory, to eliminate genuine religion from the face of the Earth. May the Entheogenic Reformation prevail over the Pharmacratic Inquisition, leading to the spiritual rebirth of humankind at Our Lady Gæa's[7] breasts, from which may ever copiously flow the *amrta*, the *ambrosia*, the *ayahuasca* of eternal life!

Jonathan Ott
Lleida, Catalunya, Espanya

The Age of Entheogens

> At that point Religion was born, religion pure
> and simple, free of Theology, free of Dogma-
> tics, expressing itself in awe and reverence and
> in lowered voices, mostly at night, when peo-
> ple would gather together to consult the Sac-
> red Element. The first entheogenic experience
> could have been the first, and an authentic,
> perhaps the only authentic miracle. This was
> the beginning of the Age of the Entheogens,
> long, long ago.
>
> R. Gordon Wasson
> *Persephone's Quest* [1986]

Two decades have passed since the American anthropologists Weston La Barre and
Peter T. Furst characterized shamanism as a pangæan 'Ur-religion' of extreme an-
tiquity, extending at least 50 millennia into our prehistoric past [Furst 1976; La
Barre 1970,1979,1980a]. As Furst noted in *Hallucinogens and Culture*:

> There is no question that shamanism has great antiquity: the archæ-
> ological evidence suggests, for example, that something very like the
> shamanistic religions of recent hunters was already present among the
> Neanderthals of Europe and Asia more than 50,000 years ago... there
> are demonstrably so many fundamental similarities between the core
> elements of the religions of the aboriginal New World and those of As-
> ia that almost certainly at least in their basic foundations the sym-
> bolic systems of American Indians must have been present already in
> the ideational world of the original immigrants from northeastern
> Asia. These foundations are shamanistic...

In *The Ghost Dance: The Origins of Religion*, La Barre had already proposed as much,
offering elaborate details, which he summarized a decade later in "Anthropological
Perspectives on Hallucination, Hallucinogens, and the Shamanic Origins of Religion" [La Barre 1970,1980a]:

> That this picture of the ancient shamanic hunters' religion is not a
> projective fantasy of our own is indicated in the fact that the religion
> of all hunting peoples known in early modern times has remained this
> same simple shamanism... In the Paleolithic Ur-culture that Kluck-

hohn discerned in the whole world, it is quite plain that there were shamans before there were gods. For gods are only charismatic power-wielding shamans, hypostatized after death and grown in stature with the increased world horizons... On the basis of culture traits universal or near-universal from Alaska to Patagonia (bow, spear-thrower, dog), it is evident that the trickling southward of post-Aurignacian, bow-using, Paleo-Siberian hunters continued on into the Mesolithic... This picture is fully confirmed archeologically, in Asiatic-American semi-subterranean houses from Siberia to Alaska and also in the American Southwest; and linguistically (tonemic Apache-Navaho is cognate with Tibeto-Burman-Chinese tone languages of Asia); and culturally (the conical tipi-wigwam extends from western Asia across Siberia to the central Algonkians of the Great Lakes, snow vehicles are of similar type from Finland to Maine, so too the sweat-lodge even beyond these limits); and in religion (the circumboreal 'bear ceremonialism,' Tungusic olonism and the Asiatic-American vision-quest complex, shamanism); and folkloristically (the Eurasiatic-American lightning-eagle, the 'magic flight' motif, the Orpheus legend); and even botanically (the absence of aboriginally shared cultigens, and domesticates beyond the Mesolithic dog).

Both Furst and La Barre acknowledged the fundamental importance of the innovative work of R. Gordon Wasson in the formulation of these astonishing insights. Wasson, a banker and pioneering 'ethnomycologist,' devoted his life to documenting the survival of shamanism "with diminishing vigor in the world's outlying communities," and to exploring a "unified field theory" of religion, of "the proto-history of our own Indo-European culture"—to establishing the connection between shamanic ecstasy and religion [Wasson 1968,1972a,1980; Wasson & Wasson 1957; Wasson et al. 1974,1978,1986]. Wasson summarized this revolutionary discovery with disarming simplicity [Wasson 1968]:

> 'Shamanism' is the convenient name that we give to the religious experience of the Stone Age, and its key is ecstasy, rapture. Fortunately for us, the cult of the entheogen did not die out in pre-history. Shamanism lingered on here and there, reaching as with fingers down the corridors of time into early history. I suggest that it survives to this day in the secret rites of the divine mushroom in Mesoamerica...

Wasson was later to characterize pre- and proto-history or, perhaps more to the point, the *preliterate history* of all peoples, as the Age of Entheogens, which lives on in Amazonia, in the remote mountains of México, and elsewhere [Wasson 1980]:

> I have sometimes asked myself whether the unlettered ages, stretching back through æons of time, were not those belonging peculiarly to the entheogens, the Age of entheogens. The Mysteries of Eleusis began in the unlettered past of the amazing Greek people, then persisted for a few centuries under an hermetic seal of secrecy into an age of glorious letters... The Soma of the Vedic Hymns knew its heyday before the Aryans learned their letters but it disappeared with the coming of the alphabet...

Although Mircea Eliade, in his exhaustive study of shamanism [Eliade 1951], conceived of the shamanic use of what he indiscriminately called 'drugs' or 'narcotics' as 'decadence,' as "a vulgar substitute for 'pure' trance," we now know this to have been a colossal error;[8] a classic example of failing to see the forest for the trees. With the blinders and tunnel-vision characteristic of academic over-specialization, alloyed with prejudice derived from western society's pharmacological Calvinism,[9] and lacking the most rudimentary knowledge of pharmacology or the history of inebriants, Eliade hamfistedly described as 'degenerate' use of the sacred plants whose visionary effects were *the very essence of shamanism*; as 'vulgar' what Gordon Wasson was to identify four years later, on the basis of his personal experience with the Mazatec shaman María Sabina, as "religion pure and simple, free of Theology, free of Dogmatics, expressing itself in awe and reverence and in lowered voices, mostly at night, when people would gather together to consult the Sacred Element" [Wasson 1968; Wasson *et al.* 1986]. Having experienced shamanic ecstasy at first hand, on the night of 29–30 June 1955 in a remote village high in the mountains of southern México,[10] Wasson astutely recognized in the humble person of the preliterate Mazatec Indian *curandera* María Sabina [Wasson 1980]:

> The Shaman, the focus for the woes and longings of mankind back, back through the Stone Age to Siberia. She was Religion Incarnate. She was the hierophant, the thaumaturge, the psychopompos, in whom the troubles and aspirations of countless generations of the family of mankind had found, were still finding, their relief. All this I saw in the light of that one match, in the shadow performance of María Sabina.

[17]

The light of that match seemed to last an æon of time, and then, suddenly, it was out.

While many scholars of early humankind, like Eliade, were made extremely uncomfortable by the Wasson Theory [Forte 1988; Ott 1990,1993]; their colleagues of greater vision descried therein a skeleton key to unlock the "hermetic seal of secrecy" veiling the spiritual world of preliterate peoples from our sight. To Claude Lévi-Strauss [1970], Wasson's was a:

> Revolutionary hypothesis... the implications of which are so widespread... of all sorts of keys to be discovered in sequence, each one governing a hidden meaning...

and La Barre saw in Wasson's work "an object lesson to all holistic professional students of man" [La Barre 1980c]. La Barre explored thoroughly Wasson's *nexus* between entheogens and shamanism, also between shamanism and religion (along with other aspects of culture), in his monumental *The Ghost Dance*, cited above [La Barre 1970]. With the passing years, the Wasson Theory has become so widely accepted by specialists as to be considered beyond serious dispute. Shamanism is the earliest manifestation of culture; the shaman the first professional and the precursor of the priest, physician, musician, and every artist alike. Visionary ecstasy is the primal heart and soul of shamanism and religious revelation [La Barre 1979], and the use of entheogenic plant sacraments is the most archaic, fundamental and pangæan (not to mention effective) technique for the induction of shamanic ecstasy. There could be no more appropriate designation for our millenary, preliterate past than the Age of Entheogens.

The Pharmacratic Inquisition

Has the famous story that stands at the beginning of the Bible really been understood? the
story of God's hellish fear of *science*? [...] Only
from woman did man learn to taste of the tree
of knowledge. What had happened? The old
God was seized with hellish fear. Man himself
had turned out to be his *greatest* mistake; he
had created a rival for himself; science makes
godlike—it is all over with priests and gods
when man becomes scientific. Moral: science
is the forbidden as such—it alone is forbidden.
Science is the *first* sin, the seed of all sin, the
original sin. *This alone is morality.* 'Thou shalt
not know'—the rest follows.

Friedrich W$^{m.}$ Nietzsche
Der Antichrist [1888/1895]

The symbolic demise of the Age of Entheogens in Palæogæa occurred at the end of
the fourth century of our era, when Alaric's Goths overran the sanctuary at Eleusis,
putting an end to an organized Mystery religion two millennia old, centered on an
annual rite in which the initiates or *mystai* imbibed the *kykeon*,[11] an entheogenic
potion which transformed them into *epoptai*, who had seen *ta hiera*, 'the holy'
[Wasson *et al.* 1978]. As Eleusinian archæologist G.E. Mylonas [1961] commented:

> When the walls of the Sanctuary were ruined by the hordes of Alaric
> in A.D. 395, they were apparently left in their ruinous state. The Em-
> peror was now a Christian who had proclaimed dire measures against
> the mystic cults... A new religion controlled the minds and actions
> of men. The old pagan rites must go and their shrines must be buried
> in their own debris. It was so decreed; it so happened.

This momentous event in human history stands as a portentous symbol of the death
of ancient religion and the inauguration of the Pharmacratic Inquisition.[12] Although
the Age of Entheogens lived on in Palæogæa for perhaps another millennium, the
demise of the Eleusinian Mysteries tolled its death-knell. The Christian enmity is
easy to explain. Since the Christians were promulgating a religion in which the core
mystery, the holy sacrament itself, was conspicuous by its absence, later transmogrified
by the smoke and mirrors of the Doctrine of Transubstantiation[13] into a specious

symbol, an inert substance, a placebo[14] entheogen, the imposture would be all-too-evident to anyone who had known the blessing of ecstasy, who had access to personal religious experiences [Ott 1993]. Thus a concerted attack on the use of sacred inebriants was mounted, and the supreme heresy was to presume to have any direct experience of the divine, not mediated by an increasingly corrupt and politicized priesthood. The Pharmacratic Inquisition was the answer of the Catholic Church to the embarrassing fact that it had taken all the religion out of religion, leaving an empty and hollow shell with no intrinsic value or attraction to humankind, which could only be maintained by hectoring, guilt-mongering and plain brute force.

While the world was to endure an incredible profusion of pogroms and organized and unorganized inquisitions throughout the millennium aptly characterized as the Dark Ages[15]—directed here against vestiges of pre-Christian pagan philosophy, there against rival faiths like Judaism, Manichæism, Islam, or against the nascent stirrings of science and rationalism—there existed continual and vigorous pressure against ecstatic religions and against practitioners of traditional herbal lore.[16] Thus diviners, healers and midwives, exponents of the shamanic arts, were dragged to the stake among the Jews, Manichæans, Muslims, alchemists, political dissidents and epileptics (or others whose behavior inspired fear), criminals, harridans, business rivals and anyone else whose misfortune it was to become a scapegoat for the problems of the day. *The Witch's Garden* was plowed under by an evil force which conceived of human beings as sheep, and used their bodies to fuel the fires of ritual purification.[17] By the advent of the sixteenth century, Europe had been beaten into submission, shamanic ecstasy virtually expunged from the memory of the survivors, and the shamanic pharmacopœia all but forgotten [Hansen 1978; Harner 1973].

The Age of Entheogens yet lived on in Neogæa, however, and European seafarers abruptly came face-to-face with their own pagan heritage, with people having direct experience of the divine mediated, not by ignorant priests, but by a bewildering array of entheogenic 'plant-teachers,' which were being smoked, snuffed, ingested, even taken in enemas![18] Troubled churchmen among those seafarers uneasily saw in this a diabolical parody of their cherished 'Holy Communion,' blissfully unaware of the fact that it was rather their *own* placebo sacrament that was a decidedly unholy parody of humankind's immemorial communion with sacred plant-teachers![19] We might date the advent of the Pharmacratic Inquisition in Neogæa to 1521, when Cortes' ragtag band of outlaw *conquistadores* established dominion over the Aztecs or Mexicas, consummate virtuosos of the entheogenic arts and sciences. Like the Chinese concept of *yin/yang*, however, the seed of the Entheogenic Reformation lay dormant in the fallow spiritual field left in the wake of this historical cataclysm.

[20]

On 19 June 1620 in México City, the Inquisition formally decreed that the use of shamanic inebriants was heretical, stating in no uncertain terms:

> The use of the Herb or Root called Peyote... is a superstitious action and reproved as opposed to the purity and sincerity of our Holy Catholic Faith... We decree that henceforth no person... may use or use of this said herb, this Peyote, or of others for said effects, nor others similar... being warned that doing the contrary, besides incurring said censures and penalties, we will proceed against whoever is rebellious and disobedient, as against persons suspect in the holy Catholic faith.

It bears witness to the sincerity and integrity of the Mesoamerican Indians that they continued to commune with their traditional sacraments in defiance of this decree, braving brutal torture and hideous execution. Over the next 265 years, there were at least 90 *autos de fe* of the Inquisition for use of *péyotl* [Aguirre Beltrán 1963; Stewart 1987]; and numerous *autos de fe* involving *teonanácatl*, the sacred mushrooms [Wasson 1980] and *ololiuhqui*, the entheogenic morning glory seeds which, even more than *péyotl* or *teonanácatl* attracted the opprobrium of Inquisitors like Hernando Ruiz de Alarcón and Jacinto de la Serna [Wasson 1963]. The Inquisition eventually ran out of steam, failing to extirpate the use of plant sacraments in México, but succeeding in driving this underground. Nevertheless, Protestant missionaries have continued the Pharmacratic Inquisition with undiminished zeal; like their Catholic predecessors blissfully ignorant of any irony involved—as one missionary noted: "the partaking of the divine mushroom poses potential problems in relation to the Christian concept of the Lord's Supper" [Pike 1960; Pike & Cowan 1959]. To say the least...[20]

Contemporary prohibition of entheogenic and other psychoactive drugs dates from 1 March 1915, when entered into force HR6282, or the Harrison Narcotic Act, which passed the U.S. Congress on 14 December 1914, to be signed three days later by President Wilson. Although the Constitution itself had to be amended to proscribe alcohol, the U.S. Supreme Court in 1919 [U.S. v. Doremus; Webb et al. v. U.S.] upheld this federal statute proscribing 'narcotics' and the arrogation of broad federal police powers in the matter of 'dangerous drugs.' The concept has achieved the status of tradition in the United States, which has exported its anti-drug crusade worldwide, and the legislation currently in force, Public Law 91–513, the Comprehensive Drug Abuse Prevention and Control Act of 1970, provides for facile proscription of any substance the government wishes to add to its 'schedules.' Indeed, Public Law 99–570, the Controlled Substance Analogue Enforcement Act of 1986, boldly pen-

[21]

etrates into areas of governmental control over research undreamed of by any National Socialist ('Nazi'), Communist or other dictatorship; presuming to declare any "human research with new drugs" unlawful unless explicitly approved by the federal government [Shulgin 1992]! The situation has degenerated to such a point that the late federal Judge J.G. Burciaga, in ruling against the United States government in a criminal case involving drug law, stated:

> The tattered Fourth Amendment right to be free from unreasonable searches and seizures and the now frail Fifth Amendment right against self-incrimination or deprivation of liberty without due process have fallen as casualties in this 'war on drugs'... today, the 'war' targets one of the most deeply held fundamental rights—the First Amendment right to freely exercise one's religion. [774 F. Supp. 1333 (D.N.M. 1991)]

While the original impetus for anti-drug legislation in the U.S. involved questions of imperialistic struggles for world dominance [Musto 1973], not to mention economics and racism [Helmer 1975], it triumphed on the tide of reformist zeal of fundamentalist religious minorities intolerant of diversity.[21] Albeit tricked-up as 'Public Health Laws' addressing so-called 'crimes against health,' contemporary drug prohibition is merely the modern expression, disguised by secular circumlocutions, of the millennial Pharmacratic Inquisition, as Justice Burciaga sagaciously noted.

We must not lose sight of the fact that, like the decree of the Spanish Inquisition in México in 1620, contemporary drug legislation, whatever its justification, inexorably has the effect of prohibiting ecstatic, experiential religion while simultaneously promoting exsanguinated, desacramentalized simulacra of religion. The secular American state is clearly comfortable with purely symbolic, Christian non-religion, but feels rightly threatened by ecstatic religion grounded in individual religious experiences, which lead people to examine their own assumptions and motivations, and those of their churches, and those of their governments—the difference is between blind obedience and eternal, sceptical questioning and distrust of authority.

Not only is the Pharmacratic Inquisition alive and well on the threshold of the new millennium, but it has been enshrined in the secular law of one of the world's most secular states, whose Constitution respects individual freedom, and is being used as a pretext, not merely to attack ecstatic religions, but to attack scientific research and the very Bill of Rights to that Constitution, destroying at once religious freedom, scientific freedom, and the juridical guarantees protecting citizens of the United States from governmental arrogance and tyranny!

[22]

The Entheogenic Reformation

> If our classical scholars were given the opportunity to attend the rite at Eleusis, to talk with the priestess, what would they not exchange for that chance? How propitious would their frame of mind be, if they were invited to partake of the potion! Well, those rites take place now, unbeknownst to the classical scholars, in scattered dwellings, humble, thatched, without windows, far from the beaten track, high in the mountains of Mexico, in the stillness of the night...
>
> **R. Gordon Wasson**
> *The Hallucinogenic Fungi of Mexico* [1961]

In history, as in physics, in the millennial struggle between governmental tyranny and human rights, no action is without an equal and opposite reaction—the reaction to the Pharmacratic Inquisition was the Entheogenic Reformation. Let us go now to the equatorial rainforests of West Africa, in present-day Gabon, where in the mid-nineteenth century the Fang people were observed by Europeans to use an entheogenic plant called *iboga* [*eboka*], known botanically as *Tabernanthe iboga* Baillon,[22] about which use, according to myths of the origin of *iboga*, they seem to have learned ultimately from the forest-dwelling Pygmies, although the Apindji, Mitsogho and Eshira peoples served as intermediaries [Pope 1969; Samorini 1993]. In response to Catholic evangelism and Protestant missionary activity in West Africa, there evolved among the Fang a syncretism between the traditional use of this entheogenic *iboga* plant and Christianity, of which the most prominent manifestation is the Bwiti cult (*iboga* use is also associated with the MBiri cult; a Fang adaptation of the Ombwiri healing tradition).[23] As Fang ethnographer James W. Fernandez [1972, 1982] noted:

> We have in the eating of *eboka* a eucharistic experience with similarities to Christian communion... For not only do members of Bwiti practice communion, employing *eboka* instead of bread, but they also boast of the efficacy of *eboka* over bread in its power to give visions of the dead. Some of the more Christian branches of Bwiti... speak of *eboka* as a more perfect and God-given representation of the body of Christ!

The Bwiti cult apparently revolves around dynamic reinterpretations of Biblical myths, with the story of Adam and Eve, the Tree of Life and the Tree of the Knowledge of Good and Evil (which is, of course, *iboga*), the Christian Trinity and the

[23]

Deluge being prominent. Giorgio Samorini became the first outsider to be initiated fully into Bwiti in Gabon, and he recently quoted a remark by a Bwitist which clearly establishes the place of Bwiti in the Entheogenic Reformation [Samorini 1993]:

> We are the true Christians. The Catholics have lost the way that leads you to Christ; the missionaries who offer us their insipid Host and ask us to abandon *Iboga*, do not know what they are talking about!

Could we ask for a more direct statement of the difference between genuine, experiential, ecstatic religion and the watered-down, exsanguinated simulacrum of religion evoked by a placebo sacrament—by an insipid Host? As Georges Balandrier pointedly commented of Bwiti ceremonies in Gabon [Pope 1969]:

> What does our civilization offer that is capable of arousing a fervor of this kind, an involvement spelling adventure for the body as well as the mind? Our churches... seem cold, devoid of supernatural presence, ill-suited to impassioned communion.

During the French colonial *régime* in Gabon, especially in the decades 1920–1940, the missionaries, with the tacit approval of the colonial government, prosecuted a vicious Pharmacratic Inquisition against Bwiti, including burning many temples and murdering religious leaders. Nevertheless, Bwiti continued to grow in the face of persecution, identifying with the nationalist, anticolonial sentiment which led to the eventual expulsion of the French and founding of the Republic of Gabon, whose first President was a Bwitist [Samorini 1993]. Indeed, Bwiti has achieved the character of state-religion in Gabon, where there are between one and two thousand Bwiti temples. The religion is spreading rapidly across national borders, "despite a great deal of missionary effort" and slander against it; taking root in Equatorial Guinea, People's Republic of Congo, Cameroon, and Zaïre. Bwiti, the African stronghold of the Entheogenic Reformation, bids fair to become, along with Christianity and Islam, one of the predominant religions of equatorial West Africa [Pope 1969; Samorini 1993]!

Meanwhile, on the North American continent, the Entheogenic Reformation was extending its roots into the scorched earth left in the wake of the brutal Union Army or United States Army raised by Abraham Lincoln to 'preserve the Union.' Having trampled the United States Constitution into the ground in the course of subduing the Confederate Army [E.A. Wasson 1965], the awesome federal military might Lincoln had amassed was turned against the hapless indigenous population of the continent. Unlike Mesoamerica and South America, where bloody conquest was followed by a gradual process of *mestizaje* or miscegenation of European and Indian blood, the United States government embarked on a 'Final Solution' involving the extermination (or imprisonment on 'reservations' which shrank increasingly to approximate concentration camps)[24] of the indigenous population, in pursuit of the nation's 'Manifest Destiny' to control the continent. Both México and the British Crown had already been forced in the 1840s to cede immense territories to the imperialistic government on the Potomac, lands that didn't 'belong' to those governments any more than the rest of the continent 'belonged' to the United States government. The Indians fought bravely against superior numbers and arms, and ultimately watched helplessly as their great chiefs and warriors, as whole tribes were exterminated... watched in stunned amazement as the great herds of buffalo, vast roiling seas of large animals, were slaughtered for their skins, the huge, meaty bodies which gave them sustenance left to rot on the dusty prairies!

As Weston La Barre detailed in *The Ghost Dance: The Origins of Religion*, the two Ghost Dance movements "represent the final catastrophe of Indian cultures in the United States" [La Barre 1970]. Although it had its antecedents in 1870, it was the Great Ghost Dance of 1890 which brought down the curtain on traditional Indian, shamanic culture. The fundamental tenets of this pan-Indian religious movement were Millenialist—a great cataclysm would destroy the whites and the Earth would sprout a new skin on which the grass would grow and the buffalo graze as before, restoring the Indians to glory. The Indians were to escape destruction by dancing the Ghost Dance wearing special 'ghost shirts.' It appears that this movement was a syncretism between ancient Northern Paiute beliefs in the cyclical renewal of the world, and Christian doctrines of the Millennium [Stewart 1987]. The futility of even this last, desperate attempt to salvage part of their culture became apparent in 1890, when the Hunkpapa Teton Dakota Sioux shaman-chief Sitting Bull was killed in South Dakota, followed by the massacre of his people at Wounded Knee, putting a sanguine end to Indian resistance to whites [La Barre 1970].

Unlike this swift and brutal military reaction against the Sioux Ghost Dance in the Dakotas, the authorities in Oklahoma allowed the movement to run its course in the first years of the 1890s. By this time, the ancient shamanic use of *péyotl*, the entheogenic cactus *Lophophora williamsii* (Lem.) Coulter,[25] had begun to diffuse to the north. An important plant sacrament of the Mexican Indians, as noted above, and having a vast range in México, *péyotl* grew in the United States only in the Río Bravo/Grande valley of southern Texas, where it may have been used traditionally by the Carrizo Indians. During the nineteenth century, sacramental use of *péyotl* began to spread to the Lipan Apache, Mescalero Apache, Tonkawa, Karankawa and Caddo, gaining a growing foothold in the United States [Stewart 1987]. In Oklahoma, 'the cradle of peyotism,' use of the cactus took root in the fertile fields of Ghost Dance fervor [La Barre 1970; McAllester 1949], and on the Kiowa-Comanche reservation of Oklahoma, the Caddo and Delaware shaman John Wilson was an important leader both in the Ghost Dance movement and in the nascent *péyotl* religion. Wilson and Comanche Chief Quanah Parker were instrumental in founding the religious movement which was to coalesce on 10 October 1918 with the establishment of the Native American Church in Oklahoma, uniting the *péyotl* religions of the Cheyenne, Otoe, Ponca, Comanche, Kiowa and Kiowa-Apache Indians. The fascinating story of the founding of this new syncretic Christian/shamanic religion has been written in detail by Omer C. Stewart, *Peyote Religion: A History* [1987].

In *The Peyote Cult*, his classic study of North American peyotlism, Weston La Barre [1938] had noted the complex interweaving of Christian elements and Mexican and Plains Indian beliefs into a new religion. La Barre characterized the syncretism with Christianity as 'superficial,' and to be sure, unlike the case of *iboga* in the Bwiti rite, *péyotl* is not here conceived of as a precise, indeed, "more perfect and God-given" equivalent of the Host. Moreover, some versions of Plains peyotlism, such as that of the Kiowa-Comanche, lack Christian elements. On the other hand, the Plains Indians were exposed more to Protestantism than Catholicism, with its comparatively reduced emphasis on sacramental communion,[13] which may explain the lack of equation between *péyotl* and the Eucharist. Furthermore, the second article of incorporation of the Native American Church states specifically that:

> The purpose... is to foster and promote the religious belief of the several tribes of Indians in the State of Oklahoma, in the Christian religion with... the Peyote Sacrament... and to teach the Christian religion...

We must not forget Comanche Chief Quanah Parker's famous *dictum*: "The white man goes into his church house and talks *about* Jesus, but the Indian goes into his tipi and talks *to* Jesus" [La Barre 1938; Stewart 1987].

As was the case with Bwiti, a latter-day *auto de fe* of the Pharmacratic Inquisition began to persecute the novel religion. It was too late for another extermination campaign—even land-hungry whites had been shocked by the brutality of the Army's 'Final Solution' to the 'Indian Problem.' Since Puritanical prohibitionist forces had already turned to the ballot-box and Congress to wage their war on inebriants, *péyotl* was included along with alcohol, tobacco and other inebriants in a general legal campaign against drugs, which began in the States on a grassroots level, and culminated in the aforementioned passage of the Harrison Narcotic Act of 1914, the 18th Amendment to the Constitution and the Volstead Act of 1919, which illegalized alcohol itself, although an exemption was made for the watered-down, vinous sacrament of the Catholics, that even a target of the prohibitionist zealots [E.A. Wasson 1914]! Omer C. Stewart's *Peyote Religion* [1987] tells the sorry tale of the sleazy attempt to take their *péyotl* away from the Indians. Although many battles were lost along the way, this time in the courts, the American Indians have successfully resisted attempts to illegalize the *péyotl* religion. The Comprehensive Drug Abuse Prevention and Control Act of 1970 classified *péyotl* and its visionary alkaloid mescaline as illicit drugs, but the American Indian Religious Freedom Act of 1978 specifically protects Indian religions, and the Amendments to this law enacted in 1994 decree that:

> Use, possession, or transportation of peyote by an Indian for bona fide traditional ceremonial purposes in connection with the practice of a traditional Indian religion is lawful, and shall not be prohibited by the United States or any State.

Despite the long-standing discrimination against Indians in the United States, and a vigorous propaganda campaign against so-called 'hallucinogenic' drugs like *péyotl* and mescaline, the Native American Church has continued its inexorable expansion north into Canada, and today has more than 250,000 members, or a quarter of the adult Indian population of North America. Several tribes admit non-Indians to the church, and in 1979 the all-race Peyote Way Church of God was incorporated in Arizona [Anderson 1980; Mount 1987]. The federal government interprets legal exemptions for religious use of *péyotl* in a racist fashion, to apply only to Indians or persons with at least 25% Indian blood! Nevertheless, recent federal court decisions [Native American Church of New York v. U.S., 468 F. Supp. 1247 (1979); U.S. v. John D. and Frances Warner, Cr. No. C2–84–51; U.S. v. Boyll, 774 F. Supp. 1333 (D.N.M. 1991)] have supported rights of non-Indians to use *péyotl* as a sacrament, and the next step for the Entheogenic Reformation in North America is to legitimize rights of *all* citizens to participate in ecstatic religions with genuine sacraments.

With far less fanfare than had accompanied its earliest manifestations in Africa and North America, the Entheogenic Reformation spread quietly in South America for more than half a century, before inspiring a counterattack by the reactionary forces of the Pharmacratic Inquisition. Starting in the 1920s and 1930s in the state of Acre in Brasilian Amazonia, syncretic Christian churches began to appear, employing the pan-Amazonian shamanic entheogenic potion *ayahuasca*[26] as the Host in decidedly Christian rituals of Communion. Today there are two major (and several minor) Christian *ayahuasca* churches in Brasil—the older Santo Daime church and the more recent, but larger, União do Vegetal or UDV.[27] Edward MacRae has outlined the history of Santo Daime in his admirable book *Guiado Pela Lua: Xamanismo e Uso Ritual da Ayahuasca no Culto do Santo Daime* [MacRae 1992], and the objectives and background of the UDV have been adumbrated by the church itself in the recent book entitled *União do Vegetal. Hoasca: Fundamentos e Objetivos* [Centro 1989].

André Lázaro has summarized Santo Daime doctrine, stating quite plainly that: "The Doctrine of Santo Daime is manifested by way of the ritual use of our sacrament, also known as Ayahuasca..." [Lázaro 1994]. MacRae noted the key role of the *ayahuasca* potion or *daime* ('gi'me') in promoting 'concentration' for those receiving Communion during Santo Daime rites, which involve dancing and singing hymns [MacRae 1992]. The potion is dispensed from a 'Fount of Wisdom' by church 'Mestres' during Mass and festivals, and is composed of aqueous infusions of *Banisteriopsis caapi* (Spr. ex Griseb.) Morton stems, known as *cipó* or *jagube* and doctrinally as the masculine, solar element; and leaves of *Psychotria viridis* Ruiz et Pavón[28] or *folha, rainha,* or *chacrona,* doctrinally representative of the feminine, lunar element conceptualized as Nossa Senhora da Conceição or Rainha da Floresta (Our Lady of Conception or Queen of the Forest). Both plants are cultivated in Amazonia and the potion prepared in large quantities which are then bottled for storage and transportation [Lowy 1987; MacRae 1992]. Chemical analysis of a *daime* sample showed it to contain typical *ayahuasca* alkaloids [Liwszyc *et al.* 1992; see Note 26] in entheogenic amounts, according to human pharmacological studies employing '*ayahuasca* capsules' (or *pharmahuasca*) and *anahuasca* or '*ayahuasca* analogues' [Ott 1994].

Although the published doctrine of the União do Vegetal or 'Herbal Union' does not specifically equate the potion known as *chá hoasca* ('vine tea') with the Christian Eucharist, it states in no uncertain terms [Centro 1989]:

> The União do Vegetal professes the fundamentals of Christianity, recovering these in their original purity and integrity, free of the distortions imprinted on them by the human mind over the course of the centuries... In ritual sessions taking place in its temples, the União do Vegetal employs a tea called Hoasca... as an instrument of mental concentration... The effect of the tea might be compared to religious ecstasy...

As is the case in Santo Daime, in the UDV the potion is administered in the course of Mass and religious festivals, and its value in promoting concentration or "a state of contemplative lucidity that places the subject in direct contact with the spiritual plane" is similarly stressed [Centro 1989]. Like *daime*, *chá hoasca* is composed of aqueous extracts of stems of the liana *Banisteriopsis caapi* or *mariri* and the leaves of *chacrona* or *Psychotria viridis*. Again, the plants are cultivated in Amazonia to supply this primarily urban church, and the potion is prepared in large quantities under the supervision of church 'Mestres.' The pharmacodynamics of the potion are conceptualized as the union of *force*, from the masculine *mariri* vine, and *light* from the feminine *chacrona* leaves [Henman 1986]. Broadly speaking, the UDV and Santo Daime have more attributes in common than they have differences, and both are emblematic of the Entheogenic Reformation of Christianity in South America.

After flourishing in obscurity for some six decades, the Amazonian Entheogenic Reformation suddenly was attacked by the Pharmacratic Inquisition of the Brasilian government, under foreign pressure to enlist in the pangæan crusade against the 'scourge of drugs.' In 1985, the Divisão de Medicamentos do Ministério da Saúde (Dimed) and Conselho Federal de Entorpecentes (Confen) of the Brasilian government added the *ayahuasca* plant to the list of proscribed drugs, prompting the UDV to petition Confen to annul the ban [Centro 1989]. After a commission appointed to study the issue found no evidence of social disruption associated with sacramental use of *ayahuasca*, which the commission members themselves tried, *ayahuasca* was removed from the controlled substances list on 26 August 1987. However, the following year an anonymous denunciation in Rio de Janeiro alleged there were ten million 'fanatics' in the *ayahuasca* churches who were "drug addicts or ex-guerrillas"; that *Cannabis* was used as 'incense' in the rites; that "LSD or a similar drug" was being mixed surreptitiously into the sacramental potions of the UDV; and that finally, adepts of the *ayahuasca* churches were being enslaved by 'urban guerrillas' [MacRae 1992]. Confen once again ordered a technical study of the issue, especially of the pharmacology of the sacramental potions. Once again, *ayahuasca* and the syncretic churches received a clean bill of health, and Confen accepted the conclusions of the technical study, which recommended that *ayahuasca* potions, as well as their constituent plants, *Banisteriopsis caapi* and *Psychotria viridis*, should be exempted from the illicit drugs list, which they summarily were in June 1992.

Now fully legitimized in Brasil, the *ayahuasca* churches continue a steady expansion. At its Céu do Mapiá commune in Amazonian Brasil, the Santo Daime church conducts 'transformational retreats' which are advertised in the United States and other countries, to introduce foreigners to the church. Some of these retreats are run by U.S. members of the church. Touring groups of Santo Daime devotees offer *ay-*

ahuasca rituals, sometimes for a fee (about 300–500 Deutschmarks), in Europe—these *ayahuasca* Masses have been celebrated in Madrid, Barcelona, Amsterdam, Munich, Frankfurt, Berlin and several other large cities. This commercial activity—sometimes the church and Christianity take a back seat in promotional literature, such as "Ayahuasca: The Legendary Shamanic Ritual of the Amazon"—has generated some negative publicity, and it appears some 'white shamans' may be using the name of the church as a cover for their strictly profit-making activity [Anon. 1994]. On the other hand, Santo Daime temples are being established in European cities like Barcelona. The UDV is far less given to evangelism, and maintains a 'Medical Studies Center' staffed by medical professionals among church devotees, to review and catalogue scientific reports on *ayahuasca* [Centro 1989]. The church has lately been collaborating with an international scientific research team on a 'Hoasca Project' to evaluate the phytochemistry and pharmacology of *chá hoasca*, as well as the psychological and physical dimensions of the long-term, chronic use of this entheogen by church members [McKenna 1994].

Given the current rabid interest in shamanism and rainforest conservation in the overdeveloped world, it would appear these *ayahuasca* churches have unlimited potential for expansion, assuming they can circumvent the problem of the DMT content of the potions, since DMT is an illicit drug in most countries. It remains to be seen whether European and United States residents are genuinely interested in the Christian doctrines of Santo Daime and UDV, or are primarily interested in obtaining *ayahuasca* for their own, non-Christian, psychonautic/shamanic self-actualization. Indeed, *aficionados* of one California underground UDV temple wrote me that "most of us have sharply curtailed our sessions with the psychedelic Catholics" after having learned how to concoct their own *ayahuasca* and/or '*ayahuasca* analogues' [Ott 1994], and some people in the contemporary entheogenic 'drug scene' of the industrialized world consider Christianity to be inimical to the ecstatic state, to be *ipso facto* the Pharmacratic Inquisition—finding in shamanism or pagan religion their cynosure. It seems to me, rather, that the bulk of my peers in these overdeveloped countries despise Christianity and regard it to be the ecological and theological enemy of 'the movement,' and that shamanism, with its emphasis on individual psychonautic vision quests, is the reigning model. Indeed, it is my impression that the contemporary interest in shamanism and entheogenic drugs in western countries is the direct counterpart of the syncretic Christian/shamanic movements we have examined in Africa and the Americas—that the so-called 'Psychedelic Age' and the 'White Shaman' movement constitute *our* version of the Entheogenic Reformation.

Besides magazines catering to *Cannabis* habitués and users of entheogenic drugs, such as *High Times* (which have been a fixture of the U.S. 'drug scene' for two decades), there are now magazines focusing on shamanism, like *Shaman's Drum* and *Magical Blend*. A novel magazine, *Psychedelic Illuminations*, represents a hybrid between drug magazine and shamanism magazine. *Shaman's Drum* in particular is a forum for advertisements by tourist operators promoting *péyotl* tourism to México ('Visions of Power,' "visit Huichol places of power... learn advanced techniques of shamanic healing...") and *ayahuasca* tourism to Perú ('The Shaman's Journey' and 'The Way of the Warrior'), Brasil ('The Healer's Journey'), Ecuador ('Shamans and Healers of Ecuador') and Bolivia [Krajick 1992; Ott 1993,1994]. Also promoted are training courses in 'shamanism' by 'white shamans' (as they are called derisively by some Indian shamans) from the industrialized world. It is interesting to note that mushroomic tourism, which happily never reached the state of organization of today's *péyotl* and *ayahuasca* tours, has waned in México, but is flourishing in Thailand, where local people with no apparent *direct* connection to traditional shamanic use of entheogenic mushrooms have learned to exploit them as a novel tourism opportunity [Allen & Merlin 1992].

It is the transformation of holy sacrament to crass tourist commodity, occasioned by this entheogenic tourism, which leads me to condemn it in no uncertain terms. In México, within two decades of Wasson's unveiling of the shamanic use of sacramental mushrooms—which required two years of patient field work in the same village to bear fruit—the mushrooms were being peddled to tourists in the streets by every urchin in that town, while tawdry and garish tourist garments festooned with crude mushroom motifs and postcards with photographs of the mushrooms and of María Sabina and other shamans were openly sold [Ott 1975,1993]. María Sabina and some of her Mazatec peers even served jail sentences in Oaxaca City for allegedly pandering to the mushroomic tourist trade [Estrada 1977]. As Wasson commented [Wasson 1961]: "For more than four centuries the Indians have kept the divine mushroom close to their hearts, sheltered from desecration by white men, a precious secret." Tourists seeking shamans or entheogens, whatever their intentions, can only hasten the end of the Age of Entheogens... as Sabina noted [Estrada 1977]:

> Before Wasson, I felt that the mushrooms exalted me. Now I no longer feel this... from the moment the strangers arrived... the mushrooms lost their purity. They lost their power. They decomposed. From that moment on, they no longer worked.

I couldn't express this more decisively or eloquently... It is unspeakably obscene that the holy sacrament be thus desecrated, nay, trivialized; that a spiritual adept of María Sabina's stature be imprisoned like a common criminal! S. Valadez, partisan of Huichol cultural survival and wife of Huichol artist Mariano Valadez, denounced "Guided Tour Spirituality: Cosmic Way or Cosmic Rip-off?" in the pages of *Shaman's Drum*, which had featured her husband's work on one of its covers [Valadez 1986]:

> Westerners who participate in peyote pilgrimages with Huichols… are endangering the Huichols who escort them. The soldiers patrolling the peyote desert are not impressed by Americans who claim they come for enlightenment. The Mexicans think the outsiders come for dope, and accuse the Huichols of dealing drugs to the 'gringo Hippies.'

Holy sacrament as trinket and souvenir is bad enough… but as dope? The true dimensions of the problem come into sharp focus… not only do we profane the sacrament, but we debase the shaman, noble practitioner of humankind's oldest profession, into a sleazy dope-dealer at the mercy of the police! And it is a distressingly short, slippery step… from the inner sanctum… to the slammer!

It is also worth noting that, while shamanism may be contributing to the Entheogenic Reformation, to the reform of Christianity in Africa and the Americas, there has been a concurrent 'Christian Deformation' of shamanism… when Wasson met María Sabina in 1955, her shamanic rites were already heavily corrupted by Christian influences. María Sabina censed her mushrooms before a crude altar bearing cheap iconic prints of the Baptism in Jordan and the Santo Niño de Atocha,[29] she said the mushrooms grew where Jesus Christ had spat on the ground, when the *holy children* spoke to her (in Mazatec) it was Jesus speaking, *etc.* [Wasson *et al.* 1974].

In order that traditional shamanism might live out its last days in peace and dignity, it is imperative that residents of the industrialized world have legal access to shamanic inebriants, and to ecstatic religions, in their own countries. We descendants of western civilization have just as much right to entheogenic drugs, as any Huichol or Mazatec or Comanche Indian—forsooth we've much more need of them as well! But we have no right to descend on what are perforce the least 'civilized' areas of the planet with our money, high-tech gear and morbid interest in 'drugs,' and if it weren't for the Pharmacratic Inquisition, if we weren't so desperate, I submit, we simply wouldn't. Could there ever be a more damning indictment of the spiritual bankruptcy of our vaunted western civilization… than the fact that it has transubstantiated the sacred fruit of the Tree of Life, the veritable well-spring of all culture… into scurvy contraband… made the truth a secret… the *Logos* a dirty word…?

[32]

Agape: Vac or Logos... The Divine Afflatus

> What we were seeing was, we knew, the only reality, of which the counterparts of every day are mere imperfect adumbrations. At the time we ourselves were alive to the novelty of this our discovery, and astonished by it. Whatever their provenience, the blunt and startling fact is that our visions were sensed more clearly, were superior in all their attributes, were more authoritative, for us who were experiencing them, than what passes for mundane reality.
>
> **R. Gordon Wasson**
> *Mushrooms Russia and History* [1957]

Perhaps history really turns in cycles as Giovanni Battista Vico proposed during the eighteenth century in *La Scienza Nuova,* but to his quadripartite[30] scheme of historical cycles—theocratic, aristocratic, democratic and chaotic—we in this chaotic post–Wasson world, with our vastly expanded knowledge of the proto- and pre-history of humankind, must needs add a fifth, primordial cycle, the *shamanic...* appropriately enough, the shamanic cycle embodies the quintessence of our culture, dealing as it does with what the Vedic priests called *Vac* and the Greek philosophers *Logos...* the Divine Afflatus. In 1872, at the age of 28, Friedrich Nietzsche gave voice to a brilliant intuition in his *The Birth of Tragedy from the Spirit of Music*:

> Dionysian stirrings arise... through the influence of those narcotic potions of which all primitive races speak in their hymns... So stirred, the individual forgets himself completely... Not only does the bond between individual men come to be forged anew by the magic of the Dionysian rite, but nature herself, long alienated or subjugated, rises again to celebrate the reconciliation with her prodigal son, man.

Lacking the most rudimentary historical or ethnobotanical data, based solely on intuition inspired by the pangæan 'sacred potion' motifs of ancient hymns, Nietzsche anticipated the Wasson Theory by the better part of a century [Ocaña 1993]. The great German genius conceived of the ancient Greek dichotomy of the Apollonian and Dionysian world-views—the former what some now call 'right-brain,' logical, analytical thinking; the latter so-called 'left-brain,' dream-like, artistic intuition. Thanks to the pioneering work of C.A.P. Ruck—who characterizes the Dionysian world-view as the 'wild' and the Apollonian as the 'cultivated'— we now know the ancient Greeks made liberal use of plant entheogens, to dissolve temporarily the artificial boundaries of ego implicit in our rational, self-conscious thought... that yawning chasm between 'self' and 'other' which isolates each individual human being, not only from her or his fellow Gæan creatures, but from other human beings as well [Ruck 1981,1982,1983]. As Albert Hofmann astutely noted [Hofmann 1980]:

> The Greek genius attempted the cure, by supplementing the... Apollonian world view created by the subject/object cleavage, with the Dionysian world of experience, in which this cleavage is abolished in ecstatic inebriation.

This is what Nietzsche meant by the reconciliation of the prodigal son, humankind, with Our Lady Gæa, from whom humankind is alienated by ego, by self-consciousness. Indeed, religion did not merely derive from ecstatic inebriation, true religion *is* ecstasy, "this inebriacyon or heuenly dronkennesse of the spiryte." The function of religion in human society, reduced to its barest essentials, is to instill in us human beings, by grace of ecstasy, the certainty of our unity with the universe and our fellow creatures, the *unio mystica*... to give us faith in the simple truth enunciated by William Blake 202 years ago, that [Kazin 1946]: "every thing that lives is Holy."

The Pharmacratic Inquisition inaugurated by Alaric in A.D. 395 has systematically attempted to annihilate the Dionysian tradition of antiquity, our source of faith and solace to temper the terrible solitude of self-consciousness. As Hofmann further noted:

> Ecclesiastical Christianity, characterized by the duality of creator and creation, has... largely obliterated the Eleusinian-Dionysian legacy of antiquity... Objective reality, the world-view produced by the spirit of scientific inquiry, is the myth of our time. It has replaced the ecclesiastical-Christian and mythical-Apollonian world view.

I would say this duality of subject/object is the *superstition* of our time, for there is overwhelming scientific and experiential evidence that reassures us we are but one strand in the warp and weft of life, biochemically kindred to every other Gæan lifeform and descended from the same primordial ancestors. This is a treacherous superstition, which has led to the objectification of our planet and all her Gæan creatures. Rather than marvel at the eternally ephemeral, living miracle that is each and every one of our furry, feathered, leafy, spiny or scaly brethren, we see only resources to be exploited; and exploit them we do... so ruthlessly that the extinction of plant

[34]

and animal species, nay, of entire habitats, is an everyday occurrence, and by the time it dawns on us (if it ever does) that we, too, are on the endangered species list, it may be a trifle too late! For scientific hypermaterialism celebrates its apocalyptic marriage to Judeo-Christian dualism in a mesmerizing last tango on the deck of the Titanic, a ghastly *danse macabre* or *Totentanz*... while we watch, awestricken.

This is where the Entheogenic Reformation comes into the picture, restoring to humankind its millennial, healing balsam for the lesions of materialism, its traditional key to ecstasy or the 'withdrawal of the soul from the body'—the ineffable, spiritual, non-materialistic state of being in which the universe is perceived more as energy or spirit than as matter... Blake's 'Eternal Delight,' the archetypal religious experience, the heart and soul of shamanism, well-spring of *all* culture [La Barre 1979]. While Christianity, with its *decretum horribile* of humankind as a special creation, separate from the rest of the universe and enjoined, moreover, to subdue and dominate the planet—with this disastrous core superstition and all of the cataclysmic ecological destruction it has wrought—seems particularly evocative of the Entheogenic Reformation, there is some evidence for a sort of 'archaic revival' in parts of the world that have largely escaped the bane of Christian evangelism.[31]

The classical scholar Mary Barnard [1963] commented on the work of Wasson:

> Looking at the matter coldly, unintoxicated and unentranced, I am willing to prophesy that fifty theo-botanists working for fifty years would make the current theories concerning the origins of much mythology and theology as out-of-date as pre-Copernican astronomy.

Although those who might call themselves *theobotanists* or, perhaps more appropriately *entheobotanists*, number fewer than fifty worldwide, and we yet have nearly two decades to go, I would say Miss Barnard's prophecy is on a sure footing. Wasson declared in 1986, just before he died, that "we are well beyond the stage of hypotheses," and a couple of years later I referred for the first time to the Wasson Theory of the genesis of religions in ecstatic states provoked by entheogenic plants; comparing Wasson rather to Charles Darwin than to Copernicus. Just as Darwin's theory of natural selection provided a natural mechanism to explain the historical *fact* of evolution, Wasson's theory suggested a natural mechanism to explain the historical *fact* that strikingly similar religious concepts arose independently in diverse parts of the terraqueous globe in protohistory, having certain pangæan motifs relating to ecstatic communion with the entheogens, the use of which has likewise been shown to be common virtually to all cultures studied... of the *Axis Mundi* or 'World Tree'

[35]

('Tree of Life,' 'Tree of the Knowledge of Good and Evil,' *etc.*) with its sacred fruit... of communion with a sacrament... of the soul's separability from the body... of the Otherworld... Just as a few fanatical believers in one or another religion to this day refuse to accept Darwin's theory of evolutionary mechanisms, in spite of the overwhelming evidence in its favor; so fanatical believers in one or another religion may refuse to accept the Wasson Theory, no matter how much evidence entheobotanists might adduce in its favor. On the other hand, as surely as scientific opinion changed to accept Darwin's theory as being more plausible than the reigning Judeo-Christian idea of 'special creation' which defied all the evidence of science and our senses, so too will scientific opinion inexorably come to accept the Wasson Theory as being more plausible than the alternative, that "the little toy-room picture of the Bible" [Campbell 1972] or the provincial 'found truth' of any other 'god' or 'chosen people' has a greater claim on reality... or the alternative of Eliade and others who, as Barnard expressed it, "put the desire for an afterlife and the belief in an imaginary nectar of immortality before the experience of actual plants and beverages used in the ceremonial communion with the gods or the ancestors," which she justifiably likened to "putting Medea's chariot before her team of serpents."

I will venture to make my own prophecy, even more polemical than Barnard's. Assuming, which is by no means assured, that our civilization survives another millennium, Christianity and suchlike symbolic, dogmatic religions will prosper only by forsaking the Pharmacratic Inquisition and embracing the Entheogenic Reformation with open arms. Only thus restoring the true sacrament, a genuine agape, the very heart and soul, yea, the central Mystery, to such exsanguinated, purely theoretical, would-be religions, might they recover their spiritual authenticity, hence their meaning and relevance for humankind. Only by abandoning what Blake called their "pale religious letchery," that "ancient curse" of the "black'ning church"... Only by ceasing their "binding with briars" of all human "joys and desires"... Only by admitting that spiritual truth is not some dogma thundered in stentorian tones from the eminence of any pulpit... but more a murmur in the heart, a whisper on the night barely heard over the sigh of the wind in the trees, or the trilling ricochet of rain in their leafy filigree... Only by letting the Word speak for itself... by ceding every pulpit to the primæval *Vac*, the primigenial *Logos*, allowing the gentle breezes of the Divine Afflatus to fill the psychonautic sails of the indomitable human spirit, perpetually embarking on Odysseys of discovery in the universe of the soul... on Gilgamesh's epic pursuit of the 'wondrous plant' of immortality... Jason's errant search for the Golden Fleece... Ponce de León's quixotic quest for the pool of living water... the quintessential elixir of life; the philosophers' stone of immortality...

NOTES

1   In 1978, R. Gordon Wasson convened an informal committee of researchers interested
in the ethnopharmacognosy of shamanic inebriants, to look for a substitute for inadequate terms like 'hallucinogenic' (which implied delusion and/or falsity, besides suggesting
pathology to psychotherapists), 'psychotomimetic' (implying also pathology) and 'psychedelic' (besides being a pejorative term prejudicing shamanic inebriants in the eyes of
persons unfamiliar with the field, this term had become so invested with connotations of
1960s western 'counterculture' as to make it incongruous to speak of a shaman ingesting
a *psychedelic* plant). I have summarized the history of *psychedelic* and *hallucinogenic* in my
recent book *Pharmacotheon*. Members of our committee were classical scholars Carl A.P.
Ruck and Danny Staples of Boston University, and independent entheobotanists Jeremy
Bigwood, Wasson and me. One of Ruck's early suggestions was *epoptic* from the Greek
epoptai to describe initiates to the Eleusinian Mysteries who had seen *ta hiera*, 'the holy.'
Wasson didn't like this term… as he said, it sounded like 'pop, goes the weasel'! I proposed *pharmacotheon*, which had the advantage of already being in the *Oxford English
Dictionary*, but it seemed too much of a mouthful, besides not adapting gracefully to the
adjectival form. We finally settled on the neologism *entheogen[ic]*, from the Greek *entheos*,
a term used in the classical world to describe prophetic or poetic inspiration. The term
means literally 'becoming divine within,' and can be seen as the user realizing that the
divine infuses all of the creation, or specifically that the *entheogenic* plant is itself infused
with the divine. It is *not* a theological term, makes no reference to any deity, and is not
meant to be a pharmacological term for designating a specific chemical class of drugs (*psychedelic*, for example, has come to be seen by some *sensu strictu* as a term to designate mes-
caline-like β-phenethylamines or DMT–like tryptamines). Rather, it is a cultural term to
include all of the shamanic inebriants—sacraments, plant-teachers, the stock-in-trade of
shamans the world over. As Bernard Ortíz de Montellano has pointed out, this word best
reflects traditional conceptions of shamanic inebriation, as indicated by ancient Náhuatl
terms *itech quinehua* 'it takes possession of him' or *itech quiza* 'it comes out in him' to describe this [Ortíz de Montellano 1990]. We launched the neologism in the *Journal of Psychedelic Drugs*, in an issue which I edited and in which I suggested the name be changed
to *Journal of Entheogenic Drugs* [Ruck *et al.* 1979]. This didn't come to pass, but I think
I influenced the editors to change the name to *Journal of Psychoactive Drugs* two years later,

consigning *psychedelic* ever more to the obscurity it deserves. By my count, our new word has appeared in print in at least seven languages; the major European languages plus Catalán, and has been widely accepted by many leading experts in the field. I expect the recent publication of my *Pharmacotheon* to establish the word more solidly in the English-, German- and Spanish-speaking worlds.

² Even with the limited availability of starting materials and chemical reagents under the modern 'War on Drugs,' LSD can be manufactured for a pittance. At the peak of its demand as the sixties gave way to the seventies, LSD sold for about U.S.$4000 *per* gram in the United States. One gram represents 10,000 doses of 100 mcg, or a wholesale cost of about $0.40 *per* dose. At this time, ergotamine tartrate, the most rational starting material for black-market manufacture of LSD, was selling for about $30,000 *per* kilogram, from which LSD could be made at about a 30% yield in primitive and large-scale conditions. Assuming 3.0 kg of ergotamine tartrate and $10,000 worth of ancillary reagents, equipment and collateral costs, one kilogram of LSD could be manufactured for roughly U.S.$100,000. This kilogram of LSD would represent 10 million doses, or a production cost of $0.01 *per* dose. Even when the wholesale value of LSD dropped below $2000 *per* gram in the late 1970s and early 1980s, this still represented 20-fold value-added, a sizable profit margin. In the early days of the LSD market, doses of 250–300 mcg were common, but the average dose quickly dropped to 100 mcg, then below; and today more likely hovers around the 50 mcg level (1.0 kg = 20 million doses!) [Brown & Malone 1973; Marnell 1993; Ratcliffe 1973].

³ As I summarized in great detail in *Pharmacotheon*, there is much confusion in lay use of terminology relating to the provenience of drugs. The term *synthetic* refers to the manner of manufacture and is not a qualitative term. Drugs may be either *natural* (if they have been found to occur in plants or animals) or *artificial* (if they have not). Even *natural* drugs may be *synthetic*, if they are manufactured by human artifice. Psilocybine and DMT are examples of *synthetic natural products*, as these have mostly been laboratory-made. Any *artificial* drug can be assumed to be so only provisionally, as *artificial* compounds, creations of the laboratory, frequently are found, with further research, to be *natural* drugs. Again, DMT is the perfect example. First synthesized in 1931, it existed as an *artificial* drug for 24 years, until it was definitively shown to be a *natural* drug and a putative active principle of *cohoba* or *yopo* snuff (see *Pharmacotheon*) [Fish *et al.* 1955; Manske 1931; Ott 1993]. It is the height of folly and presumption to embrace some drugs, on the basis of their being *natural*, and to reject others, in the naive belief they are *artificial*—we cannot know which presumably *artificial* compounds will later, like DMT, *Valium*® and polyester, be found in fact to be natural products!

⁴ In the ancient Indian *RgVeda*, the oldest of the four *Vedas* and a fundamental sacred scripture of Hinduism, which dates from the middle of the second millennium before the modern era, exalted poetry is directed to *soma* which was, at once, a god, a plant, and the juice of that plant. R. Gordon Wasson devoted the better part of a decade to the concerted study of *soma*, and his book *Soma: Divine Mushroom of Immortality*, besides being a masterpiece of the writer's and bookmaker's art, is one of the greatest and most important

[38]

scientific books of all history [Wasson 1968]. The *RgVeda* repeatedly alludes to the *soma* potion—most decidedly an entheogen, as Vedist Wendy Doniger has asserted—by the name *amrta* (sometimes written *amrita* or *amreeta*, as it would be pronounced) [Doniger O'Flaherty 1982]. This word should be translated as 'pharmacotheon' or 'entheogen,' although the *Oxford English Dictionary* gives 'immortal, ambrosial.' To be sure, the cognate term in Greek is *ambrosia*, the legendary food or, more precisely, *drink* of the Olympian gods, which was obviously in origin an entheogen like *soma*, if not identical to it (indeed, the evidence would indicate that both *soma/amrta* and *ambrosia/nectar* were originally entheogenic mushrooms). For further details, the interested reader is referred to my yet-unfinished *Pharmacotheon II: Entheogenic Plants and the Origins of Religions*.

5   In the title of my recent book *Ayahuasca Analogues: Pangæan Entheogens* [Ott 1994], I coined the term *pangæan* to describe anything of international, intercontinental, world-wide distribution. In the past, the term 'universal' has been used to refer to such, but in this era of interplanetary space-probes, our horizons have been expanded well beyond the confines of this planet, and I suggest it is rather provincial, to say nothing of presumptuous, to characterize a world-wide phenomenon as 'universal.' On the other hand, we are at a loss for words to describe ourselves in the cosmic scheme of things, as residents of this third planet in distance from the star we call the Sun. We call this planet *Earth*, and we might be *Earthians*, clumsy 'though this may sound. Some have proposed the more graceful term *Terrans*, after the Latin name for *earth* which, like that Teutonic word *earth*, in reality refers to the soil, the ground, the solid surface of the planet. Objections have been raised to the use of such a name for a planet whose most distinguishing characteristic in this solar system is its abundance of liquid water, which covers far more of the surface than solid ground—but are we then Aquans or Aquarians, we denizens of high ground; and what of the air or oxygen-rich gaseous atmosphere which is just as vital a part of the biosphere as its water and mineral composition? I need not mention that those opposed to astrology would object strenuously to calling themselves Aquarians! In Spanish there exists the lovely term *terráqueo[a]* used in common parlance to denote the planet or *Tierra* as *la faz terráquea* ('the terraqueous surface') or *el globo terráqueo* ('the terraqueous globe') which precise phrase was used in English in 1664; and *terraqueous* maintains a tenuous currency in botanical English [*Oxford English Dictionary*, Compact Edition, p. 3267]. Again, we are slighting the atmosphere here, and it seems a bit of a mouthful to call ourselves *Terraqueans*, and I might justifiably be deemed daft to propose we call ourselves *Terræroaqueans*... For the sake of simplicity, of poetic beauty and tradition, I introduced in my above-mentioned book the term *Gæan* to describe a denizen of this planet, which by analogy would be called *Gæa*, the name of the Greek earth-goddess, and the source of the name *Pangæa* to describe the primordial super-continent of plate-tectonics theory. Since Gæa was the spouse of Uranus, whose name has already been given to a planet in our solar system, this is an appropriate choice, and there is decidedly a poetic beauty in calling ourselves *Gæan* creatures. See also notes 6 and 7 below.

6   An obsolete name for the 'Old World' is *Palæogæa* [*Oxford English Dictionary*, Compact Edition, p. 2056] and the adjective *palæogæan* was introduced to the English language in

1857. I have decided to resurrect this obsolete term to replace the cumbersome binomial *Old World* which does not lend itself gracefully to the adjectival form ('Old Worldian,' 'Old Worldly'?), and to coin the parallel designations *Neogæa* and *neogæan* to refer to the so-called 'New World,' after the analogy of *Palæolithic/Neolithic* [earlier and later Stone Age; *Oxford English Dictionary*, Compact Edition, pp. 1912, 2056].

[7] The name of the ancient classical Mother Earth-Goddess is spelled either Gaia or Gæa. The former is pronounced as in German *Gäa*, '**gay** uh,' although the ugly mispronunciation '**guy** uh' has taken root in the English-speaking world, making the name of the most feminine of deities sound almost masculine! I prefer the alternate orthography, Gæa, pronounced '**jee** uh' (as in *Pangæa*, the primordial super-continent of geological [Gæa-logical] plate-tectonics theory; *Gea* or '**hay** uh' in Spanish). We thus have a satisfying family of words, based on the name of the Greek earth-goddess *Gæa* for our planet; we as *Gæan* creatures; *pangæan* as adjective to replace the shopworn and provincial 'universal' for a world-wide phenomenon; *Palæogæa* and *Neogæa* to describe what we are now obliged to call the Old and New Worlds, with the adjectives *palæogæan* and *neogæan*. Those who modernize orthography would thus use *Gea, Gean, pangean, Paleogea, Neogea, paleogean, neogean…*

[8] As R. Gordon Wasson [1968] detailed in *Soma: Divine Mushroom of Immortality*, and as I outlined in *Pharmacotheon* [Ott 1993], Eliade, in his books *Shamanism: Archaic Techniques of Ecstasy* [1951] and *Yoga: Immortality and Freedom* [1954] committed an anachronism while discussing Siberian shamanism, when he described "intoxication by drugs (hemp, mushrooms, tobacco *etc.*)" as a recent phenomenon representing "a decadence among the shamans of the present day," a point he repeated over and over again without citing any references. However, on linguistic grounds, the use of entheogenic mushrooms in Siberia can be traced back at least 6 to 8 millennia, and petroglyphs on the Pegtymel' River in the territory of the Chukotka peoples suggest mushroomic inebriation has been a feature of shamanism for at least 3 millennia. On the other hand, both alcohol and tobacco were introduced to Siberia after contact with the outside world, which commenced *circa* 1580 with Yermak's invasion. Not only were entheogenic mushrooms an ancient and integral feature of Siberian shamanism, but tobacco was, and remains, the shamanic drug *par excellence* in Neogæa [Wilbert 1987], and *Cannabis* or hemp is among humankind's oldest cultigens and inebriants. The adoption of tobacco by Siberian shamans represented, as Wasson [1968] said, "recapturing for it the religious meaning that it has always had for the American Indians"—is this degeneration? Hardly… it shows that Siberian shamanism remained healthy in historical times, living and growing by adopting a shamanic inebriant that American descendants had been using for millennia. It also shows the inquiring, experimentalist, scientific mind-set of traditional shamans, which is so evident today in Amazonia [Ott 1994]. Just before his death, Eliade evaded an interview by one of his students on the subject of 'sacred substances and the history of religion,' confessing "I do not know anything about them" and noting "I don't like these plants!" [Forte 1988]. Wasson was to penetrate to the very heart of the subject four years after the publication of Eliade's detailed study of shamanism, and the great strides made in the field subsequently have shown that Eliade missed the mark completely and that, blinded by his

moralistic prejudice against inebriants, he failed to understand the essence of a subject that he studied in exhaustive detail... failed to preceive the breathtaking vista which presented itself to Wasson, of "a prodigious miracle, inspiring... poetry and philosophy and religion" [Wasson 1961].

[9] In an interesting paper published in 1972, G.L. Klerman discussed "Psychotropic hedonism vs pharmacological Calvinism" [see *Hastings Center Report* 2(4): 1–3]. Klerman had first used the term 'pharmacological Calvinism' two years earlier ["Drugs and social values" *International Journal of the Addictions* 5: 313–319, 1970]. John Calvin or Jean Chauvin, the abstemious French Protestant, with the Swiss Huldreich Zwingli a sort of spiritual father of Puritanism, was fanatically opposed to sensualism in all its forms—not the classic pleasures of the flesh merely, but promiscuous bathing, dancing, theater... even sleeping or laughing in church, fighting, swearing, *etc*. But Calvin was no teetotaler [E.A. Wasson 1914], and 'though it be tempting to see in the intolerant Chauvin's name the origin of the word *chauvinism*, that dubious distinction rather devolves to a Napoleonic soldier, Nicolas Chauvin [*Oxford English Dictionary*, Compact Edition, p. 386]. See also Note 20.

[10] As far as can be determined, R. Gordon Wasson and his photographer Allan Richardson became the first outsiders, whites, intentionally to ingest the entheogenic mushrooms now known to contain psilocybine and related compounds, when they were initiated by the Mazatec shaman María Sabina in the village of Huautla de Jiménez in the Sierra Madre Oriental of the southern Mexican state of Oaxaca [Ott 1993]. Wasson, who had gone to México as a pilgrim "seeking the Grail," and who had marvelled as a boy about the Eleusinian Mysteries and the lost Vedic entheogen *soma*, was prepared to enter sympathetically into the ways of preliterate peoples, and was the first to recognize in shamanism the veritable "well-springs of cultural history" [Wasson 1961].

[11] From the time of the *RgVeda*, *circa* 1500 B.C. to the end of the fourth century of our era, there was celebrated an annual initiation into the sacred Mysteries of Eleusis at a temple near Athens. Anyone speaking Greek and having the price of admission was accepted for initiation, but only once in a lifetime. Most of the leading intellectuals of antiquity were initiates, and many testified to the value of the experience which was "new, astonishing, inaccessible to rational cognition." Of their experience initiates or *mystai* could only say they had see *ta hiera*, 'the holy'—it was forbidden by law, under penalty of death, to say more. From the fragmentary hints of several writers, from an anonymous seventh century B.C. poem called the *Homeric Hymn to Demeter* (which described the founding of the Mystery cult by Demeter, grief-stricken over the abduction of her daughter Persephone by Hades), from a fresco at Pompeii, we know that the initiates drank a potion called the *kykeon* or 'mixture' preparatory to experiencing a soul-shattering vision which was forever to enrich their lives and convert them into *epoptai*, those who had seen. In 1977 R. Gordon Wasson, Albert Hofmann and Carl A.P. Ruck unveiled the hoary secret of the Mysteries which had been guarded for 3500 years, when they proposed that the *kykeon* was an entheogenic potion containing LSD-like ergoline alkaloids. The reader is referred to their *The Road to Eleusis: Unveiling the Secret of the Mysteries* [Wasson *et al.* 1978,1980]

for details, and to *Pharmacotheon* [Ott 1993] for a summary of this revolutionary theory.

[12] In two tumultuous centuries, Christianity went from harried and persecuted brotherhood to state religion of the Roman Empire, or what was left of it... the Christians went from food for the lions in the Colosseum to the avenging persecutors of the pagan past. Constantine became the ruler of the western empire in A.D. 306, and decided not to observe Diocletian's persecution of the Christians (for the previous six decades, various emperors had vacillated in this persecution; Decius ordered the persecution in 249 but was killed a year later; Valerian inaugurated another persecution in 257, but was captured by the Persians two years hence; his son Gallienus rescinded the persecution and so matters stood until 303, when Diocletian annulled the edict of Gallienus), and when he reunited the fragmented empire in 324, he convened the famous Council of Nicea the following year, where some 300 Christian bishops established an orthodox creed, backed by the power of the imperial government. Thus Christianity, or a particular dogmatic form of it, became the state religion, and Constantine immediately moved the capital of the empire to 'Constantinople' in 330, and the following year decreed expropriation of the property of all pagan temples. Sixty years later, during the reign of Theodosius I, pagan worship *itself* was prohibited, all religions but Christianity outlawed. The last two decades of the fourth century proved cataclysmic for the pagan tradition of the ancient world. In 381 the Council of Constantinople declared the Doctrine of the Trinity and affirmed Christianity as the state religion; five years later the Manichæan Augustine converted to Christianity and denounced his Iranian religion of Mani; another five years later, in 391, Theodosius I banned pagan worship entirely and that year the emboldened Bishop Theophilus I led one of the great destructions of pagan books and 'lascivious' paintings and sculptures in the library of Alexandria; then four years later the Goth King Alaric sacked the sanctuary at Eleusis, spiritual beacon or *omphalos* of the ancient world. Another fifteen years later this same Alaric sacked Rome itself, prompting that same apostate Augustine to write *De Civitate Dei*, an *apologia* to explain away the embarrassing fact that Rome had prospered for a millennium under its pagan gods, but fell in a few decades under the novel Christian dispensation [Campbell 1964; Escohotado 1989; Garraty & Gay 1972; Mylonas 1961].

[13] The Doctrine of Transubstantiation was an eleventh century mediæval contribution to Catholic dogma, a key element in a total of seven 'sacraments'—baptism, confirmation, penance, Eucharist, marriage, ordination, and extreme unction. Catholic dogma and practice surrounding these 'sacraments' was the main catalyst of the Reformation, which commenced with Martin Luther's 95 theses against indulgences (sacrament of penance), nailed to the door of the castle church in Wittenberg, Saxony in October 1517. Chaucer's wicked parody of the "gentil Pardoner" among his 14th century pilgrims to Canterbury (written some 130 years before Luther's fateful theses) masterfully sets the stage: "For in his male he hadde a pilwe-beer,/Which that he seyde was Oure Lady veyl:/He seyde he hadde a gobet of the seyl/That Seint Peter hadde, whan that he wente/Upon the see, till Jhesu Crist hym hente./He hadde a croys of latoun ful of stones,/And in a glas he hadde pigges bones./But with thise relikes, whan that he fond/A povre person dwellyng upon lond,/Upon a day he gat hym moore moneye/Than that the person gat in monthes

tweye:/And thus, with feyned flaterye and japes,/He made the person and the peple his apes./But trewely to tellen atte laste,/He was in chirche a noble ecclesiaste." [Pratt 1966]. Luther attacked the Pardoner's craft, the selling or papal transferal of 'extra' merit accumulated by Jesus, Mary and the saints, to remit sins that otherwise would be paid for in purgatory! Essentially, the mediæval Church had convinced Christendom that all human beings were damned, but for god's grace through the seven sacraments, which could only be obtained from priests, who were in the habit of selling them to the highest bidder! Luther differed from Swiss Protestant Huldreich Zwingli in the matter of the Doctrine of Transubstantiation. Although both rejected this doctrine as sophistical and unscriptural, and both rejected all the sacraments but baptism and the Eucharist, in their famous debate at Marburg in October 1529, they quibbled over the interpretation of the verb *est* in Matthew 26:26, *Hoc est corpus meum*, "This is my body," of St. Jerome's fourth century Latin or Vulgate Bible, the scriptural basis for the sacrament of the Eucharist. Luther held that *est* meant *is*, while Zwingli maintained that it meant *significat*, *represents* or *stands for*. Luther redefined the sacrament of the Eucharist, elaborating his own Doctrine of Consubstantiation; that the Eucharist lacked any intrinsic power or virtue, which were functions merely of the faith of the individual, although Christ *was* present in the Eucharist, coexisting with the bread and wine, which remained simple bread and wine and were not *transubstantiated* as Church dogma had it. Zwingli, on the other hand, insisted that the Eucharist was a mere symbol, a commemoration of the Last Supper by imitation; that the bread and wine were not transubstantiated, neither was Christ present in them, however strong the believer's faith. Zwingli, to be sure, was correct as to the symbolic nature of the Eucharist, 'though neither he, nor Luther, nor Pope Leo X, nor any believing Christian to this day realized that it was symbolic of the primordial entheogen, "the original element in all the Holy Suppers of the world" which had been "gradually replaced by harmless Elements in a watering down of the original fearful sacrament"; that "mighty springboard for primitive man's imagination" that evoked "the miracle of awe in the presence of God" [Wasson 1959]. In primigenial, experiential religions, the faithful become so by virtue of their *experience* of ecstasy catalyzed by the sacrament... their faith thus derives from the awesome power of the sacrament; the sacrament does not acquire its power from their faith! The sacrament "carried its own conviction in the miracles it performed within" the communicants, who were "not obliged to accept the dogma of Transubstantiation in order to know that they had partaken of the body of Christ" [Wasson 1959]. Luther and Zwingli (not to slight Conrad Grebel, Menno Simons, John Calvin and other Protestants) brought down the mighty theocracy of mediæval Catholicism by showing its sacraments to be without substance... but they perceived only a minuscule fraction of the degree of fraud implicit in the *placebo* (see following Note) sacrament of the Eucharist and the Doctrine of Transubstantiation. We might allow ourselves to be amused by the absurdity and sophistry of Luther and Zwingli's 'monk's quarrel' (as the Pope had dismissed Luther's theses against indulgences) over the degree of activity of a *symbolic* sacrament; both failing to realize what a *real* sacrament was! On the other hand, it would be presumptuous to so ridicule truly courageous men who risked everything for their principles, for a Reformation which could be faulted only by lamenting that it didn't go far enough. Luther and Zwingli had not the benefit of our modern ethnopharmacognostical knowledge in the matter of plant sacraments. And we would do well to be humble… if we can be certain of anything, it is that *our* understanding of history and science is woefully inadequate and partial; many of *our* ideas certain to inspire the amusement and condescension of our descendants.

[14] Ironically, the term *placebo*, which today refers in pharmacology to 'a substance containing no medication and given merely to humor a patient,' comes from the Latin Vespers of the Office of the Dead in Catholic liturgy. It means in Latin 'I shall be pleasing or acceptable,' and denotes in English 'a flatterer, sycophant, parasite' after Chaucer's use of *Placebo* as a character's name in "the Marchantes tale" of his 1386 *Tales of Caunterbury* [*Oxford English Dictionary*, Compact Edition, p. 2192; Pratt 1966]. In strictly pharmacological terms, the Christian Eucharist is a classic *placebo*, and the sense of 'to humor' or 'to please' in the Latin *placebo* is apposite, in that *Eucharist* derives from the Greek ευχαριστια, 'thanksgiving, grateful' [*Oxford English Dictionary*, Compact Edition, p. 902]. Historically, given the fact that the Christian Eucharist is an imposture, a phony sacrament to dissuade the unwary believer from trying the real thing, we might choose stronger words than 'sycophant' or 'parasite' for the hieratic perpetrators of such a fraud.

[15] The so-called 'Dark Ages' are defined as 'the entire period from the end of classical civilization to the revival of learning in the West' [*The Illustrated Heritage Dictionary of the English Language*, Vol. I, p. 335]. This term was coined by intellectuals of the self-described 'Renaissance' in the fifteenth to sixteenth centuries, to disparage the millennium that separated them from the fall of the classical world which, as we discussed in Note 12 above, took place decisively in the final two decades of the fourth century [Garraty & Gay 1972]. The fact is inescapable that the millennium-long crepusculum of the Dark Ages commenced with the extinction of pagan religion grounded in personal, ecstatic experiences of the divine, and its replacement by purely symbolic religion free of ecstasy, devoid of religious experiences, which prospered only when backed by imperial force—creed and rote dogma in place of that faith-inspiring ecstasy which 'carried its own conviction,' inflexible theocracy instead of that religious democracy which had characterized the pagan world [Escohotado 1989]. We define the end of the Dark Ages and the dawning of the Renaissance by the rebirth and rejuvenation of the arts and sciences, *somewhat* liberated by political and economic changes, not to slight the Reformation discussed in Note 13, from the rigid, iron control of a theocratic empire. In other words, the forced imposition of Christianity as state religion in the reign of Constantine, far from being a progressive change, as Christians would have us think, plunged Europe into a millennium of atavism and book burning, of barbarous destruction and desecration of classical art and literature, in which the torch of science and learning, lit in such a promising fashion by the Greek philosophers, was all but extinguished, and during which the hard-won pharmacognostical and other scientific knowledge of the ancients was forgotten, if not lost completely. The secret of Demeter's potion, her *kykeon*, was entombed as surely as the geometry of Euclid, in the wake of one barbaric conflagration after another. I suggest that, as far as religion goes, we are *still* in the Dark Ages, and that the Entheogenic Reformation at last heralds the dawning of the Entheogenic Renaissance, a *spiritual* Renaissance which hopefully will do for religions what the mediæval Renaissance did for art and science a half-millennium ago.

[16] As Thomas Szasz and others have pointed out, autochthonous European midwives and shamans or herbalists, sometimes called 'white witches' or 'sorceresses,' were prominent targets of the Inquisition and of witch-hunts, sometimes held in higher opprobrium even than the so-called 'black witches,' for the effrontery of presuming to cure—illness was regarded to be god's punishment for sin; its cure a spiritual matter for the 'Doctors of the Church' [Forbes 1962, 1966; Szasz 1970]. For the poor, prayer or holy water would have to suffice; the rich had their Arab and Jewish physicians. While the Spanish Inquisition was established in 1478 to ferret our apostates among Jews who had been forced to convert to Catholicism (it became a capital heresy to practice Judaism in Spain), seemingly a case of religious rivalry and intolerance, the prominence of Jews among physicians is significant, and the slander of Jews as poisoners of Christians, which reverberated even into the twentieth century, points to the pharmacratic aspect of the persecution of Jews. The Inquisition was also directed against scientists, the most famous cases being the burning at the stake of Giordano Bruno in 1600 and the trial of Galileo 32 years later for the crime of teaching Copernican theory. Some persecuted scientists were medical men who transgressed prohibitions against dissection and other means of studying the human body and disease—an example is Michael Servetus, burned as a heretic in Geneva in 1553. Finally, the magician—deriving from *magos*, the Greek name for Persian priestly astrologers— was an important target of the Inquisition, and it has been argued that the witchcraft persecutions involved ancient ideas of the conjuring of spirits by magicians or thaumaturges. This theory holds that the prototype for the mediæval Inquisition is archaic persecutions, first of the Bacchanalia in Rome in B.C. 186, then of the early Christians; who were thus merely turning the tables in mediæval times and stigmatizing dissident groups as they had been stigmatized by imperial Rome, before Christianity became the state religion [Cohn 1975; Peters 1978]. Antonio Escohotado saw in the Roman persecution of the Bacchanalia the prototype for the contemporary War on Drugs [Escohotado 1989].

[17] Due to the zealotry of the bowdlerizing Christians, referred to in Note 15, we know but little of European traditional use of entheogens. From proceedings of various public trials against so-called witches, from the famous manual for witch-hunters, the 1486 *Malleus Maleficarum* of Heinrich Krämer and James Sprenger, from the 1589 *Magia Naturalis* by Giovanni Battista Della Porta and the 1536 *De Præstigiis Dæmonum* of Johann Weyer, we know that the Inquisition was especially preoccupied with the surviving use of the so-called 'witches' salves' or 'witches' ointments,' known to have contained many entheogenic plants, like *Atropa belladonna* L., henbane or *Hyoscyamus niger* L., mandrake or *Mandragora officinarum* L., *Datura* species; as well as some suspected entheogens like *Acorus calamus* L., *Nymphaea* spp. and *Lolium temulentum* L. [Clark 1921; De Vries 1991; Fletcher 1896; Gari 1987; Hansen 1978; Harner 1973; Schleiffer 1979]. These unguents were sometimes applied to vaginal mucosa with staffs or broomsticks, and were said to induce a sensation of flying, thus are known also as 'flying ointments'—the witch flying on her broomstick survives to this day in Hallowe'en folklore, and in famous artistic representations like Goya's immortal *Cocina de las Brujas* and *Linda Maestra*—the Spanish genius masterfully depicted the visionary effects of the ointments in *El Aquelarre*. Frans Francken's sixteenth century *The Witches' Kitchen* beautifully depicts the preparation, application, æronautic

and visionary properties of the ointments (see Gari 1987 and Harner 1973 for reproductions of Goya and Francken). Italian Della Porta and Spaniard Andrés Fernández de Laguna (physician to Pope Julius III) reported crude experiments with these ointments in the sixteenth century, and in modern times the effectiveness of some recorded recipes for such 'flying ointments' has been documented by intrepid psychonauts like Karl Kiesewetter, who died as a result of one such experiment, and by Siegbert Ferckel, Will-Erich Peuckert and Gustav Schenk (see Schleiffer 1979 for extracts and references). In his famous *De Nugiis Curialium* (normally translated as *Courtiers' Trifles*, *Courtly Vices* is a more appropriate translation for the title of this *exposé* of magic, witchcraft and suchlike heretical practices, written between 1181 and 1193 by Walter Map, ecclesiast and official to King Henry II), Map denounced the place for magic—conjuring, fortune-telling, sorcery, preparation of philtres or love potions—symbolized by the famous Merlin of Arthurian romances, in English courts of his day [Cohn 1975; Peters 1978]. Map made reference to surviving use in the twelfth century of 'heavenly food' or sacramental entheogens by sects of heretics, commenting "Often you will see… angelic visions… you can visit whatsoever place you wish without delay or difficulties" (cited by Lee & Shlain 1985, in their interesting social history of LSD which touched briefly on my subject). The Albigensian Crusade inaugurated by Pope Innocent [*sic*] III in 1209, and in which perhaps a million people were brutally killed in southern France, was directed against Manichæism, against followers of Mani, the third century Iranian prophet—Joseph Campbell referred to Catharism or Albigensianism as "a resurgent variant of the Manichean religion." Although the first Albigensians were burned at the stake in Orléans in 1017, it was Innocent's slave army of 200,000 foot soldiers and 20,000 cavalry that committed the major slaughter [Campbell 1964]. Now, it happens that the theatre of the Albigensian Crusade, the south of France and adjacent areas of Euzkadi (Basque Country) and Catalunya, constitutes an enclave of *mycophilia* within generally *mycophobic* Europe (neologisms devised by Valentina P. and R. Gordon Wasson for cultures loving and hating mushrooms, respectively) [Wasson & Wasson 1957]. There exists intriguing evidence that the Cathars or Albigensians may have utilized *Amanita muscaria* (L. ex Fr.) Pers. ex Gray as sacrament. Recalling, as mentioned in Note 12 above, that St. Augustine had been a Manichæan before his conversion to Christianity in 386, it is significant that after his apostasy Augustine wrote *De Moribus Manichæorum* or "On the Ways of the Manichæans," in which he denounced them for, among other vices, eating mushrooms; or more specifically, eating *Amanitas*, as he used the Latin name for *Amanitas*, *boletos*, and also disparaged their eating of truffles, *tubera* [Fericgla 1985; Wasson 1968]. He could hardly have been talking about *Amanita caesarea* (Fr.) Schw., favored food of the ancient Romans through the contemporary Italians [Wasson 1972b], and yet another clue points to *Amanita muscaria*. In China, contemporaneous with the persecution of Albigensians, a Chinese official named Lu Yu (1125–1209) denounced the Manichæans for eating *red mushrooms*. The Chinese, as is well known, are hardly mycophobes, and surely there must have been something special about those *red* mushrooms to have attracted the opprobrium of Lu Yu (Manichæism was introduced into China in the late seventh and early eighth centuries, and had considerable impact on the Taoists, with their famous icon of the *ling chih*, or the 'divine mushroom of immortality') [Wasson 1968]. In this context, it is important to note that ludible use of *Amanita muscaria* survives to this day in Catalunya

[Fericgla 1992]! While it is true we have no direct proof that the European Manichæans used *Amanita muscaria* as a sacrament, as Joseph Campbell pointed out, "since the writings of the Albigensian Cathari have been destroyed, and our knowledge of their practice comes mainly from their enemies, little can be said of the fine points." [Campbell 1964]. Inasmuch as the Christians were determined to efface all memory of religious ecstasy, it is logical that details of sacramental communion by a rival faith might be suppressed. Given the very ferocity of the Albigensian Crusade, the testimony of Augustine and Lu Yu, and the surviving use of *Amanita muscaria* in Catalunya, we are justified in suspecting the sacramental use of entheogenic mushrooms among the Cathars, and there is no question subsequent witch-hunts were, at least in part, pharmacologically motivated. Shortly after the Albigensian Crusades, around 1250, German Albertus Magnus made reference to the visionary properties of *A. muscaria* and referred to yet another mushroom capable of producing 'insanity.' The linguistic fossil *Narrenschwamm* or 'fool's mushroom' survives in contemporary German, in Hungarian, as *bolond gomba* and in Slovakian as *salené huby*. Just as an Austrian might ask of one behaving strangely *hast du denn die verrückten Schwammerln gegessen?* ("have you perchance eaten the crazy mushrooms?") [Wasson & Wasson 1957], a contemporary Catalán might question whether the oddball were *tocat del bolet* ("touched by the mushroom" or rather "touched by the *Amanita*") [Fericgla 1985].

[18] For a review of the botany, phytochemistry and ethnopharmacognosy of the hundreds of neogæan entheogenic plants, see *The Botany and Chemistry of Hallucinogens* [Schultes & Hofmann 1980] and *Pharmacotheon: Entheogenic Drugs, Their Plant Sources and History* [Ott 1993]. For more detailed treatment of individual shamanic inebriants, see: 1) (for entheogenic mushrooms) *Les Champignons Hallucinogènes du Mexique* [Heim & Wasson 1958], *Teonanácatl: Hallucinogenic Mushrooms of North America* [Ott & Bigwood 1978], and *The Wondrous Mushroom: Mycolatry in Mesoamerica* [Wasson 1980]; 2) (for *péyotl*) *Peyote: The Divine Cactus* [Anderson 1980], *The Peyote Cult* [La Barre 1938], *La Plante qui Fait les Yeux Émerveillés—Le Peyotl* [Rouhier 1927] and *Peyote Religion: A History* [Stewart 1987]; 3) (for *ayahuasca*) *Ayahuasca Visions: The Religious Iconography of a Peruvian Shaman* [Luna & Amaringo 1991], *Ayahuasca: Etnomedicina y Mitología* [Naranjo 1983] and *Ayahuasca Analogues: Pangæan Entheogens* [Ott 1994]; and 4) (for tobacco) *Tobacco and Shamanism in South America* [Wilbert 1987].

[19] It is evident that the Mesoamerican Indians, on being told of the Christian mass and being invited to take Communion, expected the Host to be a great entheogen, perhaps superior to their own, in proportion as the European military, navigational, and metallurgical technology was superior to theirs. They were severely disappointed, and they immediately realized that the Eucharist was a placebo entheogen. Some of the Spanish chroniclers from the sixteenth century noted the disquieting parallel between Christian Communion and the Indian rites they were unable to perceive as the source of this Christian symbol. As Friar Toribio de Benavente, known as Motolinía [Motolinía 1971] noted of the Aztec entheogenic mushrooms: "They called these mushrooms *teunamacatlth* in their language, which means 'flesh of god,' or of the devil that they worshipped, and in this manner, with this bitter food, they received their cruel god in communion."

[47]

[20] While the Inquisition as a juridical branch of the Vatican is justifiably infamous, I must stress that the so-called 'Reformed' churches also celebrated *autos de fe*, and burned their share of witches and heretics. Martin Luther himself was a prominent anti-Semite who wrote ominously in 1543: "if the Jews refuse to convert, we ought not to suffer them or bear with them any longer." John Calvin led a pogrom against witches in Geneva in 1545, culminating in the execution of 31 people [Szasz 1970]. Nazi Germany was hardly a Catholic country. The Reformation started by Luther in 1517 was as much political and ethical as religious and spiritual... it had more to do with the political and lucrative aspects of religion than with the authenticity, or lack thereof, of religious experiences.

[21] During the administration of Theodore Roosevelt, the United States attempted to embarrass the government of Great Britain (which had been financing its importation of tea and silks from China by trading opium from its Indian colonies, having waged several 'Opium Wars' to force the Chinese to accept opium instead of gold and silver), by convening a series of international conferences on the 'opium problem,' thus advancing the cause of the U.S. as a moral beacon for the world's masses [Beeching 1975; Musto 1973]. Since opium was legal in the United States, it suddenly became necessary to illegalize it, so to strengthen the U.S. position at the talks. Unemployment and racism, fueling the nascent labor movement, resulted in stigmatizing minorities and foreign immigrants—the Chinese *via* opium, the blacks *via* cocaine, and the Mexicans *via* marijuana—leading to propaganda campaigns associating these groups with 'dangerous drugs' and to the eventual illegalization of said drugs [Helmer 1975]. See: *Religion and Drink* [E.A. Wasson 1914], *Historia General de las Drogas* [Escohotado 1989], *Drugs and Minority Oppression* [Helmer 1975], *Ceremonial Chemistry: The Ritual Persecution of Drugs, Addicts and Pushers* [Szasz 1974] and *The American Disease: Origins of Narcotic Control* [Musto 1973] for the story of this 'American disease' of prohibition.

[22] The Bwiti ritual involves periodic (weekly or quarterly) nocturnal ceremonies of group communion, called *ngozé*, in which the initiates to the cult ingest low to moderate doses of powdered *iboga* root to achieve a state of *nlem myore* or 'one heart,' passing the night dancing and singing. To become an initiate, devotees must undergo a three-day ordeal involving massive doses of *iboga* root which lead to a state of unconsciousness and physical insensibility approximating death, culminating in a beatific vision and a subsequent spiritual and literal rebirth [Samorini 1993]. The visionary and stimulating properties of *iboga* root are due to its high content (up to 6%) of indole alkaloids, especially ibogaine, and secondarily tabernanthine (an isomer of ibogaine), ibogamine, iboluteine and others [Gaignault & Delourme-Houdé 1977]. Related apocynaceous species such as *Voacanga* spp. and *Tabernaemontana* spp., some of which are used as stimulants and perhaps as visionary drugs [Ott 1993] contain some of the *iboga* alkaloids and variants, notably voacangine or carbomethoxy-ibogaine (see Ott 1993 for a review of phytochemistry of these plants). Although ibogaine is considered to be the principal visionary agent of *iboga*, tabernanthine and ibogamine (as well as the *Voacanga* alkaloid voacangine), have shown ibogaine-like properties in animal experiments [Bert *et al.* 1988; Gaignault & Delourme-Houdé 1977; Zetler *et al.* 1970], indicating a need for human psychonautic bioassays of these alkaloids.

[48]

[23] The traditional cult of Bieri would appear to be the predecessor of Bwiti. Bieri involves an *iboga*–like initiation with powdered roots of *Alchornea floribunda* Muel.–Arg., like *iboga*, said to 'break open the head' in high doses. Present-day use of this euphorbiaceous plant, *alan*, is especially associated with the Eshira of Gabon, but it is also used by the Fang, and it may be mixed with *iboga* [Fernandez 1972; Pope 1969; Samorini 1993]. Another euphorbiaceous plant, *Elaeophorbia drupifera* Muel.–Arg., which may be psychoactive, is associated with the use of *alan*, and in some branches of Bwiti, *Cannabis* or *yama* may be smoked after ingestion of *iboga* [Fernandez 1972]. Also of possible pharmacological importance in the Bwiti rites may be the *duna* mushroom, yet unidentified and likely a psychoactive species [Samorini 1993]. Finally, in the MBiri (Ombwiri) cult, which focuses on healing, there is the ingestion of *iboga* as well as a mixture of ten or more plants called *ekasso*, of unknown composition and properties [Pope 1969; Samorini 1993].

[24] While public-school history courses in the United States stress the horrors of the German Nazi murder of 6 million Jews and Josef Stalin's pogroms against racial minorities and political dissidents in the Soviet Union, the facts that the U.S. Army's solution to the 'Indian Problem' was the prototype for the Nazi 'Final Solution' to the 'Jewish Problem' and that the North American Indian Reservation was the model for the twentieth century *gulag* and concentration camp, are conveniently overlooked.

[25] The spineless cactus *péyotl* was one of the most important sacred plants of pre-Columbian México. Growing from San Luis Potosí north to the Río Bravo/Grande valley, the cactus has been associated with humankind for at least two and a half millennia, and remains important in contemporary shamanism, particularly among the Huichol and Tarahumara of northwestern México [Benítez 1968; Furst 1972; Myerhoff 1974; Rouhier 1927]. This diminutive cactus was an important entheogen to the ancient Aztecs, who came from the north to settle in the Valley of México [Ott 1993]. The cactus is a veritable factory of alkaloids, containing up to 8% of a mixture of more than 50 compounds, the most important of which is mescaline, first isolated in 1896 and the first entheogenic principle to be available as a pure compound, to be synthesized (in 1919) and to be ingested by a human being, thereby inaugurating the modern era of entheogenic psychopharmacology [Anderson 1980; Heffter 1896; Ott 1993; Späth 1919].

[26] *Ayahuasca* is a pan-Amazonian complex of entheogenic potions based on aqueous extracts of stems, stem bark, or stem shavings of malpighiaceous lianas of the genus *Banisteriopsis* (also *Callaeum*, *Lophanthera* and *Tetrapterys*). Characteristic of *ayahuasca* potions is the addition of an extensive ethnopharmacopœia of plant additives or '*ayahuasca* admixtures'— nearly 100 such *ayahuasca* admixture plants in some 40 plant families have been identified [Luna 1984a, 1984b; Luna & Amaringo 1991]. The ethnobotany of these admixtures has been reviewed [Ott 1993]; and they have been described as a 'traditional pharmacopœia' [McKenna *et al.* 1986]. Curiously, the *ayahuasca* liana itself is not entheogenic or vision-producing—it contains β-carboline alkaloids which have a sedative effect and are inhibitors of the enzyme monoamine-oxidase (MAO). Some of the admixture plants contain entheogenic tryptamines like DMT (*N,N*-dimethyltryptamine) which are inactive orally, but are

rendered orally entheogenic by combination with the enzyme-inhibitors from *ayahuasca* stem! The human pharmacology of this interaction—which represents the most sophisticated pharmacognostical discovery of all antiquity—has been elucidated. A number of other chemical types of entheogenic plants are used as *ayahuasca* additives, as are caffeine- and cocaine-containing stimulants, but the rationale for the use of most of these additive plants remains obscure, pending further research [McKenna *et al.* 1986; Ott 1994].

[27] The predecessor of contemporary *ayahuasca* churches is the Círculo de Regeneração e Fé, founded in the 1920s by Antonio and André Costa, who had been initiated into the use of the potion by Peruvian shaman Don Crescêncio Pizango. The Costa brothers in turn introduced this Christian sacramental use of *ayahuasca* to Raimundo Irineu Serra, who founded the modern Santo Daime church. By 1940, Mestre Irineu had started his own church, the Centro de Iluminação Cristã Luz Universal, also known as 'Alto Santo,' in the town of Rio Branco in Acre, Brasil. One of Mestre Irineu's prominent disciples, Sebastião Mota de Melo or Padrinho Sebastião founded a branch of the church called Céu do Mapiá in the 1980s. By 1982, the first urban branch of the church, the Chamou-se Centro Ecléctico Fluente Luz Universal Sebastião Mota de Melo or Céu do Mar, was started in Rio de Janeiro. An ecumenical movement within the church led to the founding in May 1989 of the Centro Ecléctico de Fluente Luz Universal Raimundo Irineu Serra, of which the late Padrinho Sebastião was head [MacRae 1992]. The Santo Daime church is the most visible today, as it actively engages in evangelism, and *Daimista* temples are cropping up in Europe, for example in Barcelona, and touring church groups have celebrated Mass in various European cities. On 22 July 1961, José Gabriel da Costa founded an independent *ayahuasca* church in Acre, Brasil, which soon moved its headquarters to Brasília and became primarily an urban church. Costa's Centro Espírita Beneficente União do Vegetal (UDV) is today the largest *ayahuasca* church in Brasil [Centro 1989; Henman 1986].

[28] As mentioned in Note 26, *ayahuasca* potions often have plant admixtures containing the potent entheogen *N,N*-dimethyltryptamine or DMT. The most common DMT–rich *ayahuasca* admixture plant is *Psychotria viridis* in the coffee family, Rubiaceae [Ott 1993]. Leaves of various species of *Psychotria* are added to *ayahuasca* potions in western Amazonia, where *P. viridis* is known as *amirucapanga* (in Ecuador) or *chacruna* (in Perú). Leaves of this species, which are used to prepare both *daime* and *chá hoasca*, contain from 0.16 up to 0.66% DMT, a potent entheogen when smoked or injected, but inactive orally in human subjects at doses as high as 1.0 gram [Shulgin 1976]. The Amazonian shamanic psychonauts discovered that DMT–containing leaves became potent entheogens when mixed with extracts of *ayahuasca* stem, and it has recently been shown that oral doses as low as 30 mg of DMT (the average content of the doses of *ayahuasca* which have been analyzed chemically) are entheogenic when combined with a sufficient dose of the enzyme-inhibitors found in *ayahuasca* stem [Ott 1994]!

[29] As R. Gordon Wasson noted, the Spanish Catholic Santo Niño de Atocha or 'child saint,' a conception of Jesus as a young boy from the basilica of Nuestra Señora de Atocha in Madrid, Spain, has become the patron saint of Catholicized shamans throughout Meso-

america. Wasson proposed that the boy Jesus is the closest Catholic iconography comes to the pre-Columbian child-god Piltzintli, an *avatar* of Xochipilli, the 'Prince of Entheogens' [Wasson 1973]. Piltzintli is often depicted as the 'diving god,' in the murals of Teotihuacan, for instance, or in the *Codex Borgia*... even seen diving down to the altar in the phantasmagoric Mexican church Santa María Tonantzintla near Cholula, in the Valley of Puebla. Wasson also discerned the diving child god in some of the Mayan mushroom stones [Wasson 1980]. During his first shamanic *velada* with María Sabina in 1955, María had asked Wasson not to sit in a particular corner, because 'the Word' would come down there, later telling Álvaro Estrada: "I see the Word fall; it comes from above, as though tiny luminous objects were falling from heaven. The Word falls on the holy table, it falls on my body. Then I catch it with my hands, Word by Word." [Estrada 1977]. Wasson descried in Santo Niño de Atocha/Piltzintli a personification of the *Logos* which is primordial in Biblical cosmology, and 'children' was the primary trope for the entheogenic mushrooms in María Sabina's 12–13 July 1958 'Mazatec Mushroom Velada' recorded, transcribed and translated by Wasson and collaborators for eventual publication 16 years later [Wasson *et al.* 1974]. To María, the sacred mushrooms were the 'dear little ones that leap forth,' little clowns, imps, tykes that spoke through her; to the Nahua on the volcano Popocatépetl, they were *apipiltzin*, 'little children of the waters,' or on the volcano Nevado de Toluca, *mujercitas*, or 'little women' [Wasson & Wasson 1957; Wasson *et al.* 1974]. To Aurelio Carreras, Mazatec colleague of María Sabina, the mushroom was 'the Word,' *es habla* [Wasson & Wasson 1957], and Henry Munn designated 'the dear little ones that leap forth' *The Mushrooms of Language* [Munn 1973].

[30] Vico was elaborating the classical Greek conception of Four Ages—Gold, Silver, Bronze and Iron. Their counterparts in classical India were the four Yugas—the Krita Yuga of 1,728,000 years; the Tretâ Yuga of 1,296,000 years; the Dvâpara Yuga of 864,000 years and the Kali Yuga of 432,000 years. In Hindu philosophy, each cycle thus lasts 4,320,000 years. According to contemporary Hindu belief, we are presently in the Kali Yuga which commenced at the conclusion of the great war chronicled in the epic *Mahabharata*, supposedly in B.C. 18 February 3102—accordingly the new cycle will be inaugurated on 18 February A.D. 428,898. The basic unit of time is thus 432,000 years, and each Age is a multiple of that figure. Vico's idea has been all but forgotten, with the exception of its superb artistic expression in James Joyce's linguistic/historical/mythological extravaganza, *Finnegans Wake* [Burgess 1967; Campbell & Robinson 1944; Frédéric 1987; Joyce 1939].

[31] In the world of Hinduism, the primordial Vedic entheogen *soma* [see Note 4] was replaced in the liturgy of the *soma* sacrifice by various substitutes or placebo sacraments some 3000 years ago [Doniger O'Flaherty 1968; Kramrisch 1975; Wasson 1968]. As was the case in the West, a sort of Pharmacratic Inquisition ensured that the *tabu* against the Sacred Element would not be transgressed. The 'Laws of Manu,' dating back some 2000 years, and the commentary of Yama, made it a capital crime, tantamount to the murder of a Brahman, for any Brahman or member of the priestly caste to ingest *any* mushroom [Wasson 1982], thus ensuring that the ecstasy induced by the *soma* mushroom would be forever beyond the reach of the 'faithful' thus forced to accept the Hindu equivalent of the Doctrine of

Transubstantiation—that the non-entheogenic *putika* mushroom [and later, manifold other placebo sacraments] was transubstantiated into *soma* in the firing of the Mahavira Vessel during the Pravargya sacrifice [Kramrisch 1975]. While today the true identity of *soma* seems completely unknown to Hindu Brahmans [Wasson 1968], nonetheless, there remains a prominent ritual role for *Cannabis* in Hinduism. In the forms of *bhangas* (leaf), *ganja* (flower-tops) and *charas* (resin, more commonly known as *hashish*), this tetrahydro-cannabinol-rich visionary drug, along with preparations of tropane-alkaloid rich *Datura* species with which it may be mixed, remains especially associated with the dancing god Shiva, who seems to embody the survival of autochthonous shamanism and shamanic inebriants which the fair-skinned Aryans encountered in the Indian subcontinent they invaded 3500 years ago. The *RgVeda*, the earliest of the four Vedas, deals primarily with *soma*, which the Aryans brought into India with them, but the subsequent *AtharvaVeda* also describes how the gods churned the oceans to obtain *amrta*, the *soma* potion [see Note 4], and in the process obtained also *Cannabis* [Aldrich 1977; Sharma 1977]. Since this plant originated in northern Asia, it may have been brought into India along with *soma* by the Aryans. In contrast to the mushroom *soma*, which did not lend itself to cultivation, *Cannabis* is quite easily cultivated, which perhaps helps explain how it survived the Hindu Pharmacratic Inquisition. In the seventh century syncretism of the *Cannabis*–using Shiva cult in India with Tibetan Buddhism, there resulted the cult of Tantric Yoga, in which *Cannabis* has traditionally been a key entheogenic element [Aldrich 1977; Tuow 1981]. Gautama the Buddha, of course, was said to have subsisted on one *Cannabis* achene daily for the six years leading up to his enlightenment. It is also worth mentioning that Gautama died *circa* B.C. 483, after ingesting what was probably the *putika* mushroom, primary *soma* substitute—in this Mahaparinirvana, was he inviting fellow Brahmans to an Indian Entheogenic Reformation [Wasson 1982]? *Cannabis* plays a key role in the worship of the pre–Vedic Indian god Jagannath at the Jagannath Mandir in Puri, Orissa [Marglin 1985]. Similarly, in Zoroastrianism, use of the primal entheogen *haoma* (=*soma*, brought into Iran by the Aryans in Vedic times, and extolled in the *Avesta* 2500 years ago) was long associated with devotees of the shaman/psychopomp Zoroaster, although today it seems a substitute plant, *Peganum harmala* L., bears the name *haoma* [Ott 1993; Wasson 1968], and which is, in any case, now used as an incense rather than as a sacrament [Flattery & Schwartz 1989]. It has been argued that the root for the Latin name *Cannabis* is not Finno-Ugrian or Scythian, as has been thought, but Semitic, and that the plant is characterized as a sacred inebriant in the Old Testament [Benet 1975; La Barre 1980b]. In this context it is important to mention the Afro-Caribbean Jamaican syncretic cult of Rastafari. *Cannabis*, known by its Sanskrit name *ganja*, is considered to be the 'burning bush' of Moses (from which 'the Word' issued forth) in the Old Testament, and is the key sacramental element for Rastafarians, yet another example of the Entheogenic Reformation of Christianity [Rubin 1975; Rubin & Comitas 1975]. In the Moslem world, a curious inversion as to inebriants has occurred, with the Pharmacratic Inquisition focusing mostly on alcohol, which has been roundly condemned and generally prohibited. Meanwhile other inebriants such as opium (exudate of capsules of *Papaver somniferum* L.), *hashish* [Gelpke 1966] and *qat* (the leafy buds of *Catha edulis* [Vahl] Forskal) [Kennedy 1987] have found their place in Muslim society, even a religious role [Gelpke 1966]. While *qat* is today mainly used as a sort of social stimulant in Somalia, Ethiopia and North Yemen, it enjoyed in the past a prominent role in the Muslim religion and was known traditionally as the 'flower of paradise,' although some religious authorities condemned the drug [Getahun & Krikorian 1973; Kennedy 1987]. It was recently proposed that *qat* was an important sacred plant in ancient Egypt, and that the name derives from an ancient Egyptian word *kht* (an alternate spelling for *qat* is *khat*) [Musès 1989]. If this is true, then the historical use of *qat* as an adjunct to the Muslim religion may indeed constitute a sort of Entheogenic Reformation. The Swiss Persian scholar Rudolf Gelpke reviewed the prominent role of *Cannabis* and opium in Islamic spiritual practice [Gelpke 1966].

INTERLUDE

Nezahualcóyotl's Ode to Entheogens

There are entheogenic songs: may they say
I drink the flowers that inebriate,
The flowers that provoke vertigo have arrived
Come, and be thou exalted.

These flowers have arrived on panicles:
Diverse flowers of pleasure that are strewn,
That rain down and intertwine.

Let the drum resound: let there be dance:
My heart is tinted with lovely entheogenic flowers.

I am a poet: I am gathering flowers
To disseminate: enjoy.

The flower of my song breaks inside my heart:
I disseminate entheogens.

With songs one day I must be enshrouded,
My heart with entheogens must be intertwined:
They are the princes, the kings!

Thus I weep at times and say:

Someday I shall leave behind
The fame of my entheogens, the renown of my songs:
My heart with entheogens must be intertwined:
They are the princes, the kings!

Nezahualcóyotl's Monologue, in *Song to Nezahualcóyotl*,
An elegy by an unknown pre-Columbian poet to
Acolmiztli Nezahualcóyotl, 'Lion-Strong Famished Coyote,'
Poet, warrior, Lord of Texcoco [1402–1472]
Translated from Á.M. Garibay's Spanish rendering of the Náhuatl

BIBLIOGRAPHY

Aguirre Beltrán, G. 1963. *Medicina y Magia.* Inst. Nac. Ind., Ciudad de México, México.

Aldrich, M.R. 1977. "Tantric Cannabis use in India" *Journal of Psychedelic Drugs* 9(3): 227–233.

Allen, J.W. and M.D. Merlin 1992. "Psychoactive mushrooms in Thailand: Some aspects of their relationship to human use, law and art" *Integration: Zeitschrift für Geistbewegende Pflanzen und Kultur* 2&3: 98–108.

Anderson, E.F. 1980. *Peyote: The Divine Cactus.* The University of Arizona Press, Tucson, AZ.

Anon. 1994. "Brüder im Schmerz" *Der Spiegel* 10: 110–111.

Barnard, M. 1963. "The god in the flowerpot" *American Scholar* 32(4): 578–586. Also *The Psychedelic Review* 1(2): 244–251.

Beeching, J. 1975. *The Chinese Opium Wars.* Harcourt Brace Jovanovich, New York, NY.

Benet, S. 1975. "Early diffusion and folk uses of hemp" In: Rubin, V. [Ed.] *Cannabis and Culture.* Mouton and Co., Den Haag, Nederland. pp. 39–49.

Benítez, F. 1968. *En la Tierra Mágica del Peyote.* Ediciones Era [Serie Popular Era], Ciudad de México, México.

Bert, M. *et al.* 1988. "Non-amphetamine central stimulation by alkaloids from the ibogane and vobasine series" *Planta Medica* 54: 191–192.

Brown, J.K. and M.H. Malone 1973. "Status of drug quality in the street-drug market" *Pacific Information Service on Street Drugs* 3(1): 1–7.

Burgess, A. [Ed.] 1967. *A Shorter Finnegans Wake.* The Viking Press, New York, NY.

Campbell, J. 1964. *The Masks of God: Occidental Mythology.* The Viking Press, New York, NY.

Campbell, J. 1972. *Myths to Live By.* The Viking Press, New York, NY.

Campbell, J. and H.M. Robinson 1944. *A Skeleton Key to Finnegans Wake.* The Viking Press, New York, NY.

Centro Espírita Beneficente União do Vegetal 1989. *União do Vegetal: Hoasca. Fundamentos e Objetivos.* Centro de Memória e Documentação, Brasilia, Brasil.

Clark, A.J. 1921. "Flying ointments" In: Murray, M.A. *The Witch-Cult in Western Europe: A Study in Anthropology.* Clarendon Press, Oxford, England. p. 279.

Cohn, N. 1975. *Europe's Inner Demons: An Enquiry Inspired by the Great Witch-Hunt.* The New American Library, New York, NY.

De Vries, H. 1991. "Über die sogennanten Hexensalben" *Integration: Zeitschrift für Geistbewegende Pflanzen und Kultur* 1: 71–77.

Dobkin de Ríos, M. 1972. *Visionary Vine: Hallucinogenic Healing in the Peruvian Amazon.* Chandler Publishing Co., San Francisco, CA.

Dobkin de Ríos, M. 1992. *Amazon Healer: The Life and Times of an Urban Shaman.* Prism Press, Bridport, England.

Doniger O'Flaherty, W. 1968. "The post-Vedic history of the Soma plant" In: Wasson, R.G. *Soma: Divine Mushroom of Immortality.* Mouton and Co., Den Haag, Nederland. pp. 95–147.

Doniger O'Flaherty, W. 1982. "Epilogue" *Journal of the American Oriental Society* 102(4): 591–603. See: Wasson 1982.

Eliade, M. 1951. *Le Chamanisme et les Techniques Archaïques de l'Extase.* Paris, France.

Eliade, M. 1954. *Le Yoga: Immortalité et Liberté.* Payot, Paris, France.

Escohotado, A. 1989. *Historia General de las Drogas.* Three volumes. Alianza Editorial, Madrid, España.

Estrada, Á. 1977. *Vida de María Sabina: La Sabia de los Hongos.* Siglo Veintiuno, Ciudad de México, México.

Fericgla, J.M. 1985. *El Bolet i la Gènesi de les Cultures. Gnoms i Follets. Àmbits Culturals Forjats per l'*Amanita muscaria. Editorial Alta Fulla, Barcelona, Catalunya, Espanya.

Fericgla, J.M. 1992. "*Amanita muscaria* usage in Catalunya" *Integration: Zeitschrift für Geistbewegende Pflanzen und Kultur* 2 &3: 63–65.

Fernandez, J.W. 1972. "*Tabernanthe iboga*: Narcotic ecstasis and the work of the ancestors" In: Furst, P.T. [Ed.] *Flesh of the Gods: The Ritual Use of Hallucinogens.* Praeger, New York, NY. pp. 237–260.

Fernandez, J.W. 1982. *Bwiti: An Ethnography of the Religious Imagination in Africa.* Princeton University Press, Princeton, NJ.

Fish, M.S. *et al.* 1955. "Piptadenia alkaloids: Indole bases of *P. peregrina* (L.) Benth. and related species" *Journal of the American*

Chemical Society 77: 5892–5895.

Flattery, D.S. and M. Schwartz 1989. *Haoma and Harmaline: The Botanical Identity of the Indo-Iranian Sacred Hallucinogen "Soma" and its Legacy in Religion, Language, and Middle Eastern Folklore.* University of California Press, Berkeley, CA.

Fletcher, R. 1896. "The witches' pharmacopœia" *Bulletin of the Johns Hopkins Hospital* 7: 147–156.

Forbes, T.R. 1962. "Midwifery and witchcraft" *Journal of the History of Medicine.* April issue. pp. 264–283.

Forbes, T.R. 1966. *The Midwife and the Witch.* Yale University Press, New Haven, CT.

Forte, R. 1988. "A conversation with R. Gordon Wasson" *ReVision: The Journal of Consciousness and Change* 10(4): 13–30.

Frédéric, L. 1987. *Dictionnaire de la Civilisation Indienne.* Éditions Robert Laffont, Paris, France.

Furst, P.T. 1972. "To find our life: Peyote among the Huichol Indians of Mexico" In: Furst, P.T. [Ed.] *Flesh of the Gods: The Ritual Use of Hallucinogens.* Praeger, New York, NY. pp. 136–184.

Furst, P.T. 1976. *Hallucinogens and Culture.* Chandler & Sharp, Novato, CA.

Gaignault, J.C. and J. Delourme-Houdé 1977. "Les alcaloïdes de l'iboga (*Tabernanthe iboga* H. Bn.)" *Fitoterapia* 48: 243–265.

Gari, A. 1987. *El Uso de las Drogas en la Brujeria y en Algunos Relatos de Magia.* Sociedad Científica Española de Estudios sobre el Alcohol, el Alcoholismo y las otras Toxicomanías, Zaragoza, España.

Garraty, J.A. and P. Gay [Eds.] 1972. *The Columbia History of the World.* Harper & Row Publishers, New York, NY.

Gelpke, R. 1966. *Vom Rausch im Orient und Okzident.* E. Klett Verlag, Stuttgart, Deutschland. [*Drogen und Seelenerweiterung*]

Getahun, A. and A.D. Krikorian 1973. "Chat: Coffee's rival from Harar, Ethiopia. I. Botany, cultivation and uses" *Economic Botany* 27(4): 353–377.

Hansen, H.A. 1978. *The Witch's Garden.* Unity Press-Michael Kesend, Santa Cruz, CA. Originally: *Heksens Urtegård*, 1976.

Harner, M.J. 1973. "The role of hallucinogenic plants in European witchcraft" In: Harner, M.J. [Ed.] *Hallucinogens and Shamanism.* Oxford University Press, London, England. pp. 125–150.

Harris, B. 1976. *Growing Wild Mushrooms: A Complete Guide to Cultivating Edible and Hallucinogenic Mushrooms.* Wingbow Press, Berkeley, CA.

Heffter, A. 1896. "Über Cacteenalkaloïde. (II. Mittheilung)" *Berichte der Deutschen Chemischen Gesellschaft* 29: 216–227.

Heim, R. and R.G. Wasson 1958. *Les Champignons Hallucinogènes du Mexique.* Archives du Muséum National d'Histoire Naturelle, Paris, France.

Helmer, J. 1975. *Drugs and Minority Oppression.* The Seabury Press [A Continuum Book], New York, NY.

Henman, A.R. 1986. "Uso del ayahuasca en un contexto autoritario: El caso de la *União do Vegetal* en Brasil" *América Indígena* 46(1): 219–234.

Hofmann, A. [J. Ott, trans.] 1980. *LSD: My Problem Child.* McGraw-Hill, New York, NY. Orig. *LSD–Mein Sorgenkind*, 1979.

Horowitz, M. 1991. "Just say know: Gordon Wasson and the Psychedelic Revolution" *Integration: Zeitschrift für Geistbewegende Pflanzen und Kultur* 1: 4–6.

Joyce, J. 1939. *Finnegans Wake.* Paris, France.

Kazin, A. [Ed.] 1946. *The Portable Blake.* The Viking Press, New York, NY.

Kennedy, J.G. 1987. *The Flower of Paradise: The Institutionalized Use of the Drug Qat in North Yemen.* D. Reidel Publishing Co., Dordrecht, Nederland.

Krajick, K. 1992. "Vision quest" *Newsweek.* 15 June (Latin American) issue. pp. 44–45.

Kramrisch, S. 1975. "The Mahavira Vessel and the plant Putika" *Journal of the American Oriental Society* 95(2): 222–235.

La Barre, W. 1938. *The Peyote Cult.* Yale University Press, New Haven, CT.

La Barre, W. 1970. *The Ghost Dance: The Origins of Religion.* Doubleday and Co., Garden City, NJ.

La Barre, W. 1979. "Shamanic origins of religion and medicine" *Journal of Psychedelic Drugs* 11(1-2): 7–11.

La Barre, W. 1980a. "Anthropological perspectives on hallucination, hallucinogens, and the shamanic origins of religion" *Culture in Context: Selected Writings of Weston La Barre.* Duke University Press, Durham, NC. pp. 37–92.

La Barre, W. 1980b. "History and ethnography of *Cannabis*" *Culture in Context: Selected Writings of Weston La Barre.* Duke University Press, Durham, NC. pp. 93–107.

La Barre, W. 1980c. "Soma: The three-and-one-half millennia mystery" *Culture in Context: Selected Writings of Weston La Barre.* Duke University Press, Durham, NC. pp. 108–115.

Lamb, F.B. 1974. *Wizard of the Upper Amazon: The Story of Manuel Córdova-Ríos.* Houghton Mifflin, Boston, MA.

Lázaro, A. 1994. *A Luz na Doutrina do Santo Daime.* Universidade do Estado do Rio de Janeiro, Brasil.

Lee, M.A. and B. Shlain 1985. *Acid Dreams: LSD, the CIA and the Sixties Rebellion.* Grove Press, New York, NY.

Lévi-Strauss, C. 1970. "Les champignons dans la culture—À propos d'un livre de M.R.G. Wasson" *Anthropologie Structurale Deux.* Plon, Paris, France. pp. 263–279.

Liwszyc, G.E. *et al.* 1992. "Daime—A ritual herbal potion" *Journal of Ethnopharmacology* 36(1): 91–92.

Lowy, B. 1987. "Caapi revisited—In Christianity" *Economic Botany* 41(3): 450–452.

Luna, L.E. 1984a. "The healing practices of a Peruvian shaman" *Journal of Ethnopharmacology* 11(2): 123–133.

Luna, L.E. 1984b. "The concept of plants as teachers among four mestizo shamans of Iquitos, northeastern Peru" *Journal of Ethnopharmacology* 11(2): 135–156.

Luna, L.E. 1986. "Apéndices" *América Indígena* 46(1): 247–251.

Luna, L.E. 1991. "Plant spirits in ayahuasca visions by Peruvian painter, Pablo Amaringo. An iconographic analysis" *Integration: Zeitschrift für Geistbewegende Pflanzen und Kultur* 1: 18–29.

Luna, L.E. and P. Amaringo 1991. *Ayahuasca Visions: The Religious Iconography of a Peruvian Shaman*. North Atlantic Books, Berkeley, CA.

McAllester, D.P. 1949. *Peyote Music*. (Viking Fund Publication in Anthropology No. 13) Viking Fund, New York, NY.

McKenna, D.J. 1994. "The Hoasca Project update" *MAPS Newsletter* 4(4): 6–8.

McKenna, D.J. *et al.* 1986. "Ingredientes biodinámicos en las plantas que se mezclan al ayahuasca. Una farmacopea tradicional no investigada" *América Indígena* 46(1): 73–99.

McKenna, T.K. 1991. *The Archaic Revival: Speculations on Psychedelic Mushrooms, the Amazon, Virtual Reality, UFOs, Evolution, Shamanism, the Rebirth of the Goddess and the End of History*. Harper San Francisco, New York, NY.

MacRae, E. 1992. *Guiado Pela Lua: Xamanismo e Uso Ritual da Ayahuasca no Culto do Santo Daime*. Editora Brasiliense, São Paolo, Brasil.

Manske, R.H.F. 1931. "A synthesis of the methyl-tryptamines and some derivatives" *Canadian Journal of Research* 5: 592–600.

Marglin, F.A. 1985. *The Wives of the God-King: The Rituals of the Devadasis of Puri*. Oxford University Press, Oxford, England.

Marnell, T. [Ed.] 1993. *Drug Identification Bible*. Drug Identification Bible, Denver, CO.

Motolinía, F. de [E. O'Gorman, Ed.] 1971. *Memoriales o Libro de las Cosas de la Nueva España*. Universidad Nacional Autónoma de México, Ciudad de México, México.

Mount, G. [Ed.] 1987. *The Peyote Book: A Study of Native Medicine*. Sweetlight Books, Arcata, CA. Second edition, 1988.

Munn, H. 1973. "The mushrooms of language" In: Harner, M. [Ed.] *Hallucinogens and Shamanism*. Oxford University Press, London, England. pp. 86–122.

Musès, C. 1989. "The sacred plants of ancient Egypt" In: Rätsch, C. [Ed.] *Gateway to Inner Space: Sacred Plants, Mysticism and Psychotherapy—A Festschrift in Honor of Albert Hofmann*. Prism Press, Bridport, England. pp. 143–159.

Musto, D.F. 1973. *The American Disease: Origins of Narcotic Control*. Yale University Press, New Haven, CT.

Myerhoff, B.G. 1974. *Peyote Hunt: The Sacred Journey of the Huichol Indians*. Cornell University Press, Ithaca, NY.

Mylonas, G.E. 1961. *Eleusis and the Eleusinian Mysteries*. Princeton University Press, Princeton, NJ.

Naranjo, P. 1983. *Ayahuasca: Etnomedicina y Mitología*. Ediciones Libri Mundi, Quito, Ecuador.

Ocaña, E. 1993. *El Dioniso Moderno y la Farmacia Utópica*. Editorial Anagrama, Barcelona, Catalunya, Espanya.

Ortíz de Montellano, B.R. 1990. *Aztec Medicine, Health, and Nutrition*. Rutgers University Press, Brunswick, NJ.

Oss, O.T. and O.N. Oeric 1976. *Psilocybin: Magic Mushroom Grower's Guide—A Handbook for Psilocybin Enthusiasts*. And/Or Press, Berkeley, CA.

Ott, J. 1975. "Notes on recreational use of

hallucinogenic mushrooms" *Boletín de la Sociedad Mexicana de Micología* 9: 131–135.

Ott, J. 1976. *Hallucinogenic Plants of North America*. Wingbow Press, Berkeley, CA.

Ott, J. 1978. "Recreational use of hallucinogenic mushrooms in the United States" In: Rumack, B.H. and E. Salzman [Eds.] *Mushroom Poisoning: Diagnosis and Treatment*. CRC Press, West Palm Beach, FL.

Ott, J. 1990. "A twentieth century Darwin" In: Riedlinger, T.J. [Ed.] *The Sacred Mushroom Seeker: Essays for R. Gordon Wasson*. Dioscorides Press, Portland, OR. pp. 183–191.

Ott, J. 1993. *Pharmacotheon: Entheogenic Drugs, Their Plant Sources and History*. Natural Products Co., Kennewick, WA.

Ott, J. 1994. *Ayahuasca Analogues: Pangæan Entheogens*. Natural Products Co., Kennewick, WA.

Ott, J. and J. Bigwood [Eds.] 1978. *Teonanácatl: Hallucinogenic Mushrooms of North America*. Madrona Publishers, Seattle, WA.

Peters, E. 1978. *The Magician the Witch and the Law*. University of Pennsylvania Press, Philadelphia, PA.

Pike, E.V. 1960. "Mazatec sexual impurity [*sic*] and Bible reading" *Practical Anthropology* 7(2): 49–53.

Pike, E.V. and F. Cowan 1959. "Mushroom ritual versus Christianity" *Practical Anthropology* 6(4): 145–150.

Pope, H.G. 1969. "*Tabernanthe iboga*: An African narcotic [*sic*] plant of social importance" *Economic Botany* 23(2): 174–184.

Prance, G.T. 1970. "Notes on the use of plant hallucinogens in Amazonian Brazil" *Economic Botany* 24(1): 62–68.

Pratt, R.A. [Ed.] 1966. *Selections from the Tales of Canterbury and Short Poems*. Houghton Mifflin, Boston, MA.

Ratcliffe, B. 1973. "Psilocybin demand creates new drug deception" *The PharmChem Newsletter* 2(2): 1 *et seq.*

Rouhier, A. 1927. *La Plante qui Fait les Yeux*

Émerveillés—le Peyotl. Gaston Doin et Cⁱᵉ·, Paris, France.

Rubin, V. [Ed.] 1975. *Cannabis and Culture*. Mouton and Co., Den Haag, Nederland.

Rubin, V. and L. Comitas [Eds.] 1975. *Ganja in Jamaica: A Medical Anthropological Study of Chronic Marihuana Use*. Mouton and Co., Den Haag, Nederland.

Ruck, C.A.P. 1981. "Mushrooms and philosophers" *Journal of Ethnopharmacology* 4(2): 179–205. [Wasson *et al.* 1986]

Ruck, C.A.P. 1982. "The wild and the cultivated: Wine in Euripides' Bacchae" *Journal of Ethnopharmacology* 5(3): 231–270. [Wasson *et al.* 1986]

Ruck, C.A.P. 1983. "The offerings from the Hyperboreans" *Journal of Ethnopharmacology* 8(2): 177–207. [Wasson *et al.* 1986]

Ruck, C.A.P. *et al.* 1979. "Entheogens" *Journal of Psychedelic Drugs* 11(1-2): 145–146. [Wasson *et al.* 1980]

Samorini, G. 1993. "Adam, Eve and Iboga" *Integration: Zeitschrift für Geistbewegende Pflanzen und Kultur* 4: 3–10.

Schleiffer, H. [Ed.] 1979. *Narcotic Plants of the Old World: An Anthology of Texts from Ancient Times to the Present*. Lubrecht & Cramer, Monticello, NY.

Schultes, R.E. and A. Hofmann 1980. *The Botany and Chemistry of Hallucinogens*. Charles C. Thomas, Springfield, IL.

Sharma, G.K. 1977. "Ethnobotany and its significance for *Cannabis* studies in the Himalayas" *Journal of Psychedelic Drugs* 9(4): 337–339.

Shulgin, A.T. 1976. "Profiles of psychedelic drugs. 1. DMT" *Journal of Psychedelic Drugs* 8(2): 167–168.

Shulgin, A.T. 1992. *Controlled Substances: A Chemical and Legal Guide to the Federal Drug Laws*. Ronin Publishing, Inc., Berkeley, CA.

Späth, E. 1919. "Über die Anhalonium-Alkaloide. I. Anhalin und Mezcalin" *Monats-*

hefte für Chemie und Verwandte Teile An-derer Wißenschaften 40: 129–154.

Stewart, O.C. 1987. *Peyote Religion: A History.* University of Oklahoma Press, Norman, OK.

Szasz, T. 1970. *The Manufacture of Madness: A Comparative Study of the Inquisition and the Mental Health Movement.* Harper and Row Publishers, New York, NY.

Szasz, T. 1974. *Ceremonial Chemistry: The Ritual Persecution of Drugs, Addicts and Pushers.* Doubleday/Anchor, New York, NY. Second edition, 1985.

Tuow, M. 1981. "The religious and medical uses of *Cannabis* in China, India and Tibet" *Journal of Psychoactive Drugs* 13(1): 23–34.

Valadez, S. 1986. "Guided tour spirituality: Cosmic way or cosmic rip-off?" *Shaman's Drum: A Journal of Experiential Shamanism.* Fall issue. pp. 4–6.

Wasson, E.A. 1914. *Religion and Drink.* Privately printed (Burr Printing House), New York, NY.

Wasson, E.A. 1965. *That Gettysburg Address. Made by President Lincoln on the Battlefield of Gettysburg on November 19, 1863.* Privately printed (Officina Bodoni), Verona, Italia.

Wasson, R.G. 1957. "Seeking the magic mushroom" *Life.* 13 May issue. 42(19): 100 *et seq.* Watercolor paintings by R. Heim.

Wasson, R.G. 1959. "The hallucinogenic mushrooms of Mexico: An adventure in ethnomycological exploration" *Transactions of the New York Academy of Sciences* Ser. II, 21(4): 325–339.

Wasson, R.G. 1961. "The hallucinogenic fungi of Mexico: An inquiry into the origins of the religious idea among primitive peoples" *Botanical Museum Leaflets* Harvard University 19(7): 137–162.

Wasson, R.G. 1963. "Notes on the present status of *ololiuhqui* and the other hallucinogens of Mexico" *Botanical Museum Leaf-*

lets Harvard University 20(6): 161–193.

Wasson, R.G. 1968. *Soma: Divine Mushroom of Immortality.* Mouton & Co., Den Haag, Nederland; and HBJ, New York, NY.

Wasson, R.G. 1972a. *Soma and the Fly-Agaric: Mr. Wasson's Rejoinder to Professor Brough.* Botanical Museum of Harvard University, Cambridge, MA.

Wasson, R.G. 1972b. "The death of Claudius or mushrooms for murderers" *Botanical Museum Leaflets* Harvard University 23(3): 101–128. [Wasson & Wasson 1957]

Wasson, R.G. 1973. "The role of 'flowers' in Nahuatl culture: A suggested interpretation" *Botanical Museum Leaflets* Harvard University 23(8): 305–324. [Wasson 1980]

Wasson, R.G. 1980. *The Wondrous Mushroom: Mycolatry in Mesoamerica.* Harcourt Brace Jovanovich, New York, NY.

Wasson, R.G. 1982. "The last meal of the Buddha" *Journal of the American Oriental Society* 102(4): 591–603. [Wasson *et al.* 1986]

Wasson, V.P. and R.G. Wasson 1957. *Mushrooms Russia and History.* Two volumes. Pantheon Books, New York, NY.

Wasson, R.G. *et al.* 1974. *María Sabina and her Mazatec Mushroom Velada.* Harcourt Brace Jovanovich, New York, NY.

Wasson, R.G. *et al.* 1978. *The Road to Eleusis: Unveiling the Secret of the Mysteries.* Harcourt Brace Jovanovich, New York, NY.

Wasson, R.G. *et al.* 1980. *El Camino a Eleusis: Una Solución al Enigma de los Misterios.* Fondo de Cultura Económica, Ciudad de México, México. [Wasson *et al.* 1978]

Wasson, R.G. *et al.* 1986. *Persephone's Quest: Entheogens and the Origins of Religion.* Yale University Press, New Haven, CT.

Wilbert, J. 1987. *Tobacco and Shamanism in South America.* Yale University Press, New Haven, CT.

Zetler, G. *et al.* 1970. "Cerebral pharmacokinetics of tremor-producing Harmala and Iboga alkaloids" *Pharmacology* 4: 129–142.

The Angels' Dictionary:
Toward a Vocabulary
For Sacred Inebriants, Ecstatic
States and Kindred Topics

Pre-Columbian Mexican sculpture of Xochipilli, the Lord of Entheogens, unearthed near Tlalmanalco on the slopes of the volcano Popocatépetl. Pen-and-ink-drawing by Tim Girvin, Olympia, WA, 1976.

Exordium

> Thus it comes about that we are all divided
> into two classes: those who have taken the
> mushroom and are disqualified by our sub-
> jective experience, and those who have not
> taken the mushroom and are disqualified by
> their total ignorance of the subject!
>
> **R. Gordon Wasson**
> *The Hallucinogenic Fungi of Mexico* [1961]

In the summer of 1960, five years after having experienced shamanic ecstasy at first
hand, under the influence of the Divine Inebriant *Psilocybe caerulescens* Murrill, with
which he had been initiated by the Mazatec Indian shaman María Sabina, the New
York banker and pioneering 'ethnomycologist' R. Gordon Wasson endeavored to
describe his ecstatic experience to a conference of professional mycologists in Still-
water, Oklahoma. Wasson remarked:

> Here let me say a word parenthetically about the nature of the psychic
> disturbance that the eating of the mushroom causes. This disturban-
> ce is wholly different from the effects of alcohol, as different as night
> from day. We are entering upon a discussion where the vocabulary of
> the English language, of any European language, is seriously deficient.
> There are no apt words in them to characterize your state when you
> are, shall we say, 'bemushroomed.' For hundreds, even thousands, of
> years we have thought about these things in terms of alcohol, and we
> now have to break the bonds imposed upon us by the alcoholic asso-
> ciation. We are all, willy nilly, confined within the prison walls of our
> every-day vocabulary. With skill in our choice of words we may
> stretch accepted meanings to cover slightly new feelings and thoughts,
> but when a state of mind is utterly distinct, wholly novel, then all our
> old words fail. How do you tell a man born blind what seeing is like?
> [...] If we use by analogy the terms suitable for alcohol, we prejudice
> the mushroom, and since there are few among us who have been be-
> mushroomed, there is danger that the experience will not be fairly
> judged. What we need is a vocabulary to describe all the modalities
> of a Divine Inebriant. [Wasson 1961]

[63]

Noting that he was "painfully aware of the inadequacy of my words, any words, to conjure up for you an image of that state," Wasson nevertheless proceeded to regale the mycologists with a moving and poetic description of being bemushroomed, to give voice to the Word; yea, words to the ineffable. I know not whether Wasson's inspired poetry was lost on the mycologists, but it cannot be gainsaid that he came closer than anyone else has, to crafting a verbal image of "what the ineffable is, and what ecstasy means." Aldous Huxley's attempts to describe mescaline-inspired ecstasy are jejune and stilted by comparison, and most of the other writing on shamanic ecstasy does not even merit mention here. Henri Michaux strove mightily to verbalize the ineffable in French, and the Swiss Islamic scholar Rudolf Gelpke penned some of our most brilliant descriptions of ecstasy, catalyzed by his psychonautic bioassays with *Indocybin®* or psilocybine, visionary principle of María Sabina's fungal sacrament, and with *Delysid®* or LSD-25, a semi-synthetic mushroomic pharmacotheon—both visionary pharmaceuticals having been discovered by Gelpke's friend and countryman Albert Hofmann. The great German writer Ernst Jünger, both in his novels and in his personal psychonautic log-book of visionary experiments, including some in collaboration with Gelpke, Hofmann and others, likewise stands as one of the supreme linguists of the ineffable.

During the last decade of his life, Aldous Huxley was much concerned with sacred inebriants, and in a lecture given in San Francisco in January 1959, he made the following observation [quoted by Horowitz & Palmer in 1977, *Moksha*, p. 166]:

> Our problem is to adapt a language which is not now suitable to describing the continuum of mind and body, a universe of complete continuity. Somehow or other we have to invent the means of talking about these problems in an artistically varied way which shall make them accessible to the general public. Ideally, for example, we ought to be able to talk about a mystical experience simultaneously in terms of theology, of psychology and of biochemistry. This is a pretty tall order, but unless we can do something of the kind, it will remain extraordinarily difficult for people to think about this continuous web of life, to think about it as a continuum, and not in terms of the old Platonic and Cartesian dualism which so extraordinarily falsifies our picture of the world... As long ago as the beginning of the 19th Century, Wordsworth in his preface to the *Lyrical Ballads* made the statement that the time would come when the remotest discovery of the physicist and the chemist would become a suitable subject for poetry.

I would say that time has now come… when any true poet must also be an entheogenic psychonaut; when psychonauts must communicate in poetry and not jargon… when scientific discoveries, at least in the field of entheogenic ethnopharmacognosy, are a suitable subject for poetry… when we must transcend our materialistic, wordbound hallucinations of the universe…

The plethora of words coined by scholars for shamanic inebriants like the psilocybian mushrooms and the *péyotl* cactus (along with their visionary constituents, in this case psilocybine and mescaline), and the lack of agreement on terminology for such, acceptable to ethnographers, historians, phytochemists and pharmacologists alike, underscores the linguistic dilemma cited by Wasson—now that we have embarked on scholarly investigation of ecstasy-producing drugs, treading a trail he and his wife first blazed, it becomes increasingly obvious how urgently we need "a vocabulary to describe all the modalities of a Divine Inebriant." In the mid-nineteenth century, when scientists began to address the subject of visionary drugs, the operative epithet was 'narcotics' provoking 'intoxication.' Thus German pioneer Ernst Freiherr von Bibra described 'narcotic dainties' (*narkotischen Genußmittel*) while Scot James F. Johnston contemporaneously catalogued 'the narcotics we indulge in.' Briton Mordecai C. Cooke later published a *Popular History of the Seven Prevailing Narcotics of the World,* and his compatriot Richard Spruce discovered some 'remarkable narcotics' in Amazonia. *Narcotic,* of course, from Greek ναρκωτικ–υν, 'to benumb, to stupefy' refers to drugs evoking such an effect, and is properly applied to the prototypical narcotic drug opium (dried exudate of unripe capsules of the opium poppy, *Papaver somniferum* L.), its analgesic alkaloids morphine and codeine, and artificial derivatives of these, whether semi-synthetic, such as heroin, or totally artificial, like methadone. On the other hand, the visionary drugs which make up the shamans' pharmacopœia tend to be potent stimulants and sensitizing agents, anything but benumbing or stupefying! *Narcotic,* moreover, has acquired in the twentieth century a pejorative political significance, designating an illicit drug— the decidedly stimulating plant-drug *coca* (*Erythroxylum coca* Lamarck) and its stimulating alkaloid cocaine were defined as *narcotics* by the first federal anti-drug law, the Harrison Narcotic Act of 1914. Clearly, the subject of shamanic inebriants, or of non-alcoholic inebriating drugs in general, was far too complex and variegated to be subsumed under the heading of *narcotics* which, in its nineteenth century use had the general meaning 'psychoactive' or 'psychotropic,' that is, of any inebriating drug save, in this case, alcohol.

The first scientist to propose a more detailed nomenclature for the psychoactive drugs was German Louis Lewin. In his pioneering 1924 treatise *Phantastica* (translated into French, Italian and English), Lewin proposed five categories of *Stupefying and Stimulating Pleasure Drugs*: 1) *Euphorica* or *Seelenberuhigungsmittel* ('anodynes for the spirit') of which the opiate narcotics were the prototypes; 2) *Phantastica* or *Sinnestäuschungsmittel* ('sensory illusion agents'), including a goodly number of visionary drugs; 3) *Inebriantia* or *Berauschungsmittel* ('intoxicants'), alcohol and other solvents; 4) *Hypnotica* or *Schlafmittel* ('sleep agents') like chloral hydrate; and 5) *Excitantia* or *Erregungsmittel* ('stimulants'), various caffeine-containing drugs, tobacco, *etc.* With the exception of his misclassification of *coca* in the opiate category and of the visionary tobacco and *paricá* snuff of Amazonia in the stimulant group, Lewin's cataloguing was precise; and Albert Hofmann later proposed the inclusion of a sixth group, which I have called *Neuroleptica*, to encompass such drugs as reserpine and chlorpromazine, unknown in Lewin's day. Although Lewin achieved a precise subcategorization of the psychoactive drugs, it must be said that his proposed terminology, with the sole exception of *Hypnotica*, failed to be adopted in his native Germany, nor did it make headway in the French-, Italian- or English-speaking worlds. Although today we recognize Lewin's category of *hypnotics*, *Euphorica* are now generally called *narcotics*; *Inebriantia*, *intoxicants*, and *Excitantia*, *stimulants*. His eponymous *Phantastica*, the subject of this book, have been called just about anything but. Evoking as they do ecstasy, the ineffable, it is not surprising that this most mysterious (not to mention both chemically and pharmacologically variegated) group of drugs has defied nomenclature, and continues to stimulate considerable debate.

Albert Hofmann's discovery of the potent semi-synthetic visionary drug LSD in 1938–1943 catalyzed renewed interest in shamanic inebriants. Although the first (1947) publication regarding the novel drug referred to it with Lewin's terminology, as a *Phantasticum*, the generic term *hallucinogen[ic]* came into widespread use six years later, evolving into the predominant term in the phytochemical, botanical and pharmacological literature. Since psychologists and psychotherapists at one time thought these drugs produced a 'model psychosis,' terms like *psychotomimetic*, *psychosomimetic* and *psychodysleptic*, all with a connotation of pathology, came to dominate the medical literature. The strange word *psychedelic*, both a noun and an adjective, coined by Humphry Osmond in hopes the anomalous root *psyche-* would not share the pathological overtones of the psychiatrists' terminology, dominated the pharmacological literature for about a decade. Since it soon acquired secondary meanings—psychedelic art, music, culture, *etc.*—associated ineluctably with countercultural use in the 1960s, and has a decidedly pejorative flavor outside of that counterculture, *psychedelic* is now little used as a scientific term, 'though it remains the most widely-used epithet in the counterculture. Pursuant to R. Gordon Wasson's wish for a vocabulary to describe divine inebriants, Carl A.P. Ruck, Danny Staples, Jeremy Bigwood and I, in collaboration with Wasson, proposed the neologism *entheogen[ic]* in 1979, as a term "appropriate for describing states of shamanic and ecstatic possession induced by ingestion of mind-altering drugs." Noting that shamanic inebriants did not provoke hallucinations or other psychiatric pathologies, we deemed *hallucinogen[ic]*, *psychotomimetic* and its congeners to be pejorative, prejudicing "transcendent and beatific states of communion with deity" characteristic of traditional use of visionary drugs. We noted that, besides being pejorative outside of the counterculture, *psychedelic* was "so invested with connotations of the pop-culture of the 1960s that it is incongruous to speak of a shaman's taking a 'psychedelic' drug." *Entheogen[ic]* (literally 'becoming divine within') was derived from an obsolete Greek word describing religious communion with visionary drugs, prophetic seizures and erotic passion, and is cognate with the common word *enthusiasm*. Since the neologism is apposite to traditional contexts of use of shamanic inebriants, it has met with an enthusiastic reception by ethnographers and historians, and has appeared in print in all of the major European languages, plus Catalán. *Entheogen[ic]* has now become the primary term for shamanic inebriants in the Spanish-speaking world, and bids fair to become the predominant term for these drugs in the ethnographic and ethnopharmacognostical literature worldwide.

Although we have thus elegantly solved the problem of a culturally-appropriate, non-pejorative term to describe the context of use of these drugs, the phytochemists and pharmacologists have yet to agree on a term to categorize their pharmacological action. There is no facile chemical classification, as many structural types of alkaloids, terpenoids, amino acids, even coumarins are psychoactive in various shamanic inebriants. Similarly, there is considerable pharmacological variability within this class of drugs. *Hallucinogen[ic]* remains the predominant term for the older generation of scientists, despite the fact that most of these drugs usually do not produce hallucinations in the clinical sense. *Psychedelic* is still much used by younger scientists, but generally only in reference to drugs with effects like LSD or mescaline; while important shamanic inebriants like the mushroom *Amanita muscaria* (L. ex Fr.) Pers. ex Gray, the mint *Salvia divinorum* Epling et Játiva, tobacco (the shamanic drug of the Americas *par excellence*)—all likewise used culturally as *entheogens*—are said **not** to evoke *psychedelic* effects. Although we may presently speak of all these shamanic 'plant-teachers' as *entheogenic* drugs or as *entheogens*, we as yet have no single word to describe their pharmacological effects, and must still have recourse to cumbersome binomials, like *visionary effects, ecstatic effects, etc.*; and we might just as well resurrect the obscure, but quite elegant, term *psychoptic*: 'producing mental or spiritual vision.'

[67]

Three and a half decades after Gordon Wasson signaled the need for "a vocabulary to describe all the modalities of a Divine Inebriant," and Aldous Huxley called for a means to "talk about a mystical experience simultaneously in terms of theology, of psychology and of biochemistry," it seemed to me prudent at least closely to examine the extant words in the English language, many of them obsolete, for shamanic inebriants, ecstatic states and allied topics. We are not bereft of words for the appropriate concepts, but we are certainly not accustomed to speaking of the ineffable. What words we have we no longer use, or have burdened with secondary meanings, and sometimes then depaupered by overuse—the word *ecstasy* itself is an obvious example. There follows a vocabulary of the ineffable, with the *Oxford English Dictionary* as my primary authority. In emulation of that milestone of scholarship, which remains the greatest dictionary in any tongue, my definitions are supported by quotations (starting with Chaucer in 1386) from classical drug and general literature in six languages—English, French, German, Spanish, Italian and Portuguese (plus one in Mazatec)—giving the original text followed by my translation in brackets. Since we are dealing with a pangæan phenomenon, and in a conscious attempt to avoid excess Eurocentrism, I have included 70 words (22%) from 29 non-European languages—Mazatec, Huichol, Zapotec, Mayan and Náhuatl from Mesoamerica, Shuar, Quichua, Warao and Tupí from South America (those two great centers of the entheogenic arts and sciences); plus Oglala Sioux and Caribou Eskimo from North America; Kenyah Dyak, Wiradjuri Aborigine and Hawai'ian from Pacifica; Galwa-Mpongwe from central Africa; Tungusic and Uralic from Siberia (which is, as we are coming to discover, the true cradle of civilization); as well as from classical Sanskrit, Urdu, Sumerian, Arabic, Persian, Old Germanic, Irish, Welsh, Hebrew, Chinese, Russian and Japanese.

The reader will notice that 37 of 318 entries (12%) are neologisms, of which 18 or half are my own; with novel words by R. Gordon Wasson, Ernst Jünger, Thomas Szasz and 11 other linguistic pioneers. Many of these new terms are scientific, and it is only natural that we should create neologisms in our gropings toward a vocabulary for that which is, by definition, beyond words. I make no pretense of comprehensive definitions (and include neither etymologies nor pronunciations), but focus exclusively on the senses of the words apposite to my subject. Some terms are included with an eye toward highlighting significant events in the history of visionary inebriants and especially their repression. There are numerous cross-references to the definitions, leading the reader to related concepts and terms. Defined words, when used in any of the definitions, are capitalized for further convenience. Page citations to quotations generally refer to the first, original editions of the works in question.

The Angels' Dictionary

Thou paintest things with entheogens,
O, Giver of Life!
With songs you immerse them in pigments,
You blend with colors
All that must live on the Earth!
Acolmiztli Nezahualcóyotl
Poet, warrior, Lord of Texcoco [*circa* 1450]
Como una Pintura nos Iremos Borrando

Absinthe—European name for wormwood, *Artemisia absinthium* L.; and for the liqueur distilled from alcoholic macerations of wormwood leaves; both containing the inebriating volatile terpenoid thujone [absinthol, salvanol, tanacetone]. Absinthism, a neurotoxic syndrome in heavy users of absinthe liqueurs, led to their illegalization in the first two decades of the twentieth century; 'though this may have been a result of their high Alcohol content and their common adulteration with antimony trichloride and copper sulfate, rather than their content of thujone, which occurs in many ethnomedicinal species of *Artemisia*, culinary sage [*Salvia officinalis* L.] and many other commonly-used edible and medicinal plants. See: **Alcohol.**

1872 Rimbaud *Comédie de la Soif.* Come, the Wines go to the beaches./And the waves by the millions!/See the wild Bitter/Rolling from the top of the mountains!/Let us, wise pilgrims, reach/The Absinthe with the green pillars…

1881 Cros *Avec les Fleurs, Avec les Femmes.* Avec les Fleurs, avec les Femmes,/Avec l'Absinthe, avec le Feu,/On peut se divertir un peu,/Jouer son rôle en quelque drame./L'Absinthe, bue un soir d'hiver,/Eclaire en vert l'âme enfumée;/Et les Fleurs, sur la bien-aimée,/Embaument devant le Feu clair. [With Flowers, and with Women,/With Absinthe, and with Fire,/We can divert ourselves awhile,/Act out our part in any drama./Absinthe, on a winter evening,/Lights up in green the sooty soul;/And Flowers, on the beloved,/Grow fragrant before the clear Fire.]

Addiction—Devotion; the state of being given to a pursuit or habit; today largely a political rather than a medical concept, chiefly pejorative and used to denote daily use of drugs, especially compulsive use of stigmatized and illegal drugs like heroin and cocaine, as opposed to similar use of legal drugs such as tobacco and Alcohol. Hence: Addict, Addicted, Addictedness. Synonyms: **Habituation, Pharmacothymia.** See: **Habitué.**

1779 Johnson *L.P. Philips Works*, II, 291. His addiction to tobacco is mentioned by one of his biographers.

1985 Ott *The Cacahuatl Eater*, 76. 'Drug addiction' will be defined as habitual (i.e. at least once daily) use of a given drug, at such levels of dosage and for sufficient duration that abstinence from the drug will evoke specific 'withdrawal' symptoms. Characteristic of such withdrawal symptoms is that they are ameliorated by administration of the drug in question, at a sufficient dose.

Afflatus, Divine—Divine Inspiration; literally: 'being breathed upon by deity,' perhaps in origin derivative of shamanic blowing or sucking. Hence: Afflate, Afflation, Afflatitious. See: **Enthusiasm, Inspiration, Logos, Tecpillatolli, Vac, Word.**

1857 Ludlow *The Hasheesh Eater*, 124. I drank the blood of grapes like nectar... I reeled under the possession of the divine afflatus.

1957 Wasson *Mushrooms Russia & History*, 299. Our Indian friends were sitting up, amazed at being stroked by the Divine Afflatus.

1980 Wasson *The Wondrous Mushroom*, 225. The divine afflatus of poetry is the gift of the entheogen.

Agape—Early Christian love-feast; celebration of the Lord's Supper; hence: by extension, sacramental ingestion of the Pharmacotheon or Medicamentum Divinum. See: **Communion, Element, Eucharist, Host, Pharmacotheon, Sacrament.**

1954 Huxley *The Doors of Perception*, 57. A sect whose principal rite is a kind of Early Christian Agape, or Love-Feast, where slices of peyote take the place of the sacramental bread and wine.

1957 Wasson *Mushrooms Russia & History*, 287. We penetrated into the mushroom cult much more deeply than before, eating the mushrooms ourselves as participants in a communal agape.

1959 Wasson *Transactions of the New York Academy of Sciences* 21: 333. The ceremony we attended in southern Mexico was a true agape, a love-feast, a Holy Supper, in which we all felt the presence of God, in which the Element carried its own conviction in the miracles it performed within us.

Age of Entheogens *nov. verb.*—Bygone era in which shamanic ingestion of entheogenic plants was 'the highest vehicle for the expression of man's religious yearnings,' or that stage of cultural evolution in remote outposts of the contemporary world characterized by the survival and primacy of shamanism and use of entheogenic plant Sacraments. See: **Entheogen, Pagan, Shaman, Wasson Theory.**

1980 Wasson *The Wondrous Mushroom*, 221. I have sometimes asked myself whether the unlettered ages, stretching back through æons of time, were not those belonging peculiarly to the entheogens, the Age of entheogens.

Aira—See: **Darnel.**

Ajucá—See: **Vinho da Jurema.**

Albigensians—See: **Manichæans.**

Alcohol—Ethyl alcohol or ethanol; C_2H_5OH, product of fermentation and volatile active agent in beers and Wines. Originally derived from Arabic *al-kohl*, a name for powdered stibnite or antimony trisulfide used since antiquity as eye-shadow and known as *kajal* in Hindi. Paracelsus gave the name *alcohol* to the Quintessence or distillable Spirit of Wine or *alcohol of wine*. Hence: Alcoholic, Alcoholism, *etc.* See: **Absinthe, Laudanum, Quintessence, Spirit, Symposium, Wine.**

Alkaloid—Nitrogen-containing natural organic compound; which represents the pharmacologically-active principle of numerous Psychoactive and other medicinal plants; of which morphine, isolated from Opium by Sertürner in the first decade of the nineteenth century, is the prototype. Literally: alkali-like; in referrence to the weakly basic nature of such compounds, consequent of their contained nitrogen atom[s]. Hence: Alkaloidal. See: β-**Carboline, Darnel, Deadly Nightshade, Delysid,**® **Ergot, Henbane, Iboga, Indocybin,**® **Indole, Laudanum, Mandrake, Mescaline, Monoamine-Oxidase, Narcotic, Nigerine, Ololiuhqui, Opium,** β-**Phenethylamine, Syrian Rue, Tryptamine, Vinho da Jurema.**

Ambrosia—The legendary food [Homer], drink [Sappho] or unguent of the Olympian gods; which conferred immortality. Literally: immortal. Cognate with the Sanskrit Amrta, the entheogenic Soma potion, *ambrosia* referred originally to visionary Potions derived from sacred plants in the Aegean area. Hence: Ambrosiac, Ambrosiacal, Ambrosial. See: **Amrta, Elixir, Nectar, Soma.**
   1821 De Quincey *Confessions of an English Opium Eater,* 'The Pleasures of Opium.' Opium! dread agent of unimaginable pleasure and pain! I had heard of it as I had of manna or of Ambrosia, but no further...
   1993 Ott *Pharmacotheon,* 143. The *amrta,* the *Soma* potion, is etymologically identical to the Greek *ambrosia,* which we now know, thanks to Ruck, Hofmann and Wasson, to have been an entheogenic potion.

Amirucapanga—See: **Chacruna.**

Amrta [Amreeta, Amrita]—The Soma potion; aqueous extract of the entheogenic

Soma plant imbibed by the Vedic priests in the Indus Valley in the second millennium B.C. and extolled in the *RgVeda*, especially Mandala IX. Literally: deathless, immortal, ambrosial. Hence: Amrital *nov. verb.*, Amritous *nov. verb.* See: **Ambrosia, Elixir, Haoma, Nectar, Soma.**

> **1857** Ludlow *The Hasheesh Eater*, 132. The Amreeta cup of Unveiling [chapter title]
>
> **1968** Wasson *Soma*, 63. Many other names are applied to Soma in the RgVeda, all of them metaphors stressing one or another of its aspects. In passages where the drink receives the highest homage it is sometimes called *amrta*, cognate with 'ambrosia,' the liquor of immortality.
>
> **1968** Wasson *Soma*, 155. Alone among us all, he has known *amrta*, the ambrosia of the Immortals.
>
> **1968** Doniger *Soma*, 130. The *Mahabharata* relates that the gods once churned the ocean in order to obtain the *amrta*, but a terrible poison emerged and would have destroyed them all had Siva not swallowed it and saved them…
>
> **1994** Ott *Ayahuasca Analogues*, 12. May the Entheogenic Reformation prevail over the Pharmacratic Inquisition, leading to the spiritual rebirth of humankind at Our Lady Gæa's breasts, from which may ever copiously flow the *amrta*, the *ambrosia*, the *ayahuasca* of eternal life!

Anahuasca *nov. verb.*—Potion analogous to Amazonian Ayahuasca; in that it contains the Tryptamine DMT as entheogenic principle; rendered orally-active by presence of Monoamine-Oxidase inhibitors, generally β-Carbolines from Syrian Rue [*Peganum harmala*L.]. Synonyms: **Ayahuasca Analogue, Ayahuasca Borealis.** See: **Ayahuasca, β-Carboline, Congenihuasca, Endohuasca, Haoma, Monoamine-Oxidase, Nigerine, Pharmahuasca, Syrian Rue, Tryptamine.**

> **1995** Ott *The Age of Entheogens*, 28. According to human pharmacological studies employing 'ayahuasca capsules' (or *pharmahuasca*) and *anahuasca* or 'ayahuasca analogues.'

Anaktoron—The inner sanctum of the Telesterion or Initiation hall in which were celebrated the annual Eleusinian Mysteries; wherein the Hiera or the sacred objects were concealed and to which only the high priest or Hierophant, 'he who shows the Hiera' had access. See: **Deiknymena, Eleusinian Mysteries, Hiera, Kistai.**

> **1961** Mylonas *Eleusis and the Eleusinian Mysteries*, 273. The Hiera were kept in the Anaktoron, the holy of holies in the center of the Telesterion, the year round and could be revealed by no one else.

Angakoq—*Shaman*, in the language of the Caribou Eskimo of the Arctic. See: **Shaman.**

> **1979** Halifax *Shamanic Voices*, 65. When the neophyte *angakoq* was taken back to his

people after his retreat in the harsh winter solitudes, he was so emaciated that he resembled a skeleton. After a year of sexual abstinence, special diet, and other prohibitions, he finally became a shaman.

Angos—A metal vessel in which Baubo served Demeter the Kykeon or Eleusinian Potion; according to an Orphic hymn. On the Caryatids from Eleusis, this is depicted as a covered, two-handled, stemmed vessel in the shape of an Opium poppy capsule. See: **Eleusinian Mysteries, Kernos, Kykeon, Opium.**

1978 Ruck *The Road to Eleusis*, 81. In an Orphic hymn, where the *kykeon* is served by Baubo instead of Iambe, the vessel is named an *angos*...

Anodyne—An analgesic drug or Potion; drug that alleviates pain. Hence: Anodynous.

1993 Ott *Pharmacotheon*, 62. There was no effective alternative therapy for tuberculosis which people might have taken *in lieu* of the anodynes...

Apollonian—Of or pertaining to the Grecian god Apollo; the term that Friedrich Nietzsche chose for the rational, controlled, cerebral aspect of human consciousness, in contrast to the irrational, animal, sensual side; the Dionysian, in his seminal 1872 [first] book, *The Birth of Tragedy from the Spirit of Music*. See: **Dionysus.**

Aporrheta—Literally: what should not be spoken; referring to the secret of the Eleusinian and other Mysteries. See: **Arrheta, Eleusinian Mysteries, Hiera, Ineffable, Kykeon.**

1978 Ruck *The Road to Eleusis*, 84. The identity of the drug in the *kykeon* must also have been part of the secret, the *aporrheta* or things that should not be spoken...

Arcanum—Mystery; the miraculous *Elixir Vitæ* or Panacea of the alchemists; the archetypal Entheogen. Hence: Arcane, Arcanum Arcanorum. See: **Elixir, Mystery, Panacea, Philosophers' Stone, Quintessence.**

1646 Browne *Pseudodoxia Epidemica*, 135. The Philosophers Stone, potable gold, or any of these Arcana's.
1970 Jünger *Annäherungen*, 16. Er suchte den Hauptschlüssel. Muß aber nicht das stärkste Arkanum notwendig tödlich sein? [He sought the master-key. But must not the most powerful arcanum necessarily be deadly?]
1993 Ott *Pharmacotheon*, 82. Penetrating at once the *arcanum arcanorum* of New World Indian spirituality and the obscurity of modern science.

Archaic Revival *nov. verb.*—A term proposed by Terence McKenna for the anach-

ronistic revival of interest in shamanism and shamanic inebriants; coined in his 1991 book *The Archaic Revival*. See: **Entheogenic Reformation**.
1991 McKenna *Archaic Revival*, 2. Welcome to the Archaic Revival.

Archetype—See: **Idea**.

Arrheta—Unspeakable, ineffable. Greek word referring to the secret of the Eleusinian and other Mysteries. See: **Aporrheta, Eleusinian Mysteries, Hiera, Ineffable, Kykeon**.
1978 Ruck *The Road to Eleusis*, 84. The Mystery was an experience rather than something learned. Basically, it was *arrheta* or unspeakable.

Auto da Fé [Auto de Fe]—Literally: 'act of the faith,' a trial or edict of the Holy Office of the Inquisition; particularly the public execution, usually by burning, of heretics 'relaxed' or condemned. The Portuguese form, using the article *da*, entered the English language before the Spanish, with the corresponding article *de*. See: **Heresy, Inquisition, Pogrom, Scapegoat**.

Axis Mundi—The imagined axle about which the Earth as well as the heavens were thought to turn; in the classic world symbolized by the Omphalos or navel, a rounded, conical stone in the temple of Apollo at Delphi. The Axis Mundi or Pillar of the World symbolized the shamanic Tree of Life or World Tree, whose fruit is the primordial Entheogen; which was said to grow at the Navel of the Earth. See: **Delphi, Omphalos, Tree of Life, Tree of the Knowledge of Good and Evil**.

Ayahuasca—Literally: 'vine of the soul' or 'liana of the dead'; Amazonian Quechua name for the liana, *Banisteriopsis caapi* (Spr. ex Griseb.) Morton, and for a complex of entheogenic shamanic Potions consisting of aqueous extracts of the stem of this and related species of Malpighiaceae (which contain Monoamine-Oxidase-inhibiting β-Carbolines); and of other shamanic plants, particularly those containing the Tryptamine DMT. Hence: Ayahuasquero. Synonym: **Ayahuasca Australis**. See: **Anahuasca, Ayahuasca Analogue, β-Carboline, Chacruna, Congenihuasca, Daime, Endohuasca, Hoasca, Monoamine-Oxidase, Natemä, Nigerine, Peyohuasca, Pharmahuasca, Tryptamine, Vinho da Jurema**.
1857 Villavicencio *Geografía de la República del Ecuador*, 373. Yo, por mí, sé decir que cuando he tomado el *Ayahuasca*, he sentido rodeos de la cabeza, luego un viaje aereo... [As for me, I can say that when I have partaken of *Ayahuasca*, I have felt my head swimming, followed by an aerial voyage...]

Ayahuasca Analogue *nov. verb.*—An entheogenic Potion with a Tryptamine such as DMT as active principle; rendered orally-active by Monoamine-Oxidase-inhibiting β-Carbolines; but with either or both components derived from non-Amazonian, or non-traditional source plants. Synonyms: **Anahuasca, Ayahuasca Borealis**. See: **Ayahuasca, β-Carboline, Congenihuasca, Endohuasca, Huasca, Monoamine-Oxidase, Nigerine, Pharmahuasca, Syrian Rue, Tryptamine**.

    1984 McKenna *Journal of Ethnopharmacology* 10: 218. Thus, this '*ayahuasca* analogue' (as the second mixture was termed) contained 69% harmine, 26% THH and 4.6% harmaline; DMT, which comprised 6.1% of the total alkaloids, was not included in the 'analogue' mixture.

    1993 Ott *Pharmacotheon*, 245. Dennis McKenna has proposed the name *ayahuasca borealis* for temperate-zone *ayahuasca* analogues.

Ayahuasca Australis *nov. verb.*—Synonym for the traditional Amazonian Ayahuasca Potions; in contrast to Ayahuasca Borealis, the name proposed for temperate-zone Ayahuasca Analogues. See: **Anahuasca, Ayahuasca, Ayahuasca Analogue, Ayahuasca Borealis**.

    1994 Ott *Ayahuasca Analogues*, 12. These are the '*ayahuasca* analogues' of this book's title, which have also been called *ayahuasca borealis*, or the 'northern *ayahuasca*,' to distinguish them from decidedly tropical Amazonian *ayahuasca*, which we would technically have to call *ayahuasca australis*.

Ayahuasca Borealis *nov. verb.*—See: **Anahuasca, Ayahuasca Analogue, Ayahuasca Australis**.

Bacchanalia—Festivals held in honor of the Greek god of Wine and Inebriation, Bacchus. The Scandal of the Bacchanalia in Rome in 186 B.C. led to a Pogrom against the Bacchantes, and is cited by some modern scholars as the prototype for the subsequent persecution of the Christians, the mediæval witch-hunts, and the contemporary 'War on Drugs.' Hence: Bacchanal, Bacchanalian, Bacchante, Bacchic. See: **Dionysus, Mænad, Pharmacratic Inquisition, Witchcraft**.

Bacchante—See: **Mænad**.

Bacchus—The Greek god of Wine or Inebriation; comparable to the Mexican Xochipilli. Synonym: **Dionysus**. See: **Bacchanalia, Mænad**.

Bahanarotu—*Shaman* or 'light shaman,' in the language of the Warao Indians of

Venezuela. The *bahanarotu* are known to employ tobacco as a visionary aid to shamanic divination. See: **Shaman.**

1972 Wilbert *Flesh of the Gods*, 65. The radiant body of this youth, his weapons, and his shamanic rattle were all made of tobacco smoke… 'Now you possess it,' said the *Bahana*. 'You are a *bahana-rotu*.'

Bali-Dayong—*Shaman*, in the language of the Melanesian Kenyah Dyak people. Literally: one who enters the trance state to seek the spirits. See: **Shaman.**

1979 Halifax *Shamanic Voices*, 213. Balu Asong Gau, a Kenyah Dyak *bali dayong* ('one who enters a trance state to seek the spirits') was the head shaman of spirit medium activities that still survived in the longhouse. When she was a young girl, the ancient spirits had possessed her and spoke through her, and she did not know why this had happened.

Beatitude—Supreme blessedness or happiness. Hence: Beatific, Beatifical, Beatification, Beatify. See: **Bliss.**

1821 De Quincey *Confessions of an English Opium Eater*, 'The Pleasures of Opium.' He has ever since existed in my mind as the beatific vision of an immortal druggist, sent down to earth on a special mission to myself.

1838 Gautier *La Pipe d'Opium*. Une mollesse pleine de béatitude ne tarda pas à s'emparer de moi… [A sensuality full of beatitude did not tarry in overcoming me…]

1898 Ellis *Contemporary Review* 73: 130. Under the influence of mescal he experienced scarcely the slightest unpleasant reaction, but, on the contrary, a very marked state of well being and beatitude.

Beta-Carboline—See: β-**Carboline.**

Beta-Phenethylamine—See: β-**Phenethylamine.**

Bhangas—Sanskrit word for the inebriating leaves of *Cannabis indica* Lam., or Indian hemp; especially sacred to Shiva and commonly used as *bhang lassi*, a sort of blended drink with milk or curds. See: **Charas, Dawamesk, Ganja, Hashish, Kif, Majoon.**

1977 Sharma *Journal of Psychedelic Drugs* 9: 337. It is said that *Cannabis* is the favourite drink of Lord Shiva… His devotees dutifully and affectionately offer Him *Cannabis* and *Datura*, in return for earthly and sometimes not so earthly rewards! As the story goes, when the oceans were churned, 'bhanga' (*Cannabis*) was one of the nectars found for Lord Shiva's use.

1980 La Barre *Culture in Context*, 96. *Bhang* is also drunk in variously spiced *thandai* drinks infused in water or milk, eaten in the form of small balls (often as jaggery or palm-sugar candies) and in *hari* ('god') *gulfi*, native green ice cream.

Blechon—See: **Glechon.**

Bliss—Beatitude, ecstasy, rapture; mental and spiritual blessedness. Hence: Blissful, Blissfulness, Blissless. See: **Beatitude, Rapture.**
> 1629 Milton *Nativity*, 98. Such musick sweet… As all their souls in blissful rapture took.

Bwiti—Contemporary syncretic Neo-Christian religion of the Fang and of other groups in equatorial West Africa; in which the powdered roots of the traditional Entheogen Iboga [Eboka], *Tabernanthe iboga* Baillon, serve as the Eucharist in Mass. See: **Entheogenic Reformation, Eucharist, Iboga.**
> 1994 Ott *Ayahuasca Analogues*, 11. Far from being an aberration or an anachronism, these churches, and the African Bwiti religion centered on the entheogenic sacrament *eboka*, rather represent the future of Christianity, stripped of its Doctrine of Transubstantiation by the Entheogenic Reformation, and with one or another *genuine* entheogen replacing the *placebo* sacrament!

Caapi—See: **Ayahuasca.**

β-Carboline—A tricyclic Indole compound, pyrido[3,4-*b*]indole. Common plant and animal metabolites, many β-Carboline Alkaloids from plants have mild Sedative effects; in Ayahuasca-type entheogenic Potions, β-Carbolines from the Ayahuasca liana [especially harmine and *d*-leptaflorine; secondarily harmaline] serve as inhibitors of the enzyme Monoamine-Oxidase [MAO], thus rendering the entheogenic Tryptamine DMT orally-active, when it would ordinarily be metabolized and inactivated by MAO in the user's body. Also: *Beta*-Carboline. See: **Alkaloid, Anahuasca, Ayahuasca, Ayahuasca Analogue, Congenihuasca, Endohuasca, Indole, Monoamine-Oxidase, Peyohuasca, Pharmahuasca, Syrian Rue, Tryptamine.**
> 1994 Ott *Ayahuasca Analogues*, 26. Indeed, the β-carbolines function here not as specific psychotropic constituents but as enzyme inhibitors, to prevent our bodies from deactivating the DMT contained in the leaves, which is not ordinarily active orally.

Cathars [Cathari]—See: **Manichæans.**

Catholicon—See: **Panacea.**

Chacruna—Literally: 'mixture' or 'mate' or 'female complement'; an Amazonian

Quechua name for the DMT-rich leaves of *Psychotria viridis* Ruiz et Pavón and allied species of *Psychotria* [such as *huarmi chacruna*, 'women's mixture' and *supay chacruna*, 'devil's mixture'], which represent the major visionary additives to Ayahuasca in the Upper Amazon. Also: Amirucapanga or Sami Ruca [in Ecuador], Chacrona [in Brasil]. See: **Ayahuasca, Nigerine.**

    1986 Luna *Vegetalismo*, 68. **Chacruna (Psychotria viridis).** The most important additive used by vegetalistas. They recognize several types of **chacruna**…

    1994 Ott *Ayahuasca Analogues*, 24. Called *chacruna* in Perú, and *sami ruca* or *amirucapanga* in Ecuador, leaves of this shrub [*Psychotria viridis*] are similarly added to *ayahuasca* to enhance its visionary potency.

Chá Hoasca—See: **Hoasca, União do Vegetal.**

Charas—Sanskrit word for the resin of *Cannabis indica* Lamarck or Indian hemp; more commonly known by the Arabic word Hashish. In India, this is usually smoked in a straight pipe called a *chillum*, and is especially sacred to the god Shiva. See: **Bhangas, Dawamesk, Ganja, Hashish, Kif, Majoon.**

    1980 La Barre *Culture in Context*, 96. *Bhang* (hemp leaves) and *charas* (the resin that, under certain climatic conditions, occurs even on the leaves and stems) are mixed with tobacco and smoked in a *chilam* or funnel-shaped pipe, often jointly by a group on social occasions.

Chilán—A type of divinatory priest or Shaman among the ancient Maya Indians of Mesoamerica; sometimes written *chilám*, as in *Chilám Balám*, 'jaguar priest' or 'jaguar diviner.' See: **Delphic, Divination, Oracle, Pythia, Shaman, Theomancy, Vatic.**

    1946 Morley *The Ancient Maya*, 156. Another class of priests were the *chilanes* or diviners, whose duty it was to give the replies of the gods to the people. The chilanes were held in such high respect that the people carried them on their shoulders when they appeared in public.

    1986 Rätsch *Chactun*, 251. *Chilan Than* 'Die Sprache der Liegenden'; Bezeichnung für die prophetischen Texte, die der *Chilam Balam* in Trance empfangen hat. [*Chilan Than* 'The Voice of the Recumbent'; Description of the prophetic texts which the *Chilam Balam* had received in trance.]

Circean—Of or pertaining to Circe; the sorceress in Homer's *Odyssey*, who dwelt on the island of Aea, and with her magical Potions transformed Odysseus' men into swine; visionary, hallucinatory; enrapturing. Also: Circæan. See: **Henbane, Moly.**

    1649 Milton *Eikon*, xiii. Inchanted with the Circæan cup of servitude…

1821 De Quincey *Confessions of an English Opium Eater*, 'The Pains of Opium.' I have thus described and illustrated my intellectual torpor, in terms that apply, more or less, to every part of the four years during which I was under the Circean spell of opium.

Communion—A ceremonial group ingestion of a Sacrament; originally an entheogenic plant or Potion; in the Catholic Church involving the Placebo Sacrament of the Eucharist. Hence: Communal, Communally, Commune, Communicant. See: **Agape, Consubstantiation, Element, Eucharist, Host, Sacrament, Transubstantiation.**
   1857 Ludlow *The Hasheesh Eater*, 60. I dwelt in an inner communion with heaven—a communion where every language is understood, rather than where all speak the same language…

Congenihuasca *nov. verb.*—Congenital Ayahuasca; a genetic defect characterized by complete or partial lack of Monoamine-Oxidase activity, the enzyme inhibited by Ayahuasca β-Carbolines. See: **Anahuasca, Ayahuasca, Ayahuasca Analogue, β-Carboline, Endohuasca, Monoamine-Oxidase, Pharmahuasca.**
   1994 Ott *Ayahuasca Analogues*, 68. This, definitely, is *endohuasca* or, perhaps more appropriately, *congenihuasca*…

Consubstantiation, Doctrine of—Martin Luther's answer to the eleventh century Catholic Doctrine of Transubstantiation; which held that the sacramental bread and Wine of Mass were *transubstantiated* into the body and blood of Christ. Luther maintained that there was no Transubstantiation, but that Consubstantiation occurred; that the bread and Wine remained such, but that Christ was present in the Eucharist, whose power and virtue was a function of the faith of the communicant. See: **Eucharist, Host, Sacrament, Transubstantiation.**

Co-ta-ci-ne—*Shaman*, in the language of the Mazatec Indians of México. Literally: one who knows; *curandero*. See: **Shaman.**
   1957 Wasson *Mushrooms Russia & History*, 251. In the Mazatec language there seems to be no name for the occupation of the shaman or *curandero*. In the proper context one speaks of him as 'he who knows,' $co^4ta^4ci^4ne^4$.

Counter Reformation—Response of the Catholic Church to the Protestant Reformation catalyzed by Martin Luther in 1517. Commenced in force with Pope Paul III, who began to attack financial and sexual misconduct within the church in 1536, and established a commission of cardinals to investigate the church. See: **Con-**

substantiation, **Entheogenic Reformation, Reformation.**

Crusades—Various military expeditions by European Christians, from the eleventh through thirteenth centuries; with the goal of conquering the 'Holy Lands' of the Levant from Arab dominion. Also: Catholic holy wars conducted at papal initiative, against rival faiths; for example Pope Innocent [*sic*] III's Albigensian Crusade inaugurated in 1209 against the Cathari or Albigensians—European Manichæans living in southern France. See: **Inquisition, Manichæans.**

Daime—Literally: 'gi'me,' the name for Ayahuasca in the Brasilian church of Santo Daime, in which the Potion serves as the Eucharist. Hence: Daimista. See: **Ayahuasca, Entheogenic Reformation, Eucharist, Hoasca, Santo Daime, União do Vegetal.**
   1992 MacRae *Guiado Pela Lua*, 67. Foi assim que aprendeu a chamar a bebida de Daime, relacionando-a ao verbo dar e às invocações 'Dai-me amor,' 'Dai-me luz' e 'Dai-me força,' que seriam características da doutrina que surgia. [Thus he came to call the potion Daime, relating it thus to the verb 'to give' and to the invocations 'Give me love,' 'Give me light' and 'Give me power,' which were characteristic of the doctrine which evolved.]

Dark Ages—The millennium between the end of classical or Pagan civilization, which can be dated precisely from the destruction of the Eleusinian Mysteries by the Goth King Alaric in 395, to the revival of the arts and sciences in the so-called Renaissance. When the Reformation finally broke the theocratic strangle-hold, the torch of learning which had been lit in such a promising fashion by the Greek philosophers, only to be extinguished by the Christians, began to be relit, and the labor of recovering the suppressed learning of the ancients commenced. On the other hand, with regard to religion and personal ecstatic experiences, we are *still* in the Dark Ages, and the contemporary advent of the Entheogenic Reformation heralds the dawning of a religious or Entheogenic Renaissance. See: **Entheogenic Reformation, Pagan, Renaissance.**
   1995 Ott *The Age of Entheogens*, 44. The fact is inescapable that the millennium-long crepusculum of the Dark Ages commenced with the extinction of pagan religion grounded in personal, ecstatic experiences of the divine, and its replacement by purely symbolic religion free of ecstasy, devoid of religious experiences, which prospered only when backed by imperial force—creed and rote dogma in place of that faith-inspiring ecstasy which 'carried its own conviction,' inflexible theocracy instead of that religious democracy which had characterized the pagan world.

Darnel—The wild grass *Lolium temulentum* L.; known as *tares* in the Bible [Matt.

13:25]; *aira* in Greek. Names like German *Taumellolch* ('delirium grass'), French *ivraie* ('inebriating') and Spanish *borrachera* ('drunkenness') betray folk knowledge of its properties, and it was used as an inebriating additive to beers as late as the 19th century. A common host to Ergot-type fungi, darnel may contain psychoactive Ergot Alkaloids. See: **Alkaloid, Delysid,**® **Ergot, Erysibe, Kykeon.**

1855 Johnston *Chemistry of Common Life* II, 147. Long known to possess narcotic and singularly intoxicating properties… [darnel seeds] impart their intoxicating quality to the beer, and render it unusually and even dangerously heady.

Dawamesk [Dawamesc]—Inebriating confection of *Cannabis indica* Lamarck resin [Hashish] or lipid extract of *Cannabis*; seasoned at times with cinnamon, ginger, essence of rose or jasmine, *etc.* and sweetened. See: **Bhangas, Charas, Ganja, Hashish, Kif, Majoon.**

1845 Moreau *Du Hachisch et de l'Aliénation Mentale*, 7. L'électuaire le plus généralement employé est celui que les Arabes apellant DAWAMESC. [The electuary most commonly employed is that called by the Arabs DAWAMESC.]
1846 Gautier *Les Club des Hachichins*, I. Un morceau de pâte ou confiture verdâtre [*dawamesc*]… était tiré par lui au moyen d'une spatule d'un vase de cristal… "Ceci vous sera défalqué sur votre portion de paradis"… [A piece of paste or comfit [*dawamesc*] was extracted by him with a spatula from a crystal vase… "This will be deducted from your share in paradise"…]
1860 Baudelaire *Les Paradis Artificiels*, II. La plus usitée de ces confitures, le *dawamesk*, est un mélange d'extrait gras, de sucre et de divers aromates, tels que vanille, cannelle, pistaches, amandes, musc. [The most frequented of these comfits, *dawamesk*, is a mixture of lipid extract, sugar, and divers flavorings, such as vanilla, cinnamon, pistachios, almonds, musk.]

Deadly Nightshade—Common name for *Atropa belladonna* L.; source of tropane Alkaloids atropine and scopolamine, used in mediæval Soporific draughts and the famous witches' Flying Ointments. Synonym: Belladonna. See: **Alkaloid, Dwale, Flying Ointment, Henbane, Mandrake, Witchcraft.**

1993 Ott *Pharmacotheon*, 364. *Atropa belladonna*, for which **atrop**ine and **trop**ane alkaloids are named, also called 'deadly nightshade,' was widely used as an ingredient of witches' 'flying ointments' in mediæval Europe.

Deiknymena—The sacred objects, including an ear of barley, sacred cakes, poppies, pomegranates, and a Thyrsus; which were shown to the Mystai or initiates to the Eleusinian Mysteries. The Deiknymena included the Hiera or sacred objects, whose identity remains a mystery to us. The Deiknymena and Hiera were kept within containers called the Kistai, and the high priest or Hierophant was 'he who shows the Hiera.' See: **Dromena, Eleusinian Mysteries, Hiera, Kistai, Legomena, Thyrsus.**

1961 Mylonas *Eleusis and the Eleusinian Mysteries*, 273. The *Deiknymena*, the objects which were shown, remain equally unknown. Most important of these were the Hiera. The climax of the celebration was attained when the Hierophant standing in front of the Anaktoron and in the midst of a radiant light exhibited the Hiera to the initiates.

Delirient [Deliriant]—Entheogen; an obscure term derived from presumed delirious effects of these drugs. See: **Delirium.**

1967 Hoffer & Osmond *The Hallucinogens*, v. The term delirients seems no better since subjects given these compounds are seldom delirious.

Delirium—Mental derangement characterized by hallucinations; uncontrolled excitement, emotion, Rapture. Hence: Deliracy, Delirament, Delirancy, Delirant, Delirate, Deliration, Delire, Delirement, Deliriant, Deliriate, Delirifacient, Delirious, Deliriously, Deliriousness, Delirous, Deliry. See: **Delierent, Frenzy, Inebriation, Intoxication, Paraphrenia, Paraphrosyne.**

1857 Ludlow *The Hasheesh Eater*, 149. Perhaps one of the most difficult things to convey to a mind not in the hasheesh delirium… is the interchanging of the senses.

Delphic—Of or pertaining to Delphi and especially the famed Oracle of Apollo at Delphi; on the slopes of Mount Parnassus. Hence: oracular, Vatic, of the nature of oracular utterances. Synonym: Delphian. Hence: Delphical. See: **Chilán, Divination, Oracle, Pythia, Theomancy, Vatic.**

1959 Wasson *Trans. New York Acad. Sci.* 21: 334. The Greeks, who were the fathers of pure reason, reserved a portion of their minds for the mystical element, the mysteries of Eleusis, the oracle at Delphi, the dæmon of Socrates.

1987 Rätsch *Curare* 10: 215. The author tries to identify herbs that helped Greek seers, as the famous Pythia of Delphi, to fall in trance, and then compares this state of trance with the drug-induced altered states of consciousness reported…

Delysid®—Sandoz Ltd. trademark for the artificial Indole Entheogen LSD-25; *d*–lysergic acid diethylamide tartrate, from Ergot Alkaloids. See: **Alkaloid, Ergot, Indocybin,® Indole, Ololiuhqui, Psychedelic, Tryptamine.**

1979 Hofmann *LSD: Mein Sorgenkind*, 58. Sandoz stellte daher den neuen Wirkstoff, der auf meinen Vorschlag hin die Marken-bezeichnung 'Delysid' (*D-Lys*erg-säurediäthylam*id* [tartrate]) erhielt… zur Verfügung. [Sandoz therefore made the new active substance available… giving it the trade name Delysid (*D-Lys*ergsäure-diäthylam*id* [tartrate]) which I had proposed.]

Dionysus—The Greek god of Inebriation and Wine; literally, the 'lord [Zeus] of Nysa,' who in the beginning of Euripides' *Bacchæ*, introduced the vine into Greece from Asia Minor. Erroneously regarded to be the god only of alcoholic Inebriation, owing to a misunderstanding of the nature of Greek Wines, potent infusions of numerous Psychoactive plants, in which the Alcohol served as preservative, rather than as inebriating principle, and which often required dilution to be drunk safely. Nietzsche characterized the 'wild' or 'animal' side of humankind as the *Dionysian*, in contrast with the rational, cerebral aspect, *Apollonian*. Dionysus represents the archaic shamanic tradition underlying Greek civilization. Hence: Dionysiac, Dionysiacal, Dionysian, Dionysic. Synonym: **Bacchus**. See: **Apollonian, Bacchanalia, Mænad, Symposium, Thyrsus, Wine**.

1958 Huxley *Drugs That Shape Men's Minds* [*Moksha*, 149]. Dionysus, or Bacchus… was a true divinity. His worshippers addressed him as… *Theoinos*, 'Godwine.'

1977 Emboden *J. Psychedelic Drugs* 9: 187. There is probably no better example of the origins and subtle changes in shamanic tradition than in the legends of Dionysus. The figure of Dionysus is clearly that of the shaman.

1978 Ruck *The Road to Eleusis*, 88. Nysa, furthermore, was the generic name for the place where mænadic rituals were enacted… These mænads were not only drunken women, but mad women. The Greek language did not distinguish between madness and inebriation because Dionysus was the god of all inebriants and not of wine alone. The reason that he was associated with all psychotropic plants is to be sought in the nature of ancient Greek wine. Like the wine of most primitive peoples, Greek wine did not contain alcohol as its sole intoxicant but was ordinarily a mixture of various inebriants.

Disembodied Eyes—Pangæan graphic art motifs representing the incorporeal, visionary eye of the seer; roving in the Psychocosmos or Visionary World; especially under the influence of entheogenic plants. Hence: Disembodied Eye Drops *nov. verb*. See: **Entheogen, Epopteia, Idea, Psychocosmos, Visionary World**.

1957 Wasson *Life* 42: 109. It seemed as though I was viewing a world of which I was not a part and with which I could not hope to establish contact. There I was, poised in space, a disembodied eye, invisible, incorporeal, seeing but not seen.

1983 Ott & Wasson *Botanical Museum Leaflets* Harvard University 29: 392. What can the 'disembodied eyes' represent, other than the visionary eye of the seer under the influence of one or other of the well-known pre-Columbian entheogens?

1994 Ott *Ayahuasca Analogues*, 94. The murals depict roving disembodied eyes, and entheogenic plants whose flowers are 'all eyes' and from which flowers exude droplets of entheogenic potion with appended disembodied eyes. Indeed, what could these 'disembodied eye drops' represent, other than the entheogenic visionary potion issuing from entheogenic flowers?

Divination—Prophesying, auguring, soothsaying; the practice of foretelling the future or revealing hidden or obscure things through visionary trance, especially by Shamans and with the aid of entheogenic plants. Hence: Divinal, Divinator, Divinatory, Divinatrice, Divine, Divinely, Divinement, Diviner, Divineress, Divinesse. See: **Chilán, Delphic, Oracle, Pythia, Theomancy, Vatic.**

 1957 Wasson *Mushrooms Russia & History*, 257. Here then is the order of the ritual of the divinatory mushroom as we witnessed and recorded it in Huautla de Jiménez.

DMT—See: **Nigerine.**

Dromena—Literally: that which was enacted; the pageants and the ritual enactments of the myth of Demeter and Persephone, which accompanied the annual Initiation to the Eleusinian Mysteries in the Telesterion or Initiation hall. See: **Deiknymena, Eleusinian Mysteries, Legomena.**

 1978 Aristides in Wasson *The Road to Eleusis*, 17. Eleusis is a shrine common to the whole earth, and of all the divine things that exist among men, it is both the most awesome and the most luminous. At what place in the world have more miraculous tidings been sung, and where have the dromena called forth greater emotion, where has there been greater rivalry between seeing and hearing?

 1978 Ruck *The Road to Eleusis*, 84. These ritual actions, the so-called *dromena* of the initiation, had been accompanied by recited words, the *legomena*. All these things were secret, and what we learn of them from late sources comes from people who did not understand, or did not care to bother with, their meaning.

Dwale—A Soporific or Sedative Potion; and also the name for the visionary Deadly Nightshade, *Atropa belladonna* L., used in such; and as a visionary ingredient in the ointment or unguent of so-called witches. See: **Deadly Nightshade, Flying Ointment, Hypnotica, Sedative, Soporific, Witchcraft.**

 1386 Chaucer *Tales of Caunterbury*, Reves Tale. Ther nas na moore,—hem nedede no dwale./This millere hath so wisly bibbed ale/That as an hors he fnorteth in his sleep,/Ne of his tayl bihynde he took no keep.

 1597 Gerarde *Herbal* II, 269. Dwale or sleeping nightshade hath round blackish stalks sixe foote high.

 1994 Piomelli & Pollio *History and Philosophy of the Life Sciences* 16: 252. Not unlike these are the components of other Medieval narcotic concoctions, whose major use was as anæsthetic medications during surgery: the *spongia soporifera*… or the *dwale*, a sleeping draft…

Dysphoria—An emotional state literally 'hard to bear,' characterized by anxiety and depression; a concomitant of Euphoria in the effects of visionary drugs. Hence:

[84]

Dysphoric, Dysphory *nov. verb.* See: **Euphoria, Euphorica.**
1958 Heim & Wasson *Les Champignons Hallucinogènes du Mexique*, 294. *La dysphorie isolée, ou succédant a l'euphorie, est, elle aussi, fréquent (69%).* [*Dysphoria* by itself, or following euphoria, is likewise frequent (69%).]

Eboka—See: **Iboga.**

Ecstasy—Literally: the withdrawal of the soul from the body; mystical or prophetic exaltation or Rapture characteristic of shamanism and visionary states, originally and *naturally* catalyzed by entheogenic plants; also, such states *artificially* induced by breath control, fasting, meditation, drumming and other shamanic and yogic practices. Hence: Ecstasied, Ecstasis, Ecstasize, Ecstatic, Ecstatical. See: **Entheogen, Enthusiasm, Inspiration, Psycholepsy, Rapture, Theolepsy, Theopneust.**
  1857 Ludlow *The Hasheesh Eater*, 55. My ecstasy became so great that I seemed to cast off all shackles of flesh.
  1957 Wasson *Mushrooms Russia & History*, 295. On both nights RGW stood for a long time… transfixed in ecstasy by the visions that he was seeing… For the first time the word 'ecstasy' took on subjective meaning for him. 'Ecstasy' was not someone else's state of mind. It was no longer a trite superlative cheapened by overuse. It signified something different and superior in kind, about which RGW could now testify as a competent witness.
  1961 Wasson *Botanical Museum Leaflets* 19: 137. At last you know what the ineffable is, and what ecstasy means. Ecstasy! The mind harks back to the origin of that word. For the Greeks *ekstasis* meant the flight of the soul from the body. Can you find a better word than that to describe the bemushroomed state? In common parlance, among the many who have not experienced ecstasy, ecstasy is fun, and I am frequently asked why I do not reach for mushrooms every night. But ecstasy is not fun. Your very soul is seized and shaken until it tingles. After all, who will choose to feel undiluted awe, or to float through that door yonder into the Divine Presence?

Eidetic—Of or pertaining to vivid mental imagery or perception. Frequently applied to the geometric or arabesque, closed-eyed visual imagery characteristic of the effects of entheogenic drugs. Hence: Eidetically. See: **Entoptic, Phosphenes.**
  1966 Klüver *Mescal and Mechanisms of Hallucinations*, 77. Eidetic images and certain types of hallucinations may vanish, change, or remain unaltered… one subject, a student, saw an eidetic image of the face of a person looking at him.
  1970 Jünger *Annäherungen*, 46. Viele Narcotica sind zugleich Phantastica. Sertürner hat, indem er 1803 das Morphium isolierte, die schmerzstillende Potenz des Opiums von der eidetischen getrennt. [Many Narcotica are also Phantastica. Sertürner separated the analgesic from the eidetic potency of opium, when he isolated morphine in 1803.]

Element—A sort of euphemism or circumlocution to describe the bread and Wine employed in the Catholic Placebo Sacrament of the Eucharist; generally capitalized. See: **Agape, Communion, Eucharist, Host, Sacrament, Teonanácatl.**

> **1959** Wasson *Trans. New York Acad. Sci.* 21: 333. How startling it is that the ancient Aztecs called this Element by the same name that we use for the Bread and Wine of the Eucharist— God's Flesh [*sic*]!

Eleusinian Mysteries—Cult of Demeter at Eleusis near Athens; spiritual beacon of the classical world, revolving around the annual springtime Initiation into the Lesser Mysteries at Agrai, followed by autumnal Initiation into the Greater Mysteries at the Eleusinian Telesterion, during which the initiates or Mystai imbibed an entheogenic Potion, the Kykeon, thus experiencing a Numinous vision which transformed them into Epoptai, those who had seen. See: **Epopt, Epopteia, Initiation, Kykeon, Mysteries, Mystes, Telesterion.**

> **1960** Wasson *Botanical Museum Leaflets* 19: 149. One writer in the 2nd century A.D., by name Aristides, pulled the curtain aside for an instant, with this fragmentary description of the Eleusinian Mystery...
>
> **1978** Wasson *The Road to Eleusis*, 9. Here lies for us the mystery of the Eleusinian Mysteries. To this mystery we three have applied ourselves and believe we have found the solution, close to 2,000 years after the last performance of the rite and some 4,000 years since the first.
>
> **1993** Ott *Pharmacotheon*, 141. The Eleusinian Mystery was an annual celebration of a fertility cult, over which the goddess Demeter presided.

Elixir—A potent extract or an alcoholic tincture of a medicinal plant; implying content of its Quintessence or hidden active principle. Literally: the Philosophers' Stone or *Elixir Stone* capable of transmuting base metals into gold; representative of the *Elixir Vitæ* or legendary 'drug of immortality'; the primigenial Entheogen of which Gilgamesh's 'herb of immortality,' the Chinese Ling Chih or 'divine mushroom of immortality' and Ponce de León's 'fountain of youth' are alike symbolic; Panacea. Hence: Elixate, Elixation, Elixed, Elixirate. See: **Arcanum, Gilgamesh, Ling Chih, Panacea, Philosophers' Stone, Potion, Quintessence.**

> **1386** Chaucer *Tales of Caunterbury*, Chanons Yemannes Tale. The philosophre stoon, Elixir clept, we sechen fast echoon.
>
> **1667** Milton *Paradise Lost*, III, 607. What wonder then if fields and regions here Breathe forth elixir pure, and Rivers run Potable Gold.
>
> **1985** Ott *The Cacahuatl Eater*, 5. De Quincey, for all his eloquence, was mistaken—chocolate and not opium is the secret drug of happiness. For my entire life I've had daily recourse to this elixir of happiness, although today a penny won't buy much of it...

Empathogen *nov. verb.*—A Psychoactive drug of the Phenethylamine class; said to have an action between the largely Stimulant/euphoric effects of the amphetamines and the mainly entheogenic or 'Psychedelic' effects of Mescaline; of which MDMA [3,4-methylenedioxymethamphetamine] is the prototype. Hence: Empathogenic *nov. verb.*, Empathogenically *nov. verb.* Synonym: **Entactogen**. See: **Mescaline, β-Phenethylamine**.

> **1993** Nichols *MAPS* IV(2): 47. Hence, the term entactogen, meaning essentially 'to produce a touching within'… is to be preferred over empathogen, at least when discussing it in a legitimate scientific or medical context.
>
> **1993** Metzner *ibid.*, 49. At least 'empathogenic'… has the virtue of using commonly understood terms. And how does 'entactogenic'… distinguish this class of drugs from the LSD-type psychedelics?
>
> **1993** Callaway *Integration* 4: 56. 'Empathogens' are very similar to entactogens but have the additional virtue of being able to engender an emotional bonding between people.

Endohuasca *nov. verb.*—Literally: endogenous Ayahuasca; in reference to J.C. Callaway's theory [*Medical Hypotheses* 26: 119, 1988] of the origins of dream visions in endogenous interactions of cerebral Tryptamines and β-Carbolines. See: **Anahuasca, Ayahuasca Analogue, Ayahuasca Borealis, β-Carboline, Congenihuasca, Mono-amine-Oxidase, Pharmahuasca, Tryptamine**.

> **1994** Ott *Ayahuasca Analogues*, 63. Callaway… has elaborated a hypothesis to explain dreams *via* nocturnal interactions of tryptamines and β-carbolines, what we might call 'endogenous *ayahuasca*' or *endohuasca*.
>
> **1994** Callaway *Kuopio University Publications A. Pharmaceutical Sciences* 15: 48. Appropriately, the endogenous version of this chemical combination has been recently termed *endohuasca*. The hypothesis is extended to include psychoses by suggesting that hallucinatory psychotic episodes may result from a desynchronized dream mechanism, where the individual essentially 'dreams' while awake.

Enlightenment—Reception of spiritual light or wisdom; whether by spontaneous grace, *naturally* through ingestion of sacramental 'Plant–Teachers,' or *artificially*, *via* ascetic meditative and/or contemplative practices. Also: the impartation of similar wisdom by a plant or human teacher. Hence: Enlighten, Enlightened, Enlightener, Enlightening. See: **Entheogen, Enthusiasm, Inspiration, Plant–Teachers**.

Entactogen *nov. verb.*—A Psychoactive drug of the Phenethylamine class; said to have an action between the largely Stimulant/euphoric effects of the amphetamines and the mainly entheogenic or 'Psychedelic' effects of Mescaline; of which MDMA

[3,4-methylenedioxymethamphetamine] is the prototype. Hence: Entactogenic *nov. verb.*, Entactogenically *nov. verb.* Synonym: **Empathogen**. See: **Mescaline, β-Phenethylamine**.

> **1993** Nichols *MAPS* IV(2): 47. Hence, the term entactogen, meaning essentially 'to produce a touching within'… is to be preferred over empathogen, at least when discussing it in a legitimate scientific or medical context.
>
> **1993** Yensen *ibid.*, 48. David Nichols' term entactogen seems a more correctly conceptualized [*sic*] word. I wish I liked the way it sounds, I don't.
>
> **1993** Callaway *Integration* 4: 56. 'Empathogens' are very similar to entactogens but have the additional virtue of being able to engender an emotional bonding between people.

Entheobotany *nov. verb.*—Entheogenic ethnobotany; the science of shamanic inebriants or visionary plant drugs. Conflation of the neologisms Entheogen and Theo-botany/Theo-botanist, the latter proposed in 1963 by Mary Barnard to characterize the study of shamanic plant Sacraments inaugurated by R. Gordon Wasson a decade earlier. Hence: Entheobotanic *nov. verb.*, Entheobotanical *nov. verb.*, Entheobotanist *nov. verb.* Synonyms: **Hierobotany, Theobotany**. See: **Entheogen**.

> **1963** Barnard *The Psychedelic Review* 1: 251. I am willing to prophesy that fifty theobotanists working for fifty years would make the current theories concerning the origins of much mythology and theology as out-of-date as pre-Copernican astronomy.
>
> **1995** Ott *The Age of Entheogens*, 35. Although those who might call themselves *theobotanists* or, perhaps more appropriately *entheobotanists*, number fewer than fifty worldwide, and we yet have nearly two decades to go, I would say Miss Barnard's prophecy is on a sure footing.

Entheogen *nov. verb.*—Plant Sacraments or shamanic inebriants evoking religious Ecstasy or vision; commonly used in the archaic world in Divination for shamanic healing, and in Holy Communion, for example during the Initiation to the Eleusinian Mysteries or the Vedic Soma sacrifice. Literally: becoming divine within. Hence: Age of Entheogens *nov. verb.*, Entheogenic *nov. verb.* See: **Enthusiasm, Hallucinogen, Phanerothyme, Phantastica, Pharmacotheon, Psychedelic**.

> **1979** Ruck *J. Psychedelic Drugs* 11: 145. In Greek the word *entheos* means literally 'god (*theos*) within'… In combination with the Greek root *-gen*, which denotes the action of 'becoming,' this word results in the term that we are proposing: *entheogen*.
>
> **1980** Wasson *The Wondrous Mushroom*, xiv. We are now rediscovering the secret and we should treat the 'entheogens' with the respect to which they were richly entitled.
>
> **1986** Wasson *Persephone's Quest*, 31. We must break down the 'Drugs' of popular parlance according to their properties and overcome our ignorance, which in this field is still monumental. 'Entheogen' is a step in that direction.

[88]

1993 Ott *Pharmacotheon*, 19. I have been privileged to be initiated into the sacred realm of the entheogens… have imbibed the *amrta* of Indra, the *ambrosia* of the Olympian gods, Demeter's potion; have for brief blessed instants gazed into Lord Shiva's blazing third eye.

Entheogenic Reformation *nov. verb.*—The anachronistic 'Archaic Revival' of shamanism and use of shamanic 'Plant–Teachers' in the contemporary 'overdeveloped' world; and the simultaneous appearance in several 'underdeveloped' countries of syncretic Neo-Christian religions in which the Placebo Sacrament of the Eucharist is replaced by entheogenic plants traditionally associated with shamanism; such as sacramental use of Péyotl by the Native American Church, similar use of Ayahuasca by Brasilian churches, and sacramental use of Iboga in the African Bwiti religion. See: **Archaic Revival, Ayahuasca, Bwiti, Daime, Entheogen, Eucharist, Hoasca, Iboga, Péyotl, Placebo, Reformation, Renaissance, Sacrament, Santo Daime, Shaman, União do Vegetal.**

1994 Ott *Ayahuasca Analogues*, 9. The resulting 'countercultural' movement of the 'Psychedelic Sixties' marked an unprecedented departure from business as usual, setting the stage for a modern Entheogenic Reformation, which promises to evoke more radical and far-reaching changes in western religion than did its predecessor. Indeed, Martin Luther's 95 theses of October 1517 packed far less punch than did Gordon Wasson's *one* thesis 440 years later—for Wasson had peeled away the ossified accretion of many, many layers of symbol and dogma which enshrouded the core mystery in impenetrable obfuscation; had laid bare before the eyes of an astonished world, in all its dazzling quotidian humility, *the holy sacrament itself,* a sacrament which 'carried its own conviction' and did not limp along encumbered by faith in an absurd Doctrine of Transubstantiation; a sacrament *which obviated the necessity of faith itself,* allowing every communicant to attest to 'the miracle he has experienced.'

Enthusiasm—Poetic or prophetic possession by deity; supernatural Inspiration. Literally: inspired by a god, from the root *entheos.* Hence: Enthusiac, Enthusian, Enthusiast, Enthusiastic, Enthusiastical. See: **Entheogen, Inspiration, Psycholepsy, Rapture, Theolepsy, Theopneust.**

1630 Pyper *History of Astrea*, 146. The Bacchanales runne thorow the streets raging and storming, full of the Enthusiasme of their god.

1931 Huxley *Treatise on Drugs* [*Moksha*, 47]. A toadstool filled the Shamans of Siberia with enthusiasm and endowed them with the gift of tongues.

1972 Wasson *Soma and the Fly-Agaric*, 17. The juice of the Soma-plant caused divine inebriation, *mada*… The 'reverential awe'… that Soma inspired permeated the Rg Veda. This reverence, this awe, prompts Brough to see an analogy with the Greek ενθουσιασμοζ [*enthusiasmos*], 'God possessed,' and rightly so.

Entoptic—Within the eye; referring to imagery perceived with closed eyes. Hence: Entoptical, Entoptically. See: **Eidetic, Phosphenes.**

  1966 Klüver *Mescal and Mechanisms of Hallucinations*, 67. Some or all of the form constants found in mescaline hallucinations are also found in certain hypnagogic hallucinations, in entoptic phenomena...

Epopt—An initiate to the Eleusinian Mysteries; who had experienced the Epopteia or vision under the influence of the entheogenic Potion Kykeon, in the darkened Telesterion at Eleusis. The Mystes [plural *mystai*] was transformed into an Epoptes [plural *epoptai*], having seen *ta hiera*, 'the holy' under the influence of the Kykeon. Hence: Epoptic, Epoptically *nov. verb.*, Epoptist. See: **Eleusinian Mysteries, Epopteia, Epoptica, Epoptician, Hiera, Kykeon, Mystes, Telesterion.**

  1978 Ruck *The Road to Eleusis*, 77. But at Eleusis, one had the vision, the *epopteia*, and became someone who had seen, an *epoptes*.

  1993 Ott *Pharmacotheon*, 638. Beneath the arboreal spirits of the forest, in the center of the chiaroscuro of the night forest... there hovers the disembodied eye of vision... or five eyes; a fifth-dimensional hyperchakra epoptically projected into space...

Epopteia—Greek name for the vision experienced in the Telesterion under the influence of the entheogenic Kykeon; at the climax of the Initiation into the Eleusinian Mysteries. Literally: the seeing. See: **Disembodied Eyes, Eleusinian Mysteries, Epopt, Epoptic, Epoptician, Kykeon.**

  1978 Ruck *The Road to Eleusis*, 77. But at Eleusis, one had the vision, the *epopteia*, and became someone who had seen, an *epoptes*.

Epoptica *nov. verb.*—Entheogens; substances capable of inducing Ecstasy or the Epopteia, the beholding of sacred visions. See: **Entheogen, Epopt, Epopteia, Epoptician.**

Epoptician *nov. verb.*—A manufacturer or merchandiser of Epoptica or Entheogens; substances capable of inducing the Epopteia or beholding of sacred visions. See: **Entheogen, Epopt, Epopteia, Epoptica.**

Ergot—Sclerotium of parasitic fungi infecting cultivated grains or wild grasses; especially ergot of rye or *secale cornutum, Claviceps purpurea* (Fr.) Tulasne; literally: 'cock's spur,' from Old French *argot*. An important source of medicinal and entheogenic Alkaloids of the lysergic acid group; of which ergonovine and ergine are examples; also source of starting materials for artificial Ergot Alkaloids like *Hyder-*

gine® and *Delysid*® or LSD-25. Hence: Ergine, Ergoline, Ergonovine, Ergotamine, Ergotized, Lysergic. See: **Alkaloid, Darnel, Delysid,**® **Erysibe, Kykeon, Ololiuhqui.**
1979 Hofmann *LSD: Mein Sorgenkind,* 17. Kaum einer anderer Droge hat eine so faszinierende Geschichte wie das Mutterkorn. In ihren Verlauf hat sich seine Rolle und Bedeutung umgekehrt: Zuerst als Giftträger gefürchtet, wandelte es sich im Laufe der Zeit in eine reiche Fundgrube von wertvollen Heilmitteln. [Ergot, more than any other drug, has a fascinating history, in the course of which its role and meaning have been reversed; once dreaded as a poison, in the course of time it has changed to a rich storehouse of valuable remedies.]

Erysibe—The Greek word for sclerotia of Ergot; the fungus *Claviceps purpurea* (Fr.) Tulasne, parasitic on grains; sometimes used as an epithet for Greek grain-goddess Demeter, to whom the Eleusinian Mysteries were sacred; strengthening the interpretation that the entheogenic properties of Demeter's Potion, the Kykeon, derived from Ergot of barley or of a wild grass such as *Lolium temulentum* L. See: **Darnel, Eleusinian Mysteries, Ergot, Kykeon.**
1978 Ruck *The Road to Eleusis,* 116. Demeter, herself, had the epithet Erysibe, as though her gift of grain could exist only through the aversion of the darker persona that was her own and its antithesis.

Eucharist—The Placebo Sacrament of the Lord's Supper or Christian Holy Communion. Literally: thanksgiving. Hence: Eucharistial, Eucharistic, Eucharistical, Eucharistize. See: **Agape, Bwiti, Communion, Consubstantiation, Daime, Element, Hoasca, Host, Iboga, Placebo, Sacrament, Santo Daime, Transubstantiation, União do Vegetal.**
1959 Wasson *Trans. New York Acad. Sci.* 21: 333. How startling it is that the ancient Aztecs called this Element by the same name that we use for the Bread and Wine of the Eucharist—God's Flesh [*sic*]!

Eudemonic—Conducive to happiness. Also: Eudæmonic. Hence: Eudæmon, Eudæmonism, Eudæmonist, Eudæmonize, Eudæmony, Eudemon, Eudemonism, Eudemonist, Eudemonize, Eudemony.
1827 De Quincey *Last Days Kant.* Ethics, braced up into stoical vigour by renouncing all effeminate dallyings with Eudæmonism...
1963 Heard *The Psychedelic Review* 1: 13. So, for all its liberating powers, LSD remains non-euphoric: as the Greeks would say, it is 'eudæmonic'—'a possession by the spirit of wholeness.'

Euphoria—Bliss, Ecstasy. Literally: bearing well. Hence, Euphoriant, Euphoric,

Euphory. See: **Beatitude, Bliss, Dysphoria, Ecstasy, Euphorica.**
1700 Jones *The Mysteries of Opium Reveald.* It [opium] causes Euphory, or eases undergoing of all Labour, Journeys, Etc....
1958 Heim & Wasson *Les Champignons Hallucinogènes du Mexique,* 293. *L'euphorie* est notée dans 81% des cas... avec loquacité, jovialité, familiarité, sens aigu des situations comiques, impression subjective de richesse idéique... [*Euphoria* is noted in 81% of the cases... with loquacity, joviality, familiarity, acute sense of comical situations, subjective impression of ideational wealth...]

Euphorica—The first of Louis Lewin's five subcategories of Psychoactive drugs set forth in his classic 1924 book *Phantastica.* Also called *Seelenberuhigungsmittel* or 'Anodynes for the spirit,' the prototype for Lewin's class of *Euphorica* was Opium and its Alkaloids [morphine, codeine] and their artificial congeners [heroin *etc.*]. See: **Euphoria, Excitantia, Hypnotica, Inebriantia, Laudanum, Narcotic, Narcotica, Nepenthes, Neuroleptica, Opium, Phantastica, Psychotica, Sedative, Theriac.**
1924 Lewin *Phantastica,* 47. Euphorica, Seelenberuhigungsmittel. Stoffe, die des Verwenders Gefühls- und Empfindungsleben... mit erhaltenem oder teilweis oder ganz geschwundenem Bewußtsein mindern... [Euphorica, anodynes for the spirit. Substances that diminish the sensory or emotional life of the user, corresponding with a partial or complete fading of consciousness ...]

Excitantia [Exzitantia]—The fifth of Louis Lewin's five subcategories of Psychoactive drugs set forth in his classic 1924 book *Phantastica.* Also called *Erregungsmittel* or 'Stimulants,' the prototypes for Lewin's class of *Excitantia* were *betel, qat, paricá* snuff, tobacco and various caffeine-containing plants. See: **Euphorica, Hypnotica, Inebriantia, Neuroleptica, Phantastica, Psychotica, Smart Drug, Stimulant.**
1924 Lewin *Phantastica,* 48. Exzitantia, Erregungsmittel. Genußmittel aus dem Pflanzenreich, die in der Regel eine... Erregung des Gehirns ohne Bewußtseinsstörungen hervorrufen. [Exzitantia, stimulants. Pleasure drugs from the plant kingdom which as a rule provoke cerebral stimulation without perturbation of consciousness.]

Færie [Fairy]—Otherworld or Visionary World said to be inhabited by Spirits; also, derivatively, a race of fairy-folk or little people said to inhabit such and sometimes perceived by Shamans and other individuals following ingestion of entheogenic plants; as, for example, María Sabina's personification of entheogenic mushrooms as mischievous, gamboling 'little clowns' or 'little tykes.' See: **Leprechaun, Menehune, Piltzintli, Spirit, Tengu, Visionary World.**
1957 Wasson *Mushrooms Russia & History,* 90. A woodcut in Olaus Magnus shows the Swedish King Hotherus paying a visit on the fairy people... Miss Margaret A. Murray may

be right that a culturally distinct people, autochthonous, unlettered, and pagan, lived side by side with the Christian world in northern Europe down into Renaissance times. But whether that people existed or not, the belief in them existed and was generally accepted...

Fantasy—Apparition, phantom, illusion, hallucination; the object of imagination. Hence: Fantaser, Fantasia, Fantasied, Fantasious, Fantasque, Fantast, Fantastic, Fantastical, Fantasticality, Fantastically, Fantasticalness, Fantasticate, Fantasticism, Fantasticize, Fantasticly, Fantasticness, Fantastico, Fantastry, Fantasying, Phantasied, Phantast, Phantasy. See: **Phantasmagorica, Phantastica, Phantasticant.**

1845 Moreau *Du Hachisch*, 67. Ceux qui font usage du hachisch, en Orient, lorsqu'ils veulent s'abandonner à l'ivresse de la *fantasia*... [Those who make use of hashish in the Orient, those who wish to abandon themselves to the inebriation of the *fantasia*...]

1855 Johnston *Chemistry of Common Life* II, 96. Taken in doses sufficient to induce the *fantasia*, as its [hashish] more remarkable effects are called...

1857 Ludlow *The Hasheesh Eater*, 261. If for a moment I yielded to the impulse, I was straightaway in the midst of sky and landscape whose splendors were only less vivid than the perfect hallucinations of the fantasia.

1966 Gelpke *Vom Rausch im Orient und Okzident*, 88. Einerseits sind die Phantasien und Träume, die er [hashish] erzeugt, eindeutig visionärer Natur, und spielt er mit Zeit und Raum... [On the one hand there are the fantasies and dreams that it [hashish] engenders, of a distinctly visionary nature, and it plays with time and space...]

Flying Ointment—Visionary unguent compounded of animal fat, hemlock, Darnel, water lilies, poppies and the entheogenic nightshades like belladonna, Henbane and Mandrake (among other ingredients); applied to the skin and vaginal mucosa by so-called witches of mediæval Europe and said to impart visions of flying. Also called Witches' Ointment, Witches's Salve. See: **Darnel, Deadly Nightshade, Dwale, Henbane, Mandrake, Moly, Opium.**

1976 Hansen *The Witch's Garden*, 90. Quite a large number of flying ointment recipes are known from the time of the witches... The well-known historian of witchcraft and magic Dr. Karl Kiesewetter—one of the first to experiment with witch's ointments in modern times—died of poisoning after one of his experiments.

1993 Ott *Pharmacotheon*, 366. Mediæval European use of *Datura* in witches' 'flying ointments' has been echoed in Castaneda's fictitious account of similar use, supposedly among the Yaqui of northern Mexico.

Frenzy—Mental derangement or Delirium, wild Enthusiasm. Hence: Frenetic, Frenzic, Frenzical, Frenzied, Frenzily, Frenziness, Phrensy. See: **Delirium, Inebriation,**

Intoxication, Paraphrenia, Paraphrosyne.
1846 Gautier *Les Club des Hachichins,* v. La frénésie joyeuse était à son plus haut point…
[The joyous frenzy had reached its highest point…]
1857 Ludlow *The Hasheesh Eater,* 66. I have taken at one time a pill of thirty grains, which hardly gave a perceptible phenomenon, and at another, when my dose had been but half that quantity, I have suffered the agonies of a martyr, or rejoiced in a perfect phrensy.

Gæa—Ancient Earth-mother goddess; mother and spouse of Uranus; also mother of the Titans, the Furies and the Cyclopes. Under the variant spelling *Gaia,* a name for the biosphere, as in Lovelock's 'Gaia Hypothesis.' Has been proposed as a name for the planet Earth; known figuratively as 'Our Lady Gæa.' Also: Gea. Hence: Gæan, Gean. See: **Gaia, Neogæa, Palæogæa, Pangæan.**
1994 Ott *Ayahuasca Analogues,* 88. Planet Earth, Our Lady Gæa, is suffering mightily the consequences of our materialistic world-view, especially the Judæo-Christian tendency to see humankind as a special creation, apart from all other Gæan life-forms, and as enjoined, moreover, to subdue and dominate all other creatures.
1995 Ott *The Age of Entheogens,* 40. We thus have a satisfying family of words, based on the name of the Greek earth-goddess *Gæa* for our planet; we as *Gæan* creatures; *pangæan* as an adjective to replace the shopworn and provincial 'universal' for a worldwide phenomenon; *Palæogæa* and *Neogæa* to describe what we are now obliged to call the Old and New Worlds, with the adjectives *palæogæan* and *neogæan.*

Gaia—Variant of **Gæa.** This spelling should be avoided, as it is usually mispronounced in English as *guy-uh* [as opposed to the proper pronunciation, *gay-uh*]. Moreover, Gæa or *jee-uh,* gives us the sound of the common prefix, e.g. *geology.*

Ganja—Sanskrit name for the flower-tops of Indian hemp; *Cannabis indica* Lamarck, especially sacred to Shiva and commonly smoked in a straight pipe called a *chillum.* In contemporary argot, known as *sinsemilla,* 'flower-tops' or simply 'tops.' See: **Bhangas, Charas, Dawamesk, Hashish, Kif, Majoon.**
1980 La Barre *Culture in Context,* 96. *Ganja,* made of the dried pistillate tops from cannabis races rich in resin, is usually smoked, such smoking being probably a post-Columbian practice from the New World.
1993 Ott *Pharmacotheon,* 386. *Cannabis* preparations, sometimes called *vijaya* or 'victory' in Sanskrit, are especially sacred to Shiva, and occur in three forms: *bhang,* a preparation of leaves used in beverages such as *bhang lassi* and taken by devout Hindus before visiting important temples, *ganja* or flower-tops and *charas* or pure resin, both of which are smoked, typically in a *chillum*… *Cannabis* preparations figured prominently in ritual worship of the pre-Vedic Indian tribal god Jagannath in the Jagannath Mandir in Puri…

[94]

Gilgamesh, Epic of—Ancient Sumerian saga of the quixotic quest for the 'herb of immortality'; a red plant which 'shimmered like the satin of Byzantium,' associated with water—in all likelihood the primordial Eurasian entheogenic mushroom, *Amanita muscaria* (L. ex Fr.) Pers. ex Gray. Considered to be the oldest written epic we possess, impressed into cuneiform tablets around the seventh century B.C., the *Epic of Gilgamesh* is thought to have been composed around 2000 B.C. See: **Arcanum, Elixir, Philosophers' Stone, Quintessence.**

    1968 Wasson *Soma*, 221. And Ponce de León early in the 16th century was still seeking in Florida the pool of living water that he might have discovered in the Siberian taiga, the pool where Gilgamesh finally found his Herb of Immortality thousands of years earlier, only to lose it again to the Serpent who was more subtle than any beast of the field, the very same Serpent who engaged Eve in pleasant conversation, whose habitation is in the roots of the towering Siberian birch.

Glechon—A plant, thought to be the mint *Mentha pulegium* L. or pennyroyal; added as a flavoring or inebriating admixture to the entheogenic Kykeon Potion given to initiates or Mystai during the Eleusinian Mysteries. Also: Blechon. See: **Eleusinian Mysteries, Kykeon.**

    1978 Staples *The Road to Eleusis*, 64. Metaneira offered her a cup filled with wine, as sweet as honey, but she refused it, telling her the red wine would be a sacrilege. She asked instead for barley and water to drink mixed with tender leaves of *glechon*.

    1978 Ruck *The Road to Eleusis*, 52. In the initiation hall, there was a final ceremonial dance of the priestesses carrying the chalice of grain upon their heads as they mixed and distributed the sacred potion: fragrant *blechon*, the despised herb associated with the illicit nature of abduction, immersed in water to which was added a sprinkling of flour from barley grown in the Rarian plain.

    1978 Ruck *ibid.*, 100. It has been suggested that *glechon* (or *blechon*) was the active psychotomimetic agent in the *kykeon*. The plant is commonly identified as pennyroyal, *Mentha Pulegium*, a mint with mild psychotropic properties.

Grail, Holy—Literally: the platter supposedly used by Jesus during the Last Supper, then by Joseph of Arimathea to catch the blood of the crucified prophet. Figuratively: the elusive object of spiritual quests. See: **Philosophers' Stone.**

    1961 Wasson *Botanical Museum Leaflets* 19: 147. When we first went down to Mexico, we felt certain, my wife and I, that we were on the trail of an ancient and holy mystery, and we went as pilgrims seeking the Grail.

    1993 Ott *Pharmacotheon*, 324. The philosophers' stone of alchemy and the Holy Grail, as well as Aladdin's famous magic lamp, are all considered to be metaphors for *Amanita muscaria*.

Habituation—Formation of habit; the act of becoming habitual as, for example, habitual taking of drugs; with less of a pejorative flavor than Addiction. Synonyms: **Addiction, Pharmacothymia.** See: **Habitué.**

> **1985** Ott *The Cacahuatl Eater*, 76. There is considerable individual variation in the type and degree of such [withdrawal] symptoms among habitués of a particular drug, due to the duration and extent (i.e. accustomed dose level) of the habituation, metabolic individuality, and doubtless other factors.

Habitué—One who practices a habit, an addict; the combination *drug habitué* is devoid of the pejorative connotations of *drug addict*. See: **Addiction, Habituation, Pharmacothymia.**

> **1985** Ott *The Cacahuatl Eater*, 76. There is considerable individual variation in the type and degree of such [withdrawal] symptoms among habitués of a particular drug, due to the duration and extent (i.e. accustomed dose level) of the habituation, metabolic individuality, and doubtless other factors.

Hallucinogen—Entheogen; sacramental Plant–Teacher, or the active agent of same and their artificial congeners; of which Mescaline is the natural prototype; LSD the artificial. See: **Delysid,**® **Entheogen, Mescaline, Phanerothyme, Phantastica, Pharmacotheon, Psychedelic.**

> **1968** Wasson *Soma*, 175. 'Hallucinogen' and 'hallucinogenic' were words coined by a group of physicians preoccupied with these mysterious drugs—Abram Hoffer, Humphrey [*sic*] Osmond, and John Smythies in America, and Donald Johnson in England... The word quickly took hold and now trips off everyone's tongue as though it had been used for generations.
> **1979** Ruck *J. Psychedelic Drugs* 11: 145. A drug that effects such a change became known as an 'hallucinogen.' The verb 'hallucinate,' however, immediately imposes a value judgment upon the nature of the altered perceptions, for it means 'to be deceived or entertain false notions.'
> **1993** Ott *Pharmacotheon*, 91. Inadequate terms like 'hallucinogenic' (which implied delusion and/or falsity, besides suggesting pathology to psychotherapists.

Haoma—The archaic Aryan/Iranian entheogenic plant described in the *Avesta* of Iran and probably in origin identical with the Indo-Aryan Soma of the *Rg Veda*. Although today *haoma* is identified with Syrian Rue, *Peganum harmala* L., this is almost certainly a substitute in the Iranian plains for the original Soma, a denizen of the mountains. Accumulating ethnobotanical, linguistic and other evidence is summing up to proof that the original Soma/*haoma* was some entheogenic mushroom. See: **Amrta, Anahuasca, Soma, Syrian Rue, Zoroastrianism.**

1974 Gershevitch *Mémorial Jean de Menasce*, 49. The ancient texts define haoma/soma as a hallucinogen… if one knew nothing of Mr. Wasson's book and the controversy, one could still, by cool reasoning, have arrived at a hallucinogenic mushroom.
1989 Flattery *Haoma & Harmaline*, 3. I intend to demonstrate that harmel or wild rue, *Peganum harmala* L. (Zygophyllaceae)… was the original intoxicant [*sic*] plant represented in the Iranian religious tradition by the term *haoma*…

Hashish [Hasheesh]—Arabic name for the resin of Indian hemp; *Cannabis indica* Lamarck, known as Charas in Sanskrit; ordinarily smoked but sometimes eaten in confections, like Dawamesk and Majoon. See: **Bhangas, Charas, Dawamesk, Ganja, Kif, Majoon.**
1855 Taylor *Land of the Saracen*, 'The Visions of Hasheesh.' I had passed through the Paradise of Hasheesh, and was plunged at once into its fiercest Hell.
1857 Ludlow *The Hasheesh Eater*, 11. The resin of the Cannabis Indica is hasheesh. From time immemorial it has been known among all the nations of the East as possessing powerful stimulant and narcotic properties… The forms in which it is employed are various. Sometimes it appears in the state in which it exudes from the mature stalk, as a crude resin; sometimes it is manufactured into a conserve with clarified butter, honey and spices; sometimes a decoction is made.
1857 Ludlow *ibid.*, 269. True, the Syrian has his hasheesh, the Chinaman his opium; he must be a poverty-stricken Siberian who lacks his ball of narcotic fungus, an impossible American who goes without tobacco…
1860 Baudelaire *Les Paradis Artificiels*, IV. Le haschisch [*dawamesk*] s'étend alors sur toute la vie comme un vernis magique… [Hashish [*dawamesk*] spreads itself over the whole of life like a magical veneer…]

Heffter Technique *nov. verb.*—Psychonautic bioassay or self-experiment by scientist studying the phytochemistry or pharmacology of entheogenic plants; named in honor of Arthur Heffter of Germany, who isolated 4 Alkaloids from Péyotl and then ascertained *via* bioassay on 23 November 1897 that Mescaline was the main visionary principle. See: **Mescaline, Péyotl, Psychonaut.**
1994 Ott *Ayahuasca Analogues*, 50. I resolved to employ the 'Heffter Technique,' to don the venerable mantle of the human guinea pig… to auto-pharmacize. In short, I employed the 'intact Jonathan Ott preparation,' my most rational bioassay in the alembic of my own brain, and plunged headlong into the phantasmagoric world of *ayahuasca*…

Henbane—The visionary solanaceous plant *Hyoscyamus niger* L.; source of tropane Alkaloids such as scopolamine and hyoscyamine; said to have been used as an inebriating ingredient in witches' Flying Ointments; reputed to have been the legendary Moly, Hermes' antidote to the Potions of Circe in Homer's *Odyssey*. Spanish: *beleño*; French: *jusquiame*; German: *Bilsenkraut*. See: **Alkaloid, Circean, Deadly Nightshade, Flying Ointment, Majoon, Mandrake, Moly.**

1855 Johnston *Chemistry of Common Life* II, 147. The roots of black henbane (*Hyoscyamus niger*) are strongly narcotic and inebriating.

1860 Cooke *Seven Sisters of Sleep*, 332. Henbane (*Hyoscyamus niger*) is another of these powerful narcotic agents, educing symptoms analogous to insanity.

1868 Coleridge in Day *The Opium Habit, With Suggestions as to the Remedy*, 141. I will give a fair trial to Opium, Henbane, and Nepenthe. By the bye, I always considered Homer's account of the Nepenthe as a *Banging* lie.

1924 Lewin *Phantastica*, 177. Bei der Dämonenbeschwörung durch Nekromanten die Eigenschaft des Bilsenkrautes eine Rolle spiele. [The property of henbane played a role in the exorcism of dæmons by necromancers.]

1992 Rätsch *Dictionary of Sacred and Magical Plants*, 100. Apparently, henbane (*Hyoscyamus albus*) was the active ingredient in the incense which the Pythia, the prophetess of Delphi, used to induce her clairvoyant ecstasy.

Heresy—A belief, creed, action or an opinion which is contrary to that of any established, orthodox church or religious dogma. Hence: Heresiarch, Heresiography, Heresiologist, Heretic, Heretical, Hereticate, Hereticize. See: **Auto da Fé, Inquisition, Witchcraft.**

1993 Ott *Pharmacotheon*, 278. For this was the age of witchcraft, and in 1620 the Holy Office of the Inquisition formally decreed in Mexico City that the ingestion of inebriating plants was a heresy.

Hiera—Literally: the holy; in reference both to the Epopteia or holy vision at the climax of the Eleusinian Mysteries under the influence of the entheogenic Kykeon in the Telesterion; and the name for the holy objects concealed within the Kistai in the Anaktoron or inner sanctum of the Telesterion, and shown to the Mystai or initiates at the climax. See: **Anaktoron, Deiknymena, Eleusinian Mysteries, Epopteia, Hierobotany, Kistai, Kykeon, Mystes, Telesterion.**

1978 Ruck *The Road to Eleusis*, 77. To have seen the holy, *ta hiera*: it was in that way that one could speak safely of the Mystery. Up to that moment, the initiate was a *mystes*, with his eyes closed to the world… Yet archæologists have not found the holy, *ta hiera*, at Eleusis, although they did actually expect that they would; and in the absence of any excavated object, scholars have been free to fantasize whatever they wanted these mysterious *hiera* to be: relics, according to some, from the Mycenæan past or phallic symbols…

Hieratic—Of or pertaining to a priesthood; sacred; sacerdotal. Hence: Hieratical,

Hierocracy. See: **Hiera, Hierobotany, Hierophant.**

Hierobotany *nov. verb.*—The study of entheogenic plant Sacraments; conflation of 'hieratic botany.' Hence: Hierobotanic *nov. verb.*, Hierobotanical *nov. verb.*, Hierobotanist *nov. verb.* Synonyms: **Entheobotany, Theobotany.** See: **Hiera.**
    1995 Pagani *Altrove* 2: 69. La classe prelatizia… con suo potenziale repressivo nei confronti dei culti ierobotanici… [The prelate class… with its repressive potential when confronted with hierobotanical cults…]

Hierophant—Priest of the Eleusinian and other archaic Mysteries; initiator. Literally: he who reveals the Hiera or sacred objects. Hence: Hierophancy, Hierophantic. Synonym: **Mysteriarch.** See: **Anaktoron, Deiknymena, Eleusinian Mysteries, Hiera, Hierobotany, Kistai, Mystagogue.**
    1978 Wasson *The Road to Eleusis*, 9. The initiates lived through the night in the telesterion of Eleusis, under the leadership of two hierophantic families, the Eumolpids and the Kerykes and they would come away all wonderstruck by what they had lived through: according to some, they were never the same as before.

Hoasca—Brasilian Portuguese erosion of Ayahuasca; as in *chá hoasca* or 'vine tea,' name for the Potion in the syncretic Brasilian church União do Vegetal [Herbal Union], in which it serves as the Eucharist. See: **Ayahuasca, Daime, Entheogenic Reformation, Eucharist, Santo Daime, União do Vegetal, Vegetalista.**
    1989 Anon. *União do Vegetal: Hoasca*, 29. Nas suas sessões ritualísticas, realizadas em seu templo, a União do Vegetal faz uso de um chá, de nome Hoasca… O chá facilita a interiorização mental, produzindo clareza de consciência e aguçando a percepcão… O efeito do chá pode ser comparado ao êxtase religioso… [In its ritualistic sessions, conducted in its temples, the União do Vegetal makes use of a tea called Hoasca… This tea facilitates mental interiorization, leading to clarity of consciousness and heightening of perception… The effect of the tea might be compared to religious ecstasy…]

Host—Consecrated bread or wafer; magically transmogrified into the body of Christ by the Mass, according to the Doctrine of Transubstantiation, and offered sacrificially at the altar. See: **Agape, Communion, Consubstantiation, Element, Eucharist, Placebo, Sacrament, Transubstantiation.**

Huasca—Suffix used in nonce-words to describe specific botanical subtypes of Ayahuasca Analogues; as: Acaciahuasca, Mimosahuasca, *etc.*; or of cultural subtypes, as: Mayahuasca. See: **Anahuasca, Ayahuasca, Ayahuasca Analogue.**

Hyperesthesia—Hypersensitivity of the various senses. Also: Hyperæsthesia. Hence: Hyperæsthetic, Hyperesthetic. See: **Synesthesia**.

1958 Heim & Wasson *Les Champignons Hallucinogènes du Mexique*, 305. L'hyperesthésie sensorielle (auditive ou visuelle) a été notée dans 17% de cas. [Sensory hyperesthesia (auditory or visual) has been noted in 17% of the cases.]

Hypnagogic—Of or pertaining to drowsiness, or preceding sleep, or early, light stage of sleep. Also: Hypnogogic. See: **Entoptic, Oneirogen, Phosphenes**.

1966 Klüver *Mescal and Mechanisms of Hallucinations*, 67. Some or all of the form constants found in mescaline hallucinations are also found in certain hypnagogic hallucinations, in entoptic phenomena...

Hypnotica—The fourth of Louis Lewin's five subcategories of Psychoactive drugs set forth in his classic 1924 book *Phantastica*. Also called *Schlafmittel* or 'sleep agents,' the prototype for Lewin's class of *Hypnotica* was chloral hydrate, and it included the plant drug *kava* [*Piper methysticum* Forster]. See: **Dwale, Euphorica, Excitantia, Inebriantia, Neuroleptica, Phantastica, Psychotica, Sedative**.

1924 Lewin *Phantastica*, 48. Hypnotica, Schlafmittel. [Hypnotica, sleep-inducing agents.]

Iboga [Eboka]—Name in the Fang Bwiti cult of equatorial West Africa for the entheogenic roots of *Tabernanthe iboga* Baillon; taken in powdered form as the Eucharist in syncretic Christian rites of Communion; from which the Indole Alkaloid ibogaine was isolated in 1901, becoming the second entheogenic compound isolated in pure form. Hence: Ibogaine, Ibogaline, Ibogamine, Ibogane, Iboluteine. See: **Alkaloid, Bwiti, Communion, Entheogenic Reformation, Eucharist, Indole**.

1972 Fernandez *Flesh of the Gods*, 243. *Eboka* is the Fang name for *Tabernanthe*. The species name, as well as the Fang name, is taken from the Galwa-Mpongwe (Miene) term *iboga*.
1993 Samorini *Integration* 4: 4. 'We are the true Christians. The Catholics have lost the way that leads you to Christ; the missionaries who offer us their insipid Host and ask us to abandon *Iboga*, do not know what they are talking about.'

Icaro—A magical chant or melody with presumed healing properties; learned from 'Plant–Teachers' by Amazonian Shamans under the influence of Ayahuasca and other entheogenic Potions; from Quechua *ikaray*, 'to blow [tobacco] smoke,' as done in the course of shamanic healing. See: **Ayahuasca, Plant–Teachers, Vegetalista**.

1984 Luna *J. Ethnopharmacology* 11: 146. There are *icaros* for increasing or decreasing the strength of the hallucinations. For calling defenders or *arkana*, for curing specific illnesses, for reinforcing the effect of medicinal plants, for attracting the love of a woman (*huarmi icaro*), for calling the spirits of dead shamans...

1986 Luna *Vegetalismo*, 99. Learning **icaros**—magic songs or melodies—is an essential element in becoming a **vegetalista**. In fact, being a **vegetalista** is almost synonymous with being capable of mastering an often large repertoire of **icaros**.

Idea—In Platonic philosophy: patterns or Archetypes of material things, eternally existing in some visionary Otherworld. Hence: Ideal, Idealism, Idealist, Idealistic, Ideality, Idealization, Idealize, Ideally, Ideate, Ideation, Ideational, Ideative. See: **Disembodied Eyes, Psychocosmos, Psychonaut, Visionary World.**

1603 Holland *Plutarch's Philosophie*, 813. Socrates and Plato suppose, that these Ideæ bee substances separate and distinct from Matter, howbeit, subsisting in the thoughts and imaginations of God—that is to say, of Minde and Understanding.

1959 Wasson *Trans. New York Acad. Sci.* 21: 334. May this [the sacred mushroom] not be the explanation of the Archetypes, the Ideas, of Plato?

1961 Wasson *Botanical Museum Leaflets* 19: 155. Plato tells us that beyond this ephemeral and imperfect existence here below, there is another Ideal world of Archetypes, where the original, the true, the beautiful Pattern of things exists for evermore... It is clear to me where Plato found his Ideas; it was clear to his contemporaries too. Plato had drunk of the potion in the Temple of Eleusis and had spent the night seeing the great Vision.

1961 Huxley *Visionary Experience* [*Moksha*, 192]. Well, here again is another indication that a great metaphysical idea, the platonic Idea, the platonic system of an ideal world, is also based upon a world of vision.

Illumination—See: **Enlightenment.**

Indocybin®—Sandoz Ltd. trademark for the Indole Alkaloid psilocybine or 4-phosphoryloxy-*N,N*-dimethyltryptamine; first isolated by Albert Hofmann from cultured *Psilocybe mexicana* Heim; also called CY-39. See: **Alkaloid, Delysid,® Indole, Magic Mushroom, Nigerine, Teonanácatl, Tryptamine, Xochinanácatl.**

1978 Hofmann *Teonanácatl*, 60. In order to express our gratitude to María Sabina for this gala performance, I gave her a bottle of the pills, labelled 'Indocybin,' which is the generic name for psilocybin. The prefix 'Indo-' refers to the Indians, the original discoverers of this drug, or to the chemical indole, of which psilocybin is a derivative.

Indole—2,3-Benzopyrrole; a two-ringed heterocycle with conjoined benzene and pyrrolidine rings; indole rings form the nucleus of many Alkaloids, especially of Psychoactive compounds; the β-Carbolines, LSD and Tryptamines such as psilocybine and DMT are all indole Alkaloids. Hence: Indolic. See: **Alkaloid, β-Carboline, Darnel, Delysid,® Ergot, Iboga, Indocybin,® Monoamine-Oxidase, Nigerine, Ololiuhqui, Psychedelic, Syrian Rue, Teonanácatl, Tryptamine, Xochinanácatl.**

Inebriantia—The third of Louis Lewin's five subcategories of Psychoactive drugs set forth in his classic 1924 book *Phantastica*. Also called *Berauschungsmittel* or 'intoxicants,' the prototype for Lewin's class of *Inebriantia* was Alcohol and other solvents. See: **Alcohol, Euphorica, Excitantia, Hypnotica, Neuroleptica, Phantastica, Psychotica, Sedative, Spirit, Wine.**

> 1924 Lewin *Phantastica*, 48. Inebriantia, Berauschungsmittel. Stoffe, die nach einer primären Erregung vom Gehirnzentren... eventuell bis zum zeitlichen Versagen derselben verursachen. [Inebriantia, Intoxicants. Substances which, after an initial stimulation of brain centers, lead eventually to temporary failure of these.]

Inebriation—Extravagant exhilaration or emotion, Ecstasy; commonly misused as 'though a synonym for [alcoholic] Intoxication. Equivalent to French *ivresse* or *ébriété*, Spanish *embriaguez*, and German *Rausch*. Hence: Inebriate, Inebriating, Inebriation, Inebriative, Inebriety, Inebrious. See: **Ecstasy, Intoxication.**

> 1526 W. de W. *Pilgrim's Perfection*, 291. This inebriacyon or heuenly dronkennesse of the spiryte.
> 1860 Baudelaire *Les Paradis Artificiels*, v. Il n'a pas besoin de vendre son âme pour payer les caresses enivrantes et l'amite des houris. [He has no need to sell his soul to pay for the inebriating caresses and affections of houris.]
> 1927 Rouhier *La Plante qui Fait les Yeux Émerveillés: Le Peyotl*, 267. 0 gr.,20 de mescaline pure ou 0 gr.,75 d'alcaloïdes totaux, représentés par leur équivalent en drogue sèche ou en extrait, sont nécessaires pour obtenir les manifestations visuelles de l'ivresse sacrée... [0.20 g of pure mescaline or 0.75 g of total alkaloids, or their equivalent in the dried drug or in an extract, are necessary to evoke the visual manifestations of sacred inebriation...]
> 1936 De Félice *Poisons Sacrés* [title]. *Poisons Sacrés, Ivresses Divines: Essai sur Quelques Formes Inférieures de la Mystique* [*Sacred Poisons, Divine Inebriations: An Essay on Certain Inferior Forms of Mysticism*]
> 1960 Wasson *Botanical Museum Leaflets* 19: 145. What we need is a vocabulary to describe all the modalities of a Divine Inebriant.
> 1963 Benn [trans. Metzner] *The Psychedelic Review* 1: 50. God is a substance, a drug! An inebriating substance with affinity for the human brain. [Metzner gave *intoxicating*]
> 1970 Jünger *Annäherungen*, 51. Wie Goethe die Farben als eines der Abenteuer des Lichtes betrachtet, könnten wir den Rausch als einen Siegeszug der Pflanze durch die Psyche ansehen. [Just as Goethe regarded colors as a sort of adventure of light, so might we view inebriation as a triumphal march of plants through the psyche.]
> 1993 Ott *Pharmacotheon*, 15. Similarly, I eschew use of the word *intoxicant* in favor of the more appropriate supposed synonym *inebriant*.

Ineffable—Unutterable, transcending language, unspeakable. Hence: Ineffability,

Ineffableness, Ineffably. See: **Aporrheta, Arrheta.**
>1978 Wasson *The Road to Eleusis*, 18. And he [Aristides the Rhetor] goes on to speak of the 'ineffable visions' that it had been the privilege of many generations of fortunate men and women to behold.

Initiation—Admission into knowledge; especially of sacred Mysteries. Hence: Initiant, Initiary, Initiate, Initiating, Initiative, Initiatively, Initiator, Initiatory, Initiatress, Initiatrix, Inition. See: **Eleusinian Mysteries, Epopt, Mystagogue, Mysteriarch, Mysteries, Mystes.**
>1993 Ott *Pharmacotheon*, 19. I have become an initiate to the sacred Mysteries of antiquity, what the ancient Greeks called an *epoptes*, one who has seen the holy.

Inquisition, Holy Office of the—Juridical branch of the Vatican inaugurated in thirteenth century by Pope Innocent [*sic*] III and administered by the Congregation of the Holy Office; for the suppresion of Heresy and castigation of heretics in Italy, France, the Netherlands; as well as Spain and Portugal and their colonies. The Spanish Inquisition reorganized in 1478 was infamous. Hence: Inquisitional, Inquisitor, Inquisitorial, Inquisitorious, Inquisitory, Inquisitress, Inquisitrix. See: **Auto da Fé, Bacchanalia, Crusades, Heresy, Pharmacratic Inquisition, Pogrom, Scapegoat, Witchcraft.**
>1994 Ott *Ayahuasca Analogues*, 12. May the Entheogenic Reformation prevail over the Pharmacratic Inquisition, leading to the spiritual rebirth of humankind at Our Lady Gæa's breasts, from which may ever copiously flow the *amrta*, the *ambrosia*, the *ayahuasca* of eternal life!

Inspiration—The action of imparting or infusing with spiritual feeling or divine influence; the action of blowing into as *via* the Divine Afflatus; of imparting Vatic or oracular knowledge. Hence: Inspirant, Inspirate, Inspirational, Inspirative, Inspirator, Inspiratory, Inspiratrix, Inspire, Inspirement, Inspirer, Inspiring. See: **Afflatus, Delphic, Enlightenment, Enthusiasm, Oracle, Psycholepsy, Pythia, Rapture, Theolepsy, Theopneust, Vatic.**
>1526 W. de W. *Pilgrim's Perfection*, 99. It is to suppose that all ye rules of religion were inspired to the holy sayntes & fathers by the holy goost.

Intoxication—Poisoning in general; or by a spiritous liquor or alcoholic inebriant. Hence: Intoxicable, Intoxicant, Intoxicate, Intoxicating, Intoxicative, Intoxicator. The barbarous term 'sacred intoxicant' is an oxymoron. See: **Alcohol, Inebriation.**
>1960 Wasson *Botanical Museum Leaflets* 19: 144. Now virtually all the words describing

the state of drunkenness, from 'intoxicated' (which, as you know, means 'poisoned') through the scores of current vulgarisms, are contemptuous, belittling, pejorative. How curious it is that modern civilized man finds surcease from care in a drug for which he seems to have no respect!

1989 Flattery *Haoma & Harmaline*, 101. In other words, if the use of a sacred intoxicant [*sic*], that is, of sauma, had not already been deduced from the Indo-Iranian texts and rituals themselves, it would be necessary to propose it on the basis of the properties and cultural history of harmel in Iran.

Kernos—The pottery bowl surrounded by attached, smaller cups, in which the Kykeon or Eleusinian Potion was mixed. Plural: *kerna*. Evidently the Eleusinian Hierophant gave the *kernos* to priestesses called *kernos* bearers, who danced, balancing the *kernos* on their heads, perhaps with lighted lamps in the accessory bowls. The actual Potion was mixed in *kernoi*, evidently large *kerna*. A special type of *krateres* or bowl for mixing Wine with Psychoactive plant additives. Also: Kerchnos. See: **Angos, Eleusinian Mysteries, Kykeon, Potion, Symposium, Wine.**

1978 Ruck *The Road to Eleusis*, 82. The mixing of the potion was part of the ceremony performed after the initiates had entered the initiation hall. There, another vessel, the *kernos*, was involved; its shape and symbolism help us recapture the meaning of the ritual and the potion.

Kif [Kief]—Moroccan and Arabic term for the *Cannabis* plant and products; especially dried flower-tops; also: said to refer to the initial pleasant effects of the drug. See: **Bhangas, Charas, Dawamesk, Ganja, Hashish, Majoon.**

1846 Gautier *Le Club des Hachichins*, VI. J'étais dans cette période bienheureuse du hachich que les Orientaux appellent le *kief*. [I was in that blissful phase of hashish that the Orientals call the *kief*.]

1855 Johnston *Chemistry of Common Life* II, 92. Dried flowers, called in Morocco *kief*, a pipe of which… is sufficient to intoxicate…

1855 von Bibra *Die Narkotischen Genußmittel und der Mensch*, 267. Die Mauren der Sahara und eben so die Bewohner der Berberei rauchen fast alle leidenschaftlich diese trockenen Spitzen, welche sie Keef nennen. [The inhabitants of the Sahara and Berera passionately smoke the dried tops, which they call keef.]

Kistai—A type of hamper kept in the Anaktoron or inner sanctum of the Eleusinian Telesterion; in which were concealed the Deiknymena; sacred objects shown to the initiates at the climax of the Eleusinian Mystery Initiation. See: **Anaktoron, Deiknymena, Eleusinian Mysteries, Initiation.**

1978 Ruck *The Road to Eleusis*, 84. At Eleusis the final indoctrination had involved the

[104]

manipulation of the sacred objects enclosed in the *kistai*, the sealed hampers of the Mystery that had come with them along the Sacred Way to Eleusis.

Krateres—See: **Kernos.**

Küpúri—Vital energy, Spirit, soul; in the language of the Huichol Indians of México, often depicted visually in their art. See: **Mara'akáme, Nieríka, Péyotl, Spirit.**
> 1972 Furst *Flesh of the Gods*, 150. 'Now I am content, now I am happy, I will give them life... Look, my children, I am the one who embraces you. I am the one who gives you *küpúri.*'

Kykeon—Sacred entheogenic Potion given to the Mystai or initiates to the Eleusinian Mysteries; enabling them to experience the vision, the Epopteia, which transformed them into Epoptai, those who had seen *ta hiera*, 'the holy.' According to the seventh century B.C. *Homeric Hymn to Demeter*, the ingredients were barley, water and a fragrant mint, Glechon, and it has been suggested that it was Ergot Alkaloids from Ergot growing on the barley which imparted entheogenic properties to the Kykeon. Literally: mixture. See: **Delysid,® Eleusinian Mysteries, Epopt, Epopteia, Ergot, Erysibe, Glechon, Hiera, Kernos, Potion.**
> 1978 Ruck *The Road to Eleusis*, 81. And indeed, we do know that the drinking of a special potion, the *kykeon*, was an essential part of the Mystery. The ingredients for this drink are recorded in the Homeric hymn to Demeter: barley (*alphi*), water, and mint or *glechon*.
> 1994 Ott *Ayahuasca Analogues*, 11. Elucidated the unique pharmacology of the jungle *amrta*, which was found to be an ingenious *kykeon* or amalgam of one plant infusion containing harmine and related enzyme-inhibitors with a second containing *N,N*-dimethyltryptamine (DMT), an entheogen ordinarily inactive orally.

Laudanum—Alcoholic tincture or extract of Opium; containing its Narcotic Alkaloids morphine and codeine; said to have been invented by Paracelsus. See: **Alcohol, Alkaloid, Euphorica, Narcotic, Nepenthes, Opium, Theriac.**
> 1821 De Quincey *Confessions of an English Opium Eater*, 'Introduction to the Pains of Opium.' I here reckon twenty-five drops of laudanum as equivalent to one grain of opium.... Tea-spoons vary as much in size as opium in strength.
> 1855 Johnston *Chemistry of Common Life* II, 165. We are indeed feeble creatures, when a grain of haschisch can conquer, or a few drops of laudanum lay us prostrate...
> 1967 Paz *Corriente Alterna*, 91. ¿La farmacia sustituye a la gracia, la visión poética es una reacción bioquímica? Coleridge atribuye al láudano la composición de Kubla-Khan... [Does pharmacy supplant grace, is poetic vision a biochemical reaction? Coleridge attributes the composition of Kubla-Khan to laudanum...]

Legomena—The Words that were spoken during the Initiation into the Eleusinian Mysteries. See: **Deiknymena, Dromena, Eleusinian Mysteries, Initiation.**
1962 Mylonas *Eleusis and the Eleusinian Mysteries,* 273. The legomena were perhaps nothing more nor less than brief ritualistic and liturgical formulæ which supplemented and made clear to the initiate the performance he was witnessing. Because of their importance only people who spoke or understood Greek were invited... to join the initiates.

Leprechaun—Literally: small body, an Irish term for fairy-folk or 'little people,' the Spirits perceived by some under the influence of entheogenic plants and denizens of the visionary Otherworld. See: **Færie, Menehune, Spirit, Visionary World.**

Lethean—Causing oblivion or forgetfulness of the past. Literally: pertaining to the River Lethe in Hades, from which the shades drank the waters of oblivion, so to forget their past on this Earth and suffer not its irrevocable loss. See: **Psychopomp.**
1985 Ott *The Cacahuatl Eater,* 13. The *cacahuatl* eater earnestly commends to his audience the course he himself is following to ward off the lethean influence of the topic, the taking of a brisk and bracing cup of chocolate at this juncture.

Ling Chih—The 'divine mushroom of immortality' of the Chinese Taoists; known to scientists as *Ganoderma lucidum* (Fr.) Karsten, a non-entheogenic species seemingly designated by fiat as the legendary mushroom purported to revive the dead, apparently a fantastic attribution to the Vedic Soma mushroom, of which the Chinese had heard extravagant accounts. Known as *reishi* in Japanese, *G. lucidum* is important in Chinese and Japanese herbal medicine. See: **Elixir, Gilgamesh, Soma.**
1968 Wasson *Soma,* 88. Pan Ku, the chronicler of the Han Emperors, composed a second ode to the *ling chih,* more than a century after the Emperor Wu's.

Logos—The Word as primal cause of the ancient Greek philosophers; reason; inspired Divine Word. See: **Afflatus, Tecpillatolli, Vac, Word.**
1980 Wasson *The Wondrous Mushroom,* 39. We recall the words of Aurelio Carreras: the mushroom *es habla,* 'is the Word'... the *Word* is the thing, just as in Sanskrit it is the *Vac* and in Greek the *Logos.*
1980 Wasson *ibid.,* 225. The mushroom bestows on the *curandero* what the Greeks called *Logos,* the Aryans *Vac,* Vedic *kavya,* 'poetic potency' as Louis Renou put it. The divine afflatus of poetry is the gift of the entheogen.
1994 Ott *Ayahuasca Analogues,* 87. Blake spoke directly from the *logos,* casting in English words and engraved designs what he saw... nothing seen with his 'mortal and perishing' eye, but 'organized and minutely articulated' visions perceived by his 'imaginative and immortal organs' and 'in stronger and better light than his perishing eye' could see.

[106]

LSD [LSD-25]—See: **Delysid**.®

Macropsia—A visual distortion produced by some drugs; in which objects appear larger than they really are. Antonym: **Micropsia.**
> **1968** Wasson *Soma*, 158. It [*Amanita muscaria*] leads to trembling, a merry or melancholic mood according to one's disposition, and macropsia: 'a small hole appears to them as a great pit, and a spoonful of water as a lake.'

Mænad—Bacchante, female devotee of Bacchus or Dionysus; known for ecstatic possession by the lord of Inebriation. The Mænads were often associated with bees [*melissai* in Greek] and honey. Hence: Mænadic. Synonym: Bacchante. See: **Bacchanalia, Dionysus, Thyrsus.**
> **1857** Ludlow *The Hasheesh Eater*, 123. Unheard upon the sunny slopes of Mount Bermius, where I wandered Bacchus-smitten among the Mænades.
> **1857** Ludlow *ibid.*, 124. Around me in endless mazes circled beauteous shapes of men and women; with hands enclasped we danced and sang, and the Mænad houris overshadowed me with their luxuriant disheveled hair.
> **1937** Ransome *The Sacred Bee*, 101. Dionysus was usually regarded as the god of wine, but that was a later development; his worship is older than the cultivation of the vine. Wine superseded the honey-drink, yet honey was always sacred to him, and from the ivy-crowned wands of his followers, the Mænads, flowed sweet honey.
> **1978** Ruck *The Road to Eleusis*, 51. Eleusis was something for which even the mænadic ecstasy of the mountain women was only partial preparation.
> **1978** Ruck *ibid.*, 88. We should have suspected the presence of Dionysus, for he was the deity of inebriants and his female devotees, the mænads, experienced ecstatic possession during his worship. These mænads also gathered plants on mountainsides as we can know from their emblem, the *thyrsos*, a fennel stalk stuffed with ivy leaves.

Magic Mushroom—A frivolous name for sacred, entheogenic mushrooms coined by the editors of *Life* Magazine to sensationalize R. Gordon Wasson's seminal 1957 article describing his rediscovery of the fungal Pharmacotheon in México in 1955. Since *magic* has the modern connotation of prestidigitation and parlor tricks, this is an inappropriate designation for this *genuine* Sacrament; a 'magic drug' is rather the Placebo Sacrament of the Christian Eucharist, magically transmogrified into a Sacrament by the smoke and mirrors of the Doctrine of Transubstantiation See: **Eucharist, Indocybin,® Magus, Moksha-Medicine, Pangk, Sacrament, Teonanácatl, Transubstantiation, Xochinanácatl.**
> **1957** Wasson *Life* 42: 100 [title]. Seeking the Magic Mushroom
> **1960** Hofmann *Chimia* 14: 309 [title]. Die psychotropen Wirkstoffe der mexikanischen

Zauberpilze [The psychotropic principles of the Mexican magic mushrooms]

Magus—Persian priestly astrologer, conjurer or sorcerer. Hence: Magi, Magian, Magianism, Magic, Magical, Magically, Magician, Magicienne. See: **Magic Mushroom, Psychopomp, Shaman, Thaumaturge, Theurgic.**

Majoon—An inebriating confection containing leaves of *Cannabis* [Bhangas] or its resin [Hashish]; sometimes mixed with *Datura* seeds or Henbane [*Hyoscyamus niger* L.], flavorings and sweetenings. See: **Bhangas, Charas, Dawamesk, Flying Ointment, Ganja, Hashish, Henbane, Kif, Moly.**
> 1860 Baudelaire *Les Paradis Artificiels*, II. Le haschisch…porte différents noms suivant sa composition… en Algérie et dans l'Arabie heureuse, *madjound*, etc. [Hashish… bears different names according to its composition… in Algeria and in Arabia Felix [Yemen], *madjound*, etc.]
> 1860 Cooke *Seven Sisters of Sleep*, 217. The *Majoon* or hemp confection, is a compound of sugar, butter, flour, milk, and bang. The mass is divided into small lozenge-shaped pieces; one dram will intoxicate a beginner, three drams one experienced in its use.

Mandrake—Feared visionary solanaceous plant *Mandragora officinarum* L., especially the root; source of tropane Alkaloids such as scopolamine and hyoscyamine; the root was considered anthropomorphic and may have been an ingredient in the visionary unguents of the so-called witches. German: *Alraun*; French: *mandragore*; Spanish: *mandrágora*. See: **Alkaloid, Deadly Nightshade, Henbane, Flying Ointment, Moly.**
> 1846 Gautier *Le Club des Hachichins*, IV. Quant à ses jambes, je dois avouer qu'elles étaient faites d'une racine de mandragore, bifurquée, noire, rugueuse… [As for his legs, I must confess these were made of a mandrake root, bifurcated, black, rough…]
> 1924 Lewin *Phantastica*, 233. Schon Plinius berichtet… die üble Mandragora, die ja für sich allein einen Dämmerschlaf erzeugen kann, für parfümierte Weine… Verwendung fanden. [Pliny reported… that the evil mandrake, by itself capable of provoking a twilight sleep, was employed… in perfumed wines.]

Manichæans—Devotees of the third century Iranian prophet Mani; who might have used entheogenic mushrooms as a Sacrament; a survival of the archaic ritual use of the primordial Aryan/Iranian Entheogen Soma/Haoma. Manichæism spread into Europe, where Manichæans were known as Cathari or Albigensians, and were sufficiently powerful and numerous as to pose a threat to the Catholic Church, prompting Pope Innocent [*sic*] III to launch the brutal Albigensian Crusade in 1209. See: **Crusades, Haoma, Soma, Zoroastrianism.**

MAO—See: **Monoamine-Oxidase.**

Mara'akáme—*Shaman,* in the language of the Huichol Indians of México. See: **Küpúri, Nieríka, Péyotl, Shaman.**

> 1972 Furst *Flesh of the Gods,* 151. A man who would assume the enormous burden, ritual and psychological, of a *mara'akáme,* who would make himself responsible for the welfare of his community, must first complete at least five peyote pilgrimages.

Matritheistic *nov. verb.*—Societies whose spiritual life revolves around the worship of a primary female deity. Hence: Matritheism *nov. verb.,* Matritheology *nov. verb.* See: **Patritheistic.**

> 1993 Ott *Pharmacotheon,* 17. With the help of Dale Pendell, I have coined the words *matritheistic* and *patritheistic,* to refer to cultures revolving around worship of female and male deities respectively.

Mead—An alcoholic beverage made by fermenting honey and water; historically, the most primitive form of alcoholic drink. See: **Metheglin, Mimir's Well, Othrörir, Wine.**

> 1993 Ott *Pharmacotheon,* 307. In the *Poetic Eddas* of Norse mythology, we hear of Odin's *Othrörir,* the magic mead which imparted immortality, wisdom and poetry, and of *Mimir's Well* at the base of the world tree *Yggdrasil,* from which flowed a magic mead of wisdom…

Medicamentum Divinum—Entheogen or plant Sacrament; Latinized version of the Greek equivalent term, Pharmacotheon. See: **Entheogen, Sacrament.**

Medicine Man—Shaman or traditional healer; now obsolete. See: **Shaman, Witch Doctor.**

> 1992 Schultes & Raffauf *Vine of the Soul,* 5. *Medicine man,* whilst usually all-inclusive and generally understood, may perhaps exclude some very successful practitioners who rarely, if ever, use medicinal plants.

Menehune—Hawai'ian name for the 'little people,' Spirit denizens of the Visionary World perceived by some people under the influence of entheogenic plants; or perhaps a personification of such plants, especially entheogenic mushrooms. See: **Færie, Leprechaun, Spirit, Tengu, Visionary World.**

Mènjak—*Shaman,* in the language of the Zapotec Indians of México. Literally: he

[109]

who knows. Synonym: *Ngwe'dz.* See: **Ngol'njak, Shaman.**

1957 Wasson *Mushrooms Russia & History,* 310. The *curandero* in San Agustín is called *mènjak,* 'he who knows,' exactly the same figure of speech that we found in the Mazatec country.

Mescaline [Mezcalin]—Entheogenic Alkaloid from Péyotl, *Lophophora williamsii* (Lem.) Coulter, and other cacti; the first active principle of a shamanic, visionary plant to be isolated in crystalline form, by Arthur Heffter in 1896; the first purified entheogenic compound to be ingested by a human being, also by Heffter in 1897; and the second such compound to be synthesized [after nicotine], by Ernst Späth in 1919, proving thus its structure as 3,4,5-trimethoxy-β-phenethylamine; also EA-1306. See: **Alkaloid, Hallucinogen, Heffter Technique, Nieríka, Peyohuasca, Péyotl, β-Phenethylamine, Psychedelic.**

1898 Heffter *Archiv für Experimentelle Pathologie und Pharmakologie* 40: 385. Mezcalin hydrochloride, 0.15 g, produces a pattern of symptoms which differs in only a few respects from the one obtained with the drug [*péyotl*].

Metheglin—Mead; a primitive alcoholic beverage made by fermenting honey and water; particularly a medicinal Mead originally from Wales, doubtless 'medicated' with added Psychoactive plants. See: **Mead, Mimir's Well, Othrörir, Strong Drink, Wine.**

1857 Ludlow *The Hasheesh Eater,* 60. It was not water, but the most delicious metheglin... It danced and sparkled like some liquid metempsychosis of amber; it gleamed with the spiritual fire of of a thousand chrysolites. To sight, to taste it was metheglin, such as never mantled in the cups of the Valhalla.

1993 Ott *Pharmacotheon,* 307. It is most unlikely any psilocybine had survived the fermentation, but the resulting metheglin may have possessed a modest amount of ethanol! What a tragic waste... fermenting the pharmacotheon into mead... like transmuting gold to lead!

Micropsia—A visual distortion produced by some drugs; in which objects appear smaller than they really are. Antonym: **Macropsia.**

1993 Ott *Pharmacotheon,* 329. Fly-agaric ingestion provoked *macropsia* (a tendency to see objects larger than life) or the opposite effect of *micropsia,* and surely this inspired the shrinking and expanding properties of the mushroom in Alice's dream.

Mimir's Well—The 'pool of living water' at the base of *Yggdrasil,* the world ash tree of Norse mythology; from which issued forth a magic Mead of wisdom, drunk daily by Mimir, uncle of Odin. Probably a metaphor for the entheogenic mushroom *Am-*

anita muscaria (L. ex Fr.) Pers. ex Gray. See: **Mead, Metheglin, Othrörir, Pangk, Tree of Life.**
> **1993** Ott *Pharmacotheon*, 307. *Mimir's Well* at the base of the world tree *Yggdrasil,* from which flowed a magic mead of wisdom...

Moksha-Medicine—A cultivated entheogenic mushroom employed in rites of passage by the residents of the fictitious island Pala; in Aldous Huxley's 1962 novel *Island.* The name derives from Sanskrit *moksha,* 'liberation,' and Wasson recounted on page 146 of his *Soma* [1968]: "Huxley, discussing the genesis of *Island,* says that he had been thinking of 'a substance akin to psilocybin,' the active agent in the divine mushrooms of Mexico. The Wassons played a major part in the rediscovery of the Mexican psilocybin cult and Wasson himself had discussed his Mexican mushrooms and the Soma problem with Huxley in the late 1950's." See: **Amrta, Haoma, Indocybin,**® **Magic Mushroom, Soma, Teonanácatl, Xochinanácatl.**
> **1962** Huxley *Island* [*Moksha,* p. 239]. The *moksha*-medicine, the reality revealer, the truth-and-beauty pill... I say that the *moksha*-medicine does something to the silent areas of the brain which opens some kind of neurological sluice and so allows a larger volume of Mind with a large 'M' to flow into your mind with a small 'm.'

Moly—In Homer's *Odyssey*: a magical plant given by Hermes to Odysseus, to counteract the charms of the sorceress Circe, who had turned his men into swine. It is said that Henbane or *Hyoscyamus niger* L. was in Circe's charm; and that *moly* was Mandrake, *Mandragora officinarum* L. See: **Circean, Henbane, Mandrake.**
> **1977** Lehane *The Power of Plants,* 135. By means of herbs, she had turned them into pigs; and it was only by means of a god-given antidote, the mysterious *moly,* that Odysseus himself was restored.
> **1995** Camilla *Altrove* 2: 106. Nella mandragora possiamo ancora identificare con tutta probilità il *moly* omerico che Mercurio raccomanda ad Ulisse come rimedio contra la magia di Circe... [In mandrake we have again the probable identification of the Homeric *moly* which Mercury recommended to Ulysses as an antidote to the magic of Circe...]

Monoamine-Oxidase [MAO]—An enzyme common to all 'higher' animals; which functions to metabolize dietary Tryptamines and other 'monoamines,' and which renders Tryptamines like DMT inactive orally. In the case of Ayahuasca and analogues, DMT is rendered active orally by the simultaneous presence in the Potions of MAOI or Monoamine-Oxidase inhibitors, in this case β-Carboline Alkaloids from the Ayahuasca liana. Hence: Monoamine-Oxidase-Inhibitors. See: **Alkaloid, Anahuasca, Ayahuasca, Ayahuasca Analogue, β-Carboline, Congenihuasca, Endohuasca,**

Peyohuasca, Pharmahuasca, Syrian Rue, Tryptamine.
1994 Ott *Ayahuasca Analogues*, 68. A point mutation… in the gene coding for monoamine oxidase A in human beings… has been correlated with "a syndrome of borderline mental retardation and abnormal behavior"…

Mulla-mullung—*Shaman*, in the language of the Wiradjuri Aborigines of Australia. See: **Shaman.**
1979 Halifax *Shamanic Voices*, 53. The *Mulla-mullung* (shaman) of Australian Wiradjuri obtains his power from supernatural sources that he encounters on his journeys to the otherworld.

Mycolatry *nov. verb.*—Shamanic religion based on sacramental ingestion of entheogenic mushrooms. Hence: Mycolator *nov. verb.*, Mycolatrous *nov. verb.* See: **Phytolatry, Shaman.**
1980 Wasson *The Wondrous Mushroom*, xiv. Mycolatry: Worship of a mushroom; specifically, worship of entheogenic mushroom species in proto- and prehistory as a means for communicating in grave circumstances with the Almighty Powers.

Mystagogue—Hierophant who imparted preliminary instructions to Mystes or initiates to the Eleusinian Mysteries. Hence: Mystagogic, Mystagogical, Mystagogically, Mystagogy. See: **Eleusinian Mysteries, Hierophant, Initiation, Mysteriarch, Mystes.**

Mysteriarch—Person who presides over Mysteries. Synonym: **Hierophant.** See: **Eleusinian Mysteries, Mystagogue, Mysteries, Mystes.**
1839 Galt *Demon Destiny*, III 22. Anon she saw a veil'd mysteriarch come.

Mysteries—Pagan religious cults of the archaic world; to which Mystai or initiates were admitted *via* celebration of secret rites; often involving ingestion of sacramental visionary Potions; for example, the Eleusinian Mysteries of Demeter, involving the ingestion of the entheogenic Kykeon Potion. The Greek root means literally 'to close' [the lips or eyes]; referring to the compulsory secrecy. Hence: Mysterial, Mysteriosophy, Mysterious, Mysterize, Mystic, Mystical. See: **Arcanum, Eleusinian Mysteries, Epopt, Epopteia, Kykeon, Mystagogue, Mysteriarch, Mystes, Pagan, Telesiurgic.**
1954 Huxley *Doors of Perception*, 65. He will be wiser but less cocksure, happier but less self-satisfied, humbler in acknowledging his ignorance yet better equipped to understand the relationship of words to things, of systematic reasoning to the unfathomable Mystery

which it tries, forever vainly, to comprehend.

1960 Wasson *Botanical Museum Leaflets* 19: 150. The word for 'Mystery' comes from a root that means the closing of the apertures of the body... If the mushroom played a vital and secret rôle in primitive Greek religion, what could be more natural than that the standard word for 'mushroom' would fall into disuse through a religious tabu... and that the Greeks substituted an alternative fungal term that was a homonym of 'mystery'? You can hear the pun, see the gesture, 'Mum's the word,' with the index finger over the mouth...

1994 Ott *Ayahuasca Analogues*, 9. Psilocybine... together with LSD, a semi-synthetic mushroomic entheogen discovered serendipitously by Hofmann 12 years before Wasson lifted the veil of the holy mystery in México, went on to become key catalysts in an anachronistic international revival of archaic religion, which was destined to shake western society to its core.

Mysterium Tremendum—The great unexplainable Mystery of the existence of life and the universe; which underlies religion. See: **Mysteries.**

1970 La Barre *The Ghost Dance*, 366. Many religionists have subsequently seized upon his implicit argument: that for the numinous experience to occur, there must exist an objective something to cause the experience, a *mysterium tremendum et fascinosum*, the divine object or the objectively divine.

Mystes—An initiate to the Eleusinian Mysteries [plural *mystai*]; who was transformed into an Epoptes after partaking of the entheogenic Kykeon Potion and experiencing the Epopteia, or vision. See: **Eleusinian Mysteries, Epopt, Epopteia, Erysibe, Glechon, Kykeon.**

1857 Ludlow *The Hasheesh Eater*, 58. I gazed heavenward, as one fascinated by mystical eyes. And now the broad luminous belt began to be peopled with myriads of shining ones from the realm of Faëry, who plunged into the translucent lake of ether as into a sea...

1978 Ruck *The Road to Eleusis*, 77. Up to that moment, the initiate was a *mystes*, with his eyes closed to the world; he came to that state through the preparatory initiation of the Lesser Mystery at Agrai.

Nagual—Word used by Mesoamerican Indians for the Shaman's animal familiar; a tutelary animal into which the Shaman is said to be able to transform under the influence of entheogenic plants; especially jaguars and other felines, eagles, serpents, *etc.* See: **Numinous, Spirit, Theurgic, Tonal, Visionary World.**

1990 Dobkin de Ríos *Hallucinogens: Cross-Cultural Perspectives*, 115. When an individual transforms into his nagual, he demonstrates possession of a particularly powerful spiritual nature represented by the animal.

[113]

Narcotic—Literally: a Soporific drug inducing stupor, sleep or insensibility; legally: an illicit drug. In the nineteenth century, *narcotic* was used to describe any mind-altering drug, what we would now call a Psychoactive or Psychotropic drug. Properly, *narcotic* drugs (or *narcotics*) are opiates—Opium itself (dried exudate of unripe capsules of *Papaver somniferum* L.), its Alkaloids morphine and codeine, and their artificial congeners, such as heroin, methadone, *etc.* See: **Alkaloid, Dwale, Euphorica, Laudanum, Narcotica, Nepenthes, Opium, Psychoactive, Psychotropic, Theriac.**

    1386 Chaucer *Tales of Caunterbury*, Knyghtes' Tale. For he hadde yeve his gailler drynke so/Of a clarree maad of a certeyn wyn,/With nercotikes and opie of Thebes fyn,/That al that nyght, thogh that men wolde him shake,/The gailler sleep, he myghte nat awake. **1993** Ott *Pharmacotheon*, 257. A further problem with *narcotic* is that it prejudices people against the entheogens—since the word has acquired the meaning of 'addictive' and since its legal meaning is 'an illicit substance'…

Narcotica—An alternate designation in Lewin's scheme of Psychoactive drug classification; for what he called Euphorica, and what we today call Narcotics, the opiates. See: **Euphorica, Narcotic, Opium.**

    1970 Jünger *Annäherungen*, 38. Die Drogen können als Exzitantien und Stimulantien, als Somnifera, Narcotica und Phantastica begehrt werden… [Drugs can be craved as excitants and stimulants, as Somnifera, Narcotica and Phantastica…]

Natemä—Name in the language of the Amazonian Shuar [Jívaro] Indians for Ayahuasca Potions. See: **Ayahuasca.**

    1973 Harner *Hallucinogens & Shamanism*, 17. The use of the hallucinogenic *natemä* drink among the Jívaro makes it possible for almost anyone to achieve the trance state essential for the practice of shamanism.

Nectar [Nektar]—The drink of the gods which confers immortality; in reference to an entheogenic Potion. Hence: Nectareal, Nectarean, Nectared, Nectarel, Nectareous, Nectarial, Nectarian, Nectaried, Nectariferous, Nectarine, Nectarious, Nectarize, Nectarous, Nectiferous. See: **Ambrosia, Amrta, Elixir, Entheogen, Philosophers' Stone, Potion, Quintessence.**

    1579 Spenser *Shepheardes Calendar*, November 195. There lives shee with the blessed Gods in blisse,/There drincks the Nectar with Ambrosia mixt.

Neogæa *nov. verb.*—The so-called New World; derived from Palæogæa, the Old World, after the analogy of Neolithic/Palæolithic Also: Neogea. Hence: Neogæan *nov. verb.*, Neogean *nov. verb.* See: **Gæa, Palæogæa, Pangæan.**

1995 Ott *The Age of Entheogens*, 14. This War on Drugs originally started as a War on Religious Experiences, and it is nothing new—it dates back, in the Old World or Palæogæa, at least to the end of the fourth century of our era; and in the New World or Neogæa, to the second decade of the sixteenth century, when Europeans began to sow a genocidal reign of terror throughout the vast reaches of the Americas.

Nepenthes—A euphoric drug mentioned in Homer's *Odyssey*; which Helen added to Telemachus' Wine, to beguile him of his grief over the loss of his father; most likely Opium, but thought by some to have been a *Cannabis* preparation; figuratively: a Panacea. Hence: Nepenthean. See: **Laudanum, Moly, Narcotic, Opium, Panacea, Strong Drink, Theriac, Wine.**

1821 De Quincey *Confessions of an English Opium Eater*, 'The Pleasures of Opium.' Here was a panacea—αφαρμακον νηπενθεζ [*pharmakon nepenthes*] for all human woes; here was the secret of happiness, about which philosophers had disputed for so many ages, at once discovered; happiness might now be bought for a penny, and carried in the waistcoat pocket; portable ecstacies might be had corked up in a pint-bottle; and peace of mind could be sent down in gallons by the mail-coach.

1855 von Bibra *Die Narkotischen Genußmittel und der Mensch*, 269. Das Nepenthes der Alten … war wahrscheinlich irgend ein Hanfpräparat… und Homer berichtet, daß Helene im Hause des Menelaus dem Telemach die Nepenthes gereicht habe, um ihm Sorge und Traurigkeit vergessen zu machen… [The nepenthes of the ancients… was presumably some kind of hemp preparation… Homer reports that Helen administered nepenthes to Telemachus in the House of Menelaus, to make him forget sorrow and sadness…]

1860 Cooke *Seven Sisters of Sleep*, 11. Homer also makes Helen administer to Telemachus, in the house of Menelaus, a potion prepared from nepenthes, which made him forget his sorrows.

1868 Coleridge in Day *The Opium Habit*, 141. I will give a fair trial to Opium, Henbane, and Nepenthe. By the bye, I always considered Homer's account of the Nepenthe as a *Banging* lie.

1924 Lewin *Phantastica*, 53. Der Gebrauch der Nepenthes, des Vergessenheitstrankes… Nepenthes war ein Opiumpräparat. [The use of nepenthes, the drink of oblivion… Nepenthes was an opium preparation.]

Neuroleptica *nov. verb.*—Albert Hofmann's proposed sixth category of Psychoactive drugs; to accompany the five invented by Louis Lewin in his classic 1924 book, *Phantastica*. Otherwise known as neuroleptic Sedatives, the plant-drug *Rauvolfia serpentina* Benth. ex Kurz. and its active principle reserpine were the prototypes for this class. See: **Euphorica, Excitantia, Hypnotica, Inebriantia, Phantastica, Psychotica, Sedative, Tranquilizer.**

[115]

1995 Ott *Plant Intoxicants*, 248. Hofmann later added a sixth modern category of neuroleptic sedatives such as chlorpromazine and meprobamate, of which the reserpine-containing snakeroot or *Rauvolfia serpentina* Bentham ex Kurz. is the prototype. This last category Lewin might have called *Neuroleptica*.

Ngol'njak—*Shamaness*, in the language of the Zapotec Indians of México. Literally: she who knows. See: **Mènjak, Shaman.**

1957 Wasson *Mushrooms Russia & History*, 310. Women are just as good as men in this vocation, perhaps better, he said, for they are not given to alcohol; and he cited one Ebrígida Santiago, in the village, to illustrate his point. The woman who pursues this calling is a *ngol'njak*.

Nieríka—Word in language of the Huichol Indians of México to indicate the portal between worlds; symbolized by the entheogenic Péyotl cactus [*híkuri* in Huichol]; also a type of Péyotl distinguished by its size, symmetry, number of 'ribs,' *etc.* The *nieríka* may be depicted visually in Huichol art as a sort of mandala, often with a Péyotl cactus at the axis. See: **Axis Mundi, Küpúri, Mara'akáme, Mescaline, Péyotl.**

1982 Halifax *Shaman the Wounded Healer*, 71. The word *Nieríka* means also the 'face' of the deity; a mirror; and the threshold through which one passes into the transpersonal realms.

Nigerine—A poorly-characterized Alkaloid; $C_{13}H_9ON_2$, thought to have been the indolic Entheogen *N,N*-dimethyltryptamine or DMT, isolated from the roots of *Mimosa hostilis* (Mart.) Bentham, source of the Brasilian entheogenic Potion, Vinho da Jurema [or Ajucá] by O. Gonçalves de Lima in 1946. See: **Alkaloid, Ayahuasca, Chacruna, Indole, Peyohuasca, Psychotica, Tryptamine, Vinho da Jurema.**

1946 Gonçalves de Lima *Arq. Inst. Pesq. Agronom.* 4: 45. Nigerina: um alcaloide isolado da Mimosa hostilis Benth. [Nigerine: an alkaloid isolated from *Mimosa hostilis* Benth.]
1980 Schultes & Hofmann *Botany & Chemistry of Hallucinogens*, 155. An alkaloid isolated from the roots of *Mimosa hostilis* in 1946 was named nigerine. In more recent studies, a single alkaloid N,N-dimethyltryptamine was extracted in 0.57 percent yield from the roots of *M. hostilis*, and the identity of nigerine with this alkaloid was established.

Numinous [Numinal]—Divine, spiritual; of or pertaining to *numina* (singular *numen*), Spirits of places, persons or other creatures. Hence: Numinously. See: **Nagual, Spirit, Theurgic, Tonal, Visionary World.**

1970 La Barre *The Ghost Dance*, 366. Many religionists have subsequently seized upon his implicit argument: that for the numinous experience to occur, there must exist an objective something to cause the experience, a *mysterium tremendum et fascinosum*, the divine object or the objectively divine.

Odylic—Of or pertaining to so-called 'animal magnetism' or Spirit. Hence: Odyl, Odyle, Odylically, Odylism, Odylization, Odylize.

> **1855** Johnston *Chemistry of Common Life*, II, 158. She believes and describes them as real, and, like the credulous Indians, hundreds around her believe the odylic moonshine to be real too.
>
> **1885** Olcott *Theosophy*, 156. The whole starry heaven is pervaded with a subtle aura… He called it Od or Odyl.
>
> **1970** Jünger *Annäherungen*, 34. Die Physiker wollten jedoch vom Od ebensowenig wie die Psychiater und Neurologen von den Sensitiven Notiz nehmen. [Nevertheless, the physicists were willing to pay as little attention to Od as were the psychiatrists and neurologists to the sensitives.]

Ololiuhqui—Literally: round thing; name in the Náhuatl language of the Mexica or Aztec Indians of Mesoamerica for the seeds of the tropical morning glory *Turbina corymbosa* (L.) Raf. (itself known as *coaxihuitl* or 'snake plant'); aqueous extracts of which are used to this day in Mesoamerica as a visionary, shamanic drug, and which contain visionary indolic ergoline Alkaloids, especially ergine. Synonym: Cuexpalli. See: **Alkaloid, Delysid,**® **Ergot, Indole, Péyotl, Teonanácatl, Xochipilli.**

> **1963** Wasson *Botanical Museum Leaflets* 20: 176. On the one hand, the fanaticism of sincere Churchmen, hotly pursuing with the support of the harsh secular arm what they considered a superstition and an idolatry; on the other, the tenacity and wiles of the Indians defending their cherished *ololiuhqui*. The Indians seem to have won out.

Omphalos—Literally: navel; a rounded, conical stone in the temple of Apollo at Delphi; which in the classical world symbolized the Axis Mundi or axis about which the Earth and the heavens turned. See: **Axis Mundi, Nieríka, Tree of Life.**

Oneirogen *nov. verb.*—A drug stimulating dreams or Hypnagogic imagery in superficial stages of sleep. Also: Oneiromantic *nov. verb.* Hence: Oneirogenic *nov. verb.*, Oneirogenically *nov. verb.* See: **Hypnagogic.**

> **1860** Baudelaire *Les Paradis Artificiels*, III. Et encore aujourd'hui, sans parler de oneiromanciens, il existe une école philosophique qui voit dans les rêves… tantôt un reproche, tantôt un conseil… [Even today, not to mention the oneiromantics, there is a school of philosophy which sees in dreams… at times a warning, at times advice…]
>
> **1986** Mayagoitia *J. Ethnopharmacology* 18: 241. All this suggests that *Calea zacatechichi* induces episodes of lively hypnagogic imagery… psychophysiological effect that would be the basis of the ethnobotanical use of the plant as an oneirogenic and oneiromantic agent.

1993 Ott *Pharmacotheon,* 410. Known as the 'dream fish' or 'silver drummer fish,' this edible fish [*Kyphosus fuseus*] is reputed to possess *Calea zacatechichi*-like 'oneirogenic' or dream-inducing properties, for which it is reportedly eaten by Norfolk Islanders of Melanesia.

Opium—Dried exudate of unripe capsules of the opium poppy; *Papaver somniferum* L., containing many Alkaloids, mainly the euphoric, analgesic and Narcotic principle morphine, along with lesser amounts of codeine or methyl-morphine; from *opion*, the Greek name for poppy juice. Hence: Opiate, Opiatic, Opiumate, Opiumist, Opiumite, Opiumy, Utopiate. See: **Alkaloid, Euphorica, Laudanum, Narcotic, Narcotica, Nepenthes, Theriac, Utopiate.**

    1386 Chaucer *Tales of Caunterbury,* Knyghtes' Tale. For he hadde yeve his gailler drynke so/Of a clarree maad of a certeyn wyn,/With nercotikes and opie of Thebes fyn,/That al that nyght, thogh that men wolde him shake,/The gailler sleep, he myghte nat awake.

    1821 De Quincey *Confessions of an English Opium Eater,* 'The Pleasures of Opium.' Opium! dread agent of unimaginable pleasure and pain! I had heard of it as I had of manna or of Ambrosia, but no further...

    1930 Cocteau in Ebin *The Drug Experience,* 152. Opium, which changes our speeds, procures for us a very clear awareness of worlds which are superimposed on each other, which interpenetrate each other, but do not even suspect each other's existence.

Oracle—An intermediary person or agent through which a deity was supposed to speak in the classical world; at times through the agency of visionary plants; also, the place where this happened; as, for example, the oracle at Delphi or the Delphic oracle. See: **Chilán, Delphic, Divination, Pythia, Theomancy, Vatic.**

    1992 Rätsch *Dictionary of Sacred and Magical Plants,* 29. Through the aid of a magical plant, an oracle (person) enters a prophetic trance in which he or she is able to divine the future. Perhaps the most well-known example of a ritual of this type is the oracle of Delphi. Here, the Pythia, the priestesses of Apollo, inhaled *Henbane* smoke in order to induce the requisite state of consciousness.

Otherworld—See: **Psychocosmos, Visionary World.**

Othrörir—The magic Mead of immortality which Odin, beguiling Gunnloth in the form of a serpent, drank in three draughts. The Norse equivalent of Ambrosia in the Aegean and Amrta in the Indus Valley. See: **Ambrosia, Amrta, Mead, Metheglin, Mimir's Well, Nectar, Wine.**

    1880 Grimm *Teutonic Mythology,* 697. Othrörir contained the sweet drink of divine poetry, which imparted immortality, and from the exertion made by Odin to regain possession of it when it had fallen into the hands of the dwarfs and giants follows its identity with amrita, nectar, and ambrosia.

Pagan—Literally: a heathen or non-Christian person; applies more specifically to practitioners of archaic, pre-Christian naturalistic/animistic religions, now known to be based on primordial shamanic ingestion of entheogenic plants; also, contemporary exponents of the anachronistic revival of shamanism and worship through Entheogens. Hence: Pagandom, Paganic, Paganical, Paganish, Paganism, Paganity, Paganize, Paganly, Paganry, Pagany. See: **Age of Entheogens, Archaic Revival.**

Palæogæa—The so-called Old World; as opposed to the New World, Neogæa [Neogea]. Also: Paleogea. Hence: Palæogæan, Paleogean. See: **Gæa, Neogæa, Pangæan.**
   1995 Ott *The Age of Entheogens*, 14. This War on Drugs originally started as a War on Religious Experiences, and it is nothing new—it dates back, in the Old World or Palæogæa, at least to the end of the fourth century of our era; and in the New World or Neogæa, to the second decade of the sixteenth century, when Europeans began to sow a genocidal reign of terror throughout the vast reaches of the Americas.

Panacea—A universal remedy; reputed to cure all afflictions. Synonym: Catholicon. Also: Panacæa. Hence: Panacæan, Panacæist, Panacean, Panaceist. See: **Arcanum, Elixir, Panapathogen, Philosophers' Stone, Quintessence.**
   1590 Spenser *The Faerie Queene*, III. v. 32. Whether yt divine Tobacco were, Or Panachæa, or Polygony, Shee fownd, and brought it to her patient deare.
   1803 Coleridge *Letters to Southey*, 438. If the coachman do not turn Panaceist, and cure all my ills by breaking my neck.
   1821 De Quincey *Confessions of an English Opium Eater*, 'The Pleasures of Opium.' Here was a panacea—αφαρμακον νηπενθεζ [*pharmakon nepenthes*] for all human woes; here was the secret of happiness, about which philosophers had disputed for so many ages, at once discovered; happiness might now be bought for a penny, and carried in the waistcoat pocket; portable ecstacies might be had corked up in a pint-bottle; and peace of mind could be sent down in gallons by the mail-coach.

Panapathogen *nov. verb.*—A universal toxin or Scapegoat; reputed to cause all ills; the opposite of Panacea. Hence: Panapathogenic *nov. verb.*, Panapathogenically *nov. verb.*, Panapathogenicity *nov. verb.* See: **Panacea, Pharmakós, Scapegoat.**
   1974 [1985] Szasz *Ceremonial Chemistry*, 77. Some further facts concerning the anti-Chinese movement will show not only the stereotyped pattern of such persecutions but also its close connection to the transformation of opium from a panacea (cure-all) to a panapathogen ('cause-all' of disease).

Pangæan *nov. verb.*—Worldwide, throughout the entire planet Gæa; to replace the provincial *universal*. Formed from *Pangæa*, the primordial super-continent of geological plate-tectonics theory. Also: Pangean. See: **Gæa, Neogæa, Palæogæa.**
1994 Ott *Ayahuasca Analogues*, [title]. *Ayahuasca Analogues: Pangæan Entheogens*
1994 Ott *ibid.*, 87. We have here indeed, the potential for a pan–Gæan entheogen for the new millennium!

Pangk—Archaic Uralic Indo-European root for the entheogenic mushroom *Amanita muscaria* (L. ex Fr.) Pers. ex Gray; and early Siberian words for Inebriation; literally meaning 'bemushroomed.' See: **Mimir's Well, Phantastica, Soma, Tengu.**
1972 Wasson *Soma and the Fly-Agaric*, 57. I have learned that the Gilyak often wear a crudely carved little wooden figure, usually with one leg, suspended around their necks to ward off illness; they call it *pangkh*. Though my sources do not say so, I think this is obviously the Ob-Ugrian word for the fly-agaric, *pango*.
1980 Wasson *The Wondrous Mushroom*, 148. Here the little sprites, youths and maidens, are peopling the enchanted scene. Here there is no brutality—no Holy Office, no human sacrifice—only a garden that surpasses all dreams where mankind lives off the rich produce of the fields round about and on the entheogens of Mesoamerica, entheogens that the Greeks knew as ambrosia, the Aryans as *amrita*, the Siberian tribesmen as *pongo*.

Paraphrenia—Temporary mental derangement or mild Delirium. Synonym: **Paraphrosyne.** See: **Delirium, Paraphronesis.**
1966 Klüver *Mescal and Mechanisms of Hallucinations*, 91. He insists that only the whole complex of symptoms… can be profitably studied and describes four such 'complexes with hallucinatory elements'… [including] hallucinosis phantastica (paraphrenia).

Paraphronesis—See: **Paraphrenia, Paraphrosyne.**

Paraphrosyne—Temporary derangement; mild Delirium; wandering of mind. Synonym: **Paraphrenia.** See: **Delirium, Paraphronesis.**
1845 Moreau *Du Hachisch*, 12. *Nosologie*—Paraphrosynie magique. *Delirium magicum*. [*Nosology*—Magical paraphrosyne. *Delirium magicum*.]

Patritheistic *nov. verb.*—Societies whose spiritual life revolves around the worship of a primary male deity. Hence: Patritheism *nov. verb.*, Patritheology *nov. verb.* See: **Matritheistic.**
1993 Ott *Pharmacotheon*, 17. With the help of Dale Pendell, I have coined the words *matritheistic* and *patritheistic*, to refer to cultures revolving around worship of female and male deities respectively.

[120]

Payé—*Shaman*, in the Tupí language of Amazonia. Literally: one who knows. See: **Shaman, Vegetalista, Yachaj.**

1975 Reichel-Dolmatoff *The Shaman and the Jaguar*, 76. In all these aspects the role of the payé is essentially that of a mediator and moderator between superterrestrial forces and society, and between the need for survival of the individual and the forces bent upon his destruction—sickness, hunger, and the ill will of others.

Peyohuasca *nov. verb.*—A type of Ayahuasca with Mescaline, active agent of Péyotl, as visionary principle instead of DMT; inspired by the Peruvian Sharanahua Indian use of *tchai*, a species of *Opuntia* cactus likely containing Mescaline, as Ayahuasca admixture, and the observation that Ayahuasca β-Carbolines potentiate the effects of Mescaline. See: **Ayahuasca, β-Carboline, Mescaline, Monoamine-Oxidase, Nigerine, Péyotl.**

1994 Ott *Ayahuasca Analogues*, 65. This experiment suggests that *peyohuasca* is possible— a definite potentiation of the too-weak mescaline with β-carbolines.

Péyotl [Peyote]—Literally: furry thing; name in the Náhuatl language of the Mexica or Aztec Indians of Mesoamerica for the dried tops of the entheogenic cactus *Lophophora williamsii* (Lem.) Coulter, source of Mescaline; known as *híkuri* in Huichol, also known as Peyote and incorrectly called *mescal buttons*. Hence: Peyotist, Peyotlic *nov. verb.*, Peyotline, Peyotlism *nov. verb.*, Peyotlist *nov. verb.* See: **Entheogenic Reformation, Heffter Technique, Mescaline, Nieríka, Ololiuhqui, Peyohuasca, Phantastica, β-Phenethylamine, Teonanácatl.**

1620 de Ysla *Annals of Inquisition*, 19 June. El vso de la Yerba o Raiz llamada Peyote... es accion supersticiosa y reprouada oppuesta à la pureça, y sinceridad [*sic*] de nuestra Santa Fee Catholica... [The use of the herb or root called Peyote... is a superstitious action and reproved as opposed to the purity and sincerity [*sic*] of our Holy Catholic Faith...]
1927 Rouhier *Le Peyotl*, 266. La dose nécessaire pour produire 'l'ivresse peyotlique' est très supérieure à celle considérée comme thérapeutique. [The dose required to produce 'peyotlic inebriation' is much higher than that considered to be therapeutic.]
1963 Wasson *Botanical Museum Leaflets* 20: 165. *Peyotl* (which has commonly been eroded to 'peyote') is a Nahuatl word. Alonso de Molina... gives its meaning as... 'silk cocoon or caterpillar's cocoon,' which fits well the small wooly cactus that is its source.
1993 Ott *Pharmacotheon*, 83. *Peiotl* or *péyotl* was the name of this cactus in the Náhuatl language, tongue of the Mexicas (or Aztecs, as they are today known; the Chichimecas were their forefathers). The word probably meant something like 'furry thing' to the Aztecs, as it referred at once to a species of silky caterpillar and the cactus... which is crowned with tufts of silky hairs... R.G. Wasson has proposed that the name *péyotl* is the origin of a contemporary Mexicanism, *piule*, referring to entheogens in general...

Phanerothyme—Entheogen; visionary shamanic plant, plus active principles or artificial congeners of same. Hence: Phanerothymic *nov. verb.* See: **Entheogen, Hallucinogen, Phantastica, Pharmacotheon, Psychedelic.**
1956 Huxley *Moksha*, 107. Or what about phanerothymes? Thymos means soul... The word is euphonious and easy to pronounce... To make this trivial world sublime,/Take a half a gramme of phanerothyme.
1979 Ruck J. *Psychedelic Drugs* 11: 146. Greek *thymos*, however, means 'organ of passion, temper and anger,' and 'phanerothyme' would indicate a drug which made intense emotions manifest.
1993 Ott *Pharmacotheon*, 103. *Phanerothyme* was all but forgotten, which is just as well, for the word would mean 'manifester of passion, temper or anger.'

Phantasmagoria—Alternating series of phantasms or visions of Fantasy or of a fantastic natural scene; a name invented for the first 'magic lantern' light show in 1802. Hence: Phantasma, Phantasmagorical, Phantasmagorial, Phantasmagorian, Phantasmagoric, Phantasmagorical, Phantasmagorist, Phantasmagory, Phantasmal, Phantastica, Phantasticant. See: **Fantasy.**
1846 Gautier *Le Club des Hachichins*, v. Un des membres du club, qui n'avait pas pris part à la voluptueuse intoxication afin de surveiller la fantasia et d'empêcher de passer par les fenêtres ceux d'entre nous qui se seraient cru des ailes, se leva, ouvrit la caisse du piano et s'assit. [One of the club members, who had not taken part in the voluptuous inebriation, in order to oversee the phantasma and prevent those of us who fancied ourselves winged from leaping out the windows, got up, opened the piano, and sat down.]
1860 Baudelaire *Les Paradis Artificiels*, III. Lorsque je pus enfin sortir de ce caveau de ténèbres glacées, et que, la fantasmagorie intérieure se dissipant... [When I was at last able to emerge from the cave of glacial darkness, when my inward phantasmagoria had dissipated...]
1994 Ott *Ayahuasca Analogues*, 50. I... plunged headlong into the phantasmagoric world of *ayahuasca*... on some two dozen psychonautic expeditions into the surreal realm of the Amazonian *ambrosia*...

Phantastica—The second of Louis Lewin's five subcategories of Psychoactive drugs set forth in his classic 1924 book *Phantastica*. Also called *Sinnestäuschungsmittel* or 'sensory delusion agents,' the prototype for Lewin's class of *Phantastica* was Péyotl, and it included also *Cannabis, Amanita muscaria* (L. ex Fr.) Pers. ex Gray, the entheogenic nightshades and Ayahuasca. Synonyms: **Entheogen, Hallucinogen, Phanerothyme, Pharmacotheon, Psychedelic.** See: **Ayahuasca, Euphorica, Excitantia, Fantasy, Hashish, Hypnotica, Inebriantia, Mescaline, Neuroleptica, Pangk, Péyotl, Phantasmagoria, Psychotica.**

[122]

1924 Lewin *Phantastica*, 1. Ich gab ihm den Namen Phantastica, obschon unter diesen von mir formulierten Begriff nicht alles das fällt, was ich im engeren Sinne darunter verstanden wissen will. [I gave them the name Phantastica, although this concept, formulated by me, does not cover everything which, strictly speaking, I would wish to subsume thereunder.]

1947 Stoll *Schweizer Archiv für Neurologie und Psychiatrie* 60: 279. Lysergsäure-diäthylamid, ein Phantasticum aus der Mutterkorn-gruppe... [Lysergic acid diethylamide, a Phantasticum from the ergot group...] [title]

1993 Ott *Pharmacotheon*, 94. There was a chapter on *péyotl*, classified with other drugs as *Phantastica*, the word Lewin coined for entheogens.

Phantasticant—Entheogen; obscure nonce-word based on Lewin's classification. See: **Fantasy, Phantasmagoria, Phantastica.**

1979 Grinspoon & Bakalar *Psychedelic Drugs Reconsidered*, 7. Another term that conveys the range of feeling and thought produced by the drugs and also has a pleasantly poetic ring is 'phantastica' (or, in the English adjective form, 'phantasticant')...

Pharmacotheon—Entheogen or plant Sacrament; equivalent to the Latin Medicamentum Divinum. See: **Entheogen, Hallucinogen, Phanerothyme, Phantastica, Psychedelic.**

1633 Austin *Meditations*, 113. By a generall Pharmacotheon, when he gave his Body full of all these vertues in the Sacrament, to make his Sufferings ours.

1978 Ott *Teonanácatl*, 8. The Pharmacotheon is Recovered from Oblivion [subheading]

1985 Ott *The Cacahuatl Eater*, 73. And so in the fullness of time it has become the *cacahuatl* eater's lot to unveil the mysteries of this pharmacotheon, a drug so infinitely fine and subtle as to have escaped the legal persecutions which have unfortunately befallen so many other drugs...

1993 Ott *Pharmacotheon* [title]. *Pharmacotheon: Entheogenic Drugs, Their Plant Sources and History.*

1994 Ott *Ayahuasca Analogues*, 11. Introduction of home technology for the cultivation of psilocybian species conspired to put an end to this unwelcome intrusion of outsiders, allowing the villages thus influenced to return to approximate normality, and distracting unwanted official attention away from the fungal pharmacotheon.

Pharmacothymia—Drug Addiction or Habituation; erroneously regarded to be a disease. Synonyms: **Addiction, Habituation.** See: **Habitué.**

1933 Rado *Psychoanalytic Quarterly* 2:1. The Psychoanalysis of Pharmacothymia... [title]

1992 Szasz *Our Right to Drugs*, 91. Rado, devoted more than twenty pages to an exposition of the severe 'psychopathology' of the person suffering from the disease of 'pharmacothymia,' to reach this conclusion: 'By easy transitions we arrive at the normal person, who makes daily use of stimulants in the form of coffee, tea, tobacco, and the like.'

Pharmacracy *nov. verb.*—A state in which medicine takes the traditional place of religion as the right-hand of politics; in which medical rationales are used to justify specific instances of political control or intolerance. Hence: Pharmacratic *nov. verb.*, Pharmacratical *nov. verb.*, Pharmacratically *nov. verb.* See: **Pharmacratic Inquisition.**

> 1974 [1985] Szasz *Ceremonial Chemistry*, 139. Inasmuch as we have words to describe medicine as a healing art, but have none to describe it as a method of social control or political rule... I propose that we call it *pharmacracy*, from the Greek roots *pharmakon*, for 'medicine' or 'drug,' and *kratein*, for 'to rule' or 'to control.'

Pharmacratic Inquisition *nov. verb.*—The Christian persecution of archaic religions based on sacramental ingestion of entheogenic plants and the consequent personal access to ecstatic states; whose first great victory was the destruction of the Eleusinian Mysteries at the end of the fourth century; which then reached a gruesome climax in the persecution of witches in the Middle Ages; and which continues in today's Pharmacratic State in the guise of a public health 'War on Drugs.' See: **Auto da Fé, Eleusinian Mysteries, Inquisition, Pharmacracy, Pogrom, Witchcraft.**

> 1994 Ott *Ayahuasca Analogues*, 12. May the Entheogenic Reformation prevail over the Pharmacratic Inquisition, leading to the spiritual rebirth of humankind at Our Lady Gæa's breasts, from which may ever copiously flow the *amrta*, the *ambrosia*, the *ayahuasca* of eternal life!

Pharmahuasca *nov. verb.*—'Capsules of Ayahuasca'; entheogenic capsules compounded of appropriate combinations of pure DMT, 5-methoxy-DMT or other Tryptamine; plus pure harmine, harmaline or related Monoamine-Oxidase-inhibiting β-Carboline, catalyzing an entheogenic effect analogous to Ayahuasca. Also used as a synonym for Anahuasca or Ayahuasca Analogue in general. See: **Anahuasca, Ayahuasca Analogue, Ayahuasca Borealis, β-Carboline, Congenihuasca, Endohuasca, Monoamine-Oxidase, Nigerine, Tryptamine.**

> 1994 Ott *Ayahuasca Analogues*, 59. I again increased the harmine HCl to 94 mg... and in Experiment 10 ingested this quantity in a *pharmahuasca* capsule with 30 mg DMT.
> 1994 Callaway *Kuopio Univ. Publ. A. Pharmaceutical Sciences* 15: 46. Recently, this finding has been verified and expanded upon, with the resulting synthetic mixtures appropriately dubbed *pharmahuasca*.
> 1995 Anon. *Altrove* 2: 26. Il principio della *farmahuasca* è il seguente: poiché gli effetti allucinogeni dell'ayahuasca sono dovuti alla contemporanea presenza di due tipi di principi attivi ricavati da due distinte piante, e poiché in tutti i cinque continenti sono diffuse

piante che producono i medesimi principi attivi, allora è possibile ottenere, ovunque nel mondo, pozioni allucinogene dagli effetti simili a quelli dell'ayahuasca... [The principle behind *pharmahuasca* is as follows: as the entheogenic effects of *ayahuasca* are due to the simultaneous presence of two types of active principles derived from two distinct plants, and since on all five continents there exist many plants that produce these same active principles, it is thus possible anywhere in the world to obtain entheogenic potions with effects similar to those of *ayahuasca*...]

Pharmakós—Ancient Greek name for Scapegoat; the ritual sacrifice or banishment of which constituted a primitive form of 'therapy' for disease or ill fortune; transformed into the root for poison and later for words dealing with drugs. Hence: Pharmaceutic, Pharmaceutical, Pharmacist, Pharmacize, Pharmacology, Pharmacopedia, Pharmacopœia, Pharmacopœial, Pharmacopœian, Pharmacopole, Pharmacopolist. See: **Auto da Fé, Inquisition, Pogrom, Scapegoat, Witchcraft.**
    1974 [1985] Szasz *Ceremonial Chemistry*, 19. In ancient Greece, the person sacrificed as a scapegoat was called the *pharmakos*... after the practice of human sacrifice was abandoned in Greece... the word did come to mean 'medicine,' 'drug,' and 'poison.' Interestingly, in modern Albanian *pharmak* still means only 'poison.'
    1983 Ruck *J. Ethnopharmacology* 8: 177. The victim was called the *pharmakós*, a scapegoat or atonement, but a word that in Greek is derived from the same root as 'drug' or *phármakon*. A mythical tradition preserved an awareness of the obvious relationship between the two words... Pharmakos was said to have incited the god's [Apollo's] wrath by stealing his sacred drinking cups, for which reason the deity had him stoned to death.

β-Phenethylamine—Alkaloids with a benzene ring and an ethylamine side-chain; Mescaline is the prototypical entheogenic phenethylamine compound, and amphetamines are likewise phenethylamine derivatives. Also: *Beta*-Phenethylamine. See: **Alkaloid, Empathogen, Entactogen, Mescaline, Peyohuasca, Péyotl, Psychedelic.**

Philosophers' Stone—Latin: *Lapis Philosophorum*; identical with the Elixir or *Elixir Stone* reputed to be capable of transforming base metals into gold; alike representative of the *Elixir Vitæ* or legendary 'drug of immortality'; as such, symbolic of the primordial Entheogen, along with its Quintessence or active principle. See: **Ambrosia, Amrta, Arcanum, Elixir, Potion, Quintessence.**
    1386 Chaucer *Tales of Caunterbury*, Chanone Yemannes Tale. The philosophre stoon, Elixir clept, we sechen fast echoon.
    1993 Ott *Pharmacotheon*, 324. The philosophers' stone of alchemy and the Holy Grail, as well as Aladdin's famous magic lamp, are all considered to be metaphors for *Amanita muscaria*.

Philtre [Philter]—Love Potion or drug reputed to inspire or to excite sexual love in the person who is the object of unrequited love; to provoke the condition known as 'love-sickness' [thought in antiquity to affect principally men, in the Middle Ages it was seen as primarily a gynecological affliction]; feminine sex secretions especially were regarded as efficacious in philtres, containing some imaginary *virus amatorium* or 'menotoxin.' Hence: Inphiltration *nov. verb.* See: **Potion.**

1602 Newton *Tryall Man's Owne Selfe*, 116. By any secret sleight or cunning, as Drinkes, Drugges, Medicines, charmed Potions, Amatorious Philtres, Figures, Characters, or any such like paltering Instruments, Devises, or Practises.

1845 Moreau *Du Hachisch*, 130. Le hachisch, dans ce cas, peut avoir la puissance d'un véritable *philtre*... [Hashish, in this case, could have the power of a veritable *philtre*...]

1985 Ott *The Cacahuatl Eater*, 90. Various animal and vegetable ingredients were believed efficacious in philtres, but particularly feared and respected was the power of menstrual blood and other feminine secretions. Philtres were thought to derive from menstrual blood some *'virus amatorium'* which caused love-sickness, and even in 20th century textbooks of gynecology, belief in a 'menotoxin' occurring in menstrual blood survived.

1985 Ott *ibid.*, 92. At risk of putting his foot into a hornet's nest, the *cacahuatl* eater hastens to add that he has yet to see evidence of such dramatic inphiltration by theobromine in the human species.

Phosphenes—Luminous spots, lines or rings perceived with closed eyes after pressure on eye or under influence of visionary drugs. Hence: Phosphenic. See: **Entoptic.**

1927 Rouhier *Le Peyotl*, 266. L'unique hicouri frais, mangé par Lhumoltz [*sic*]... provoquant chez lui de lumineux phosphènes... [The single fresh hicouri [*péyotl*] eaten by Lumholtz... provoked in him luminous phosphenes...]

1961 Heim *Revue de Mycologie* 26: 48. L'auteur souligne l'intérêt des PERCEPTIONS SANS OBJET qu'elle décrit depuis les *phosphènes*—taches colorées, pointillés, 'couleurs bizarres perdues dans des noirs'... [The author underscores interest in PERCEPTIONS WITHOUT OBJECT that she describes following the *phosphenes*—colored and stippled spots, 'bizarre colors lost in the black'...]

1966 Osler *Psychedelic Review* 7: 39. These 'visions'... phosphenes can also be produced by applying electrical currents to the temples... LSD may prove to be an important aid...

Phytolatry *nov. verb.*—Shamanic religion based on the sacramental ingestion of entheogenic, visionary plants. Hence: Phytolator *nov. verb.*, Phytolatrous *nov. verb.* See: **Mycolatry, Shaman.**

1946 Gonçalves de Lima *Arq. Inst. Pesq. Agronom.* 4: 55. A fitolatria dos índios do Nordeste parece que foi pouco extensa, sendo no caso das Juremas resultante dos seus incontestáveis efeitos fisiológicos. [It would seem the phytolatry of the Northwest Indians was

not very extensive, and in the case of the Juremas was a result of their undeniable phys-
iological effects.]

Piltzintli—The Nahua or Aztec child god; a manifestation of Xochipilli, Lord of
the Entheogens; especially associated with shamanic use of entheogenic mushrooms,
personified as 'little saints,' 'tykes,' 'little clowns' and symbolized in Catholic iconography as the child Jesus or Santo Niño de Atocha. See: **Færie, Tengu, Teonanácatl,
Xochinanácatl, Xochipilli.**
   1980 Wasson *The Wondrous Mushroom*, 136. Is he not the 'young, well developed man'
   of María Sabina's chant, whom she by an act of religious syncretism has identified with
   Jesus Christ? Here is the *Príncipe Niño* of the Nahuatl world, the Child God of Mesoamerica, the divinity known to the Nahua under various names: *Piltzintecuhtli*, or *Teopiltzintli*,
   or *Piltzinteotl*, or *Piltzintli*, all of them embodying a different aspect of Xochipilli. But today he is also, surely, the Santo Niño de Atocha of María Sabina's *velada*, the Sacred Mushroom, and we discover him as captain of the romping children, the world of the 'dear little
   people' of the entheogens.

Placebo—A pill or other preparation containing no medication and administered
to humor a patient; from the Latin Vespers of the Office of the Dead; literally: 'I
shall be pleasing or acceptable.' The Catholic Eucharist is a *placebo* Sacrament, in
that it is merely an inactive symbol of the primoridal Element in Communion—
the entheogenic plant or Potion. See: **Communion, Consubstantiation, Element,
Eucharist, Host, Sacrament, Transubstantiation.**
   1993 Ott *Pharmacotheon*, 60. It bears witness to the sincerity and integrity of the New
   World Indians that they braved torture and death to continue with their ecstatic religion—they must have been bitterly disappointed in the 'placebo sacrament' of the Christian Eucharist, which is a placebo entheogen.
   1994 Ott *Ayahuasca Analogues*, 90. We must repudiate religions which *defend against* religious experiences, wearily celebrating communion with a *placebo* sacrament, which requires
   faith and gives none!

Plant–Teachers—Entheogens; the Amazonian Indian/mestizo conception of plants
capable of inducing Ecstasy and thus edifying their user-accolytes. See: **Ayahuasca,
Enlightenment.**
   1984 Luna *J. Ethnopharmacology* 11: 140. Some of the plant teachers produce visions only
   when associated with *ayahuasca.* Others produce only *una mareación ciega* (a blind diz-
   ziness), in which you do not see anything. Other plants teach only during the dreams.

Pogrom—Officially organized massacre or destruction of a group or class of people;

according to their race, religion, nationality, political affiliation, *etc.*; from Russian word for destruction or devastation. See: **Auto da Fé, Inquisition.**

1995 Ott *The Age of Entheogens*, 20. While the world was to endure an incredible profusion of pogroms and organized and unorganized inquisitions throughout the millennium aptly characterized as the Dark Ages…there existed continual and vigorous pressure against ecstatic religions and against practitioners of traditional herbal lore.

Potion—Literally: a drinking or draught; a drinkable aqueous medicine or Philtre; an aqueous [or vinous] extract or infusion of medicinal plants; also, to administer such. Synonym: Potation. Hence: Potionate. See: **Ambrosia, Amrta, Arcanum, Ayahuasca, Dwale, Elixir, Kykeon, Philtre, Quintessence, Soma, Vinho da Jurema, Wine.**

1994 Ott *Ayahuasca Analogues*, 10. The continuing interest in entheogenic drugs began to focus ever more on *ayahuasca*, a pan-Amazonian entheogenic potion made from tropical rainforest plants.

Psilocybine—See: **Indocybin,® Teonanácatl, Xochinanácatl.**

Psychedelic [Psychodelic]—Entheogen; plant Sacrament or shamanic inebriant evoking religious Ecstasy or vision; as well as the active principles of such and their artificial congeners; has a specifically modern connotation of the 'Psychedelic Age' of the 1960s, referring thus principally to the artificial drug LSD-25, and Indole or Phenethylamine drugs with similar effects [such as Mescaline and psilocybine], and to 'Psychedelic Art,' 'Psychedelic Music,' and other similar phenomena associated with non-traditional use of these LSD-type drugs in the 1960s. *Psychedelic* has a distinct pejorative connotation, and is taken to be a synonym for Psychotomimetic, as in *The Heritage Illustrated Dictionary*: 'Of, pertaining to, or generating hallucinations, distortions of perception, and, occasionally, states resembling psychosis.' See: **Delysid,® Entheogen, Hallucinogen, Indocybin,® Indole, Mescaline, Phanerothyme, Phantastica, Pharmacotheon, β-Phenethylamine, Psychotomimetic.**

1956 Osmond cited in *Moksha*, 107. To fathom hell or soar angelic,/Just take a pinch of psychedelic.

1979 Ruck *J. Psychedelic Drugs* 11: 145. However, not only is 'psychedelic' an incorrect verbal formation, but it has become so invested with connotations of the pop-culture of the 1960s that it is incongruous to speak of a shaman's taking a 'psychedelic' drug.

1993 Callaway *Integration* 4: 56. Since the word psychedelic is one with an established usage and history, perhaps the time has come when we can safely return to its use.

1993 Ott *Pharmacotheon*, 104. It became incongruous to speak of a traditional shaman using a *psychedelic* plant. In any case, the word is decidedly pejorative for many people unfamiliar with these drugs, and evokes unpleasant associations...

Psychoactive—Of drugs: producing Inebriation or alterations in the state of consciousness; whether stimulation, sedation, Euphoria, *etc.*; in the nineteenth century a *psychoactive* plant was called Narcotic. Synonym: **Psychotropic.** See: **Narcotic.**
   1993 Ott *Pharmacotheon*, 257. *Psychoactive* and *psychotropic* are precise, etymologically correct terms to embrace all classes of drugs with effects on consciousness, as opposed to other categories of drugs, such an antimicrobials, diuretics, *etc.*

Psychocosmos *nov. verb.*—The Visionary World or Otherworld; the mental universe in which the Psychonaut voyages; wherein exist the Archetypes or Ideas of Plato. Hence: Psychocosmic *nov. verb.* See: **Disembodied Eyes, Færie, Idea, Psychonaut, Visionary World.**
   1970 Jünger *Annäherungen*, 501. Wenn ich auf dieser oder jener Kugelschale des Psychocosmos lande, mich mit den Göttern unterhalte, die dort wohnen... so zweifle ich nichr an ihrer Kraft und Weisung; ich ließ den Schatten fallen, wir stehen im unberührten Licht. [When I land on this or that spheroid of the psychocosmos, to pass the time with the gods who dwell there... I doubt not their power and instruction; I set aside the shadows, we stand in virgin light.]

Psychodysleptic—Entheogen; a psychotherapeutic term to characterize this class of drugs, as opposed to *psychoanaleptics* or Stimulants, and *psycholeptics* or depressants; the term, however, is pejorative, inasmuch as the *dys-* prefix means 'diseased, faulty or bad,' as in *dysfunction, dyslexia, dysplasia, etc.* Thus, *psychodysleptic*, like Psychosomimetic and Psychotomimetic casts improper aspersions on this category of drugs, alleging they provoke psychosis or mental dysfunction. See: **Psychotica, Psychotogen, Psychotomimetic.**
   1979 Díaz *J. Psychedelic Drugs* 11: 71. The substances which effected qualitative modifications in the mental faculties were called *psychodysleptics*, corresponding to the *phantastica* of Lewin and what are now known as hallucinogens.
   1993 Ott *Pharmacotheon*, 103. Other terms proposed were *psychodysleptic* and *psychotomimetic* (or *psychosomimetic*), which even more than *psychodelic* suffered from the association of the drugs with psychosis (the term 'psycho' to describe a deranged criminal became current with the success of Alfred Hitchcock's film *Psycho*).

Psycholepsy—Synonym for Ecstasy or possession. Hence: Psycholeptic. See: **Ecstasy, Enthusiasm, Inspiration, Rapture, Theolepsy, Theopneust.**
   1886 Maudsley *Natural Causes & Supernatural Seemings*, 351. Theologian and philoso-

pher alike exhibit the strained functions of a sort of psycholepsy.

Psychonaut *nov. verb.*—One who 'trips' or embarks on shamanic Odysseys of discovery in the universe of the mind; a mental voyager. Hence: Psychonautic *nov. verb.*, Psychonautical *nov. verb.* See: **Epopt, Heffter Technique, Psychocosmos, Rapture, Visionary World.**

> 1970 Jünger *Annäherungen*, 430. Psychonauten [Psychonauts] [chapter title]
> 1989 Siegel *Intoxication*, 14. I trained a group of human subjects—the media [*sic*] dubbed them *psychonauts*—to take controlled trips with LSD and other drugs...
> 1994 Ott *Ayahuasca Analogues*, 98. A self-experimenter like Heffter was later aptly characterized by famed German writer Ernst Jünger, in his logbook of personal drug experimentation... as a *psychonaut*, a voyager employing entheogenic drugs as his vehicle.
> 1995 Anon. *Altrove* 2: 25. Attualmente, il termine 'psiconauta' ha subito una nuova connotazione, potendo anche designare un particolare tipo di psiconauta psichedelico: il ricercatore di nuovi composti o intrugli psicoattivi. [Presently, the term 'psychonaut' has acquired a new connotation, used also to designate a particular type of psychedelic psychonaut: the researcher of new compounds or psychoactive principles.]

Psychophoric—Entheogenic; obscure neologism attributed to Aldous Huxley, and thought to mean 'mind-moving,' but more precisely translatable as 'mind-bearing' or 'mind-carrying.' See: **Dysphoria, Euphoria.**

> 1992 De Vries *Integration* 2&3: 2. Among the other words, Huxley constructed was *psychophoric*: mind-moving [*sic*], what we translated in *geistbewegend* in German.

Psychopomp—One who guides souls to the abode of the dead; in Greek applied to Charon, the ferryman on the River Styx; also applied to Hermes, Anubis, Apollo, *etc.*; thus figuratively, a Shaman, as the intercessor between the living and the dead. Hence: Psychopompal, Psychopompous. See: **Lethean, Magus, Psychocosmos, Shaman, Thaumaturge, Visionary World.**

> 1980 Wasson *The Wondrous Mushroom*, 28. María Sabina was The Shaman, the focus for the woes and longings of mankind back, back through the Stone Age to Siberia. She was Religion Incarnate. She was the hierophant, the thaumaturge, the psychopompos, in whom the troubles and aspirations of countless generations of the family of mankind had found, were still finding, their relief.

Psychoptic—Producing mental or spiritual vision; as distinct from *psychooptic*: 'of or relating to the mental perception of sight.' *Psychoptic effects* would be characteristic of visionary, shamanic drugs, or of any substance or practice evoking shamanic trance states. Hence: Psychoptical *nov. verb.*, Psychoptically *nov. verb.*

[130]

1744 Philander [title] *The Golden Calf, the Idol Worship... with Account of the Psychoptic Looking Glass...*

Psychotica *nov. verb.*—Proposed name for aberrant products of cerebral metabolism hypothesized to provoke psychosis or schizophrenia; after Lewin's subcategories of Psychoactive drugs suggested in his 1924 book *Phantastica*; singular Psychoticum; especially applied to short-acting Tryptamines like DMT. Synonyms: **Psychotoxin, Schizotoxin.** See: **Euphorica, Excitantia, Hypnotica, Inebriantia, Neuroleptica, Nigerine, Phantastica, Tryptamine.**

1958 Sai-Halász *Psychiatria et Neurologia* 135: 285. Dimethyltryptamin: Ein neues Psychoticum. [Dimethyltryptamine: A new Psychoticum] [title]

1993 Ott *Pharmacotheon*, 184. *Psychotica*, psychotomimetics, psychotoxins... who, in any case, would wish to be poisoned by toad toxins, by bizarre compounds which would turn one's face the color of a plum or an eggplant?

Psychotogen—Entheogen; a pejorative psychotherapeutic term for characterizing this class of drug; falsely alleging that they produce or mimic psychosis or mental dysfunction. Hence: Psychotogenic, Psychotogenically. See: **Psychodysleptic, Psychotomimetic.**

1967 Jarvik in DeBold & Leaf *LSD, Man & Society*, 189. Facilitation of creativity is one argument that has been given for encouraging widespread use of the psychotogens.

Psychotomimetic [Psychosomimetic]—Entheogen; a pejorative psychotherapeutic term to characterize this class of drug; wrongly alleging that they produce or mimic psychosis or mental dysfunction. See: **Psychodysleptic, Psychotica, Psychotogen.**

1993 Ott *Pharmacotheon*, 103. Other terms proposed were *psychodysleptic* and *psychotomimetic* (or *psychosomimetic*), which even more than *psychodelic* suffered from the association of the drugs with psychosis (the term 'psycho' to describe a deranged criminal became current with the success of Alfred Hitchcock's film *Psycho*).

Psychotoxin—A hypothesized aberrant product of biochemical pathways within the brain; able to cause schizophrenia or psychosis in a manner analogous to so-called Psychotomimetic drugs; first suggested by the Osmond and Smythies 'transmethylation hypothesis' in 1952; in 1965 *O*-methyl bufotenine or 5-methoxy-DMT was suggested to be such a psychotoxin. Hence: Psychotoxic *nov. verb.* Synonyms: **Psychotica, Schizotoxin.** See: **Congenihuasca, Endohuasca, Psychotomimetic.**

1993 Ott *Pharmacotheon*, 184. It seemed that early entheogen users, like the scientists, were concluding that DMT had 'psychotic effects' and was in fact nothing but a miserable 'psychotoxin,' nothing but a novel 'Psychoticum.'

Psychotropic—Of drugs: producing Inebriation or alterations in the state of consciousness; whether stimulation, sedation, Euphoria, *etc.*; in the nineteenth century a *psychotropic* plant was called Narcotic. Synonym: **Psychoactive**. See: **Narcotic**.

1988 La Barre *Journal of Ethnobiology* 8: 222. The United Nations officially uses the impersonal term 'psychotropic'... to be recommended for all properly objective [*sic*] usage.

Pythia—Priestesses of the temple of Apollo at Delphi; who under the influence of Entheogens delivered the famed Delphic Oracle. Hence: Pythian, Pythic. See: **Chilán, Delphic, Divination, Oracle, Theomancy, Vatic**.

1860 Cooke *Seven Sisters of Sleep*, 14. It has been supposed... that the ravings of the Pythia were the consequences of a good dose of haschish, or bang.

1992 Rätsch *Dictionary of Sacred and Magical Plants*, 29. Through the aid of a magical plant, an oracle (person) enters a prophetic trance in which he or she is able to divine the future. Perhaps the most well-known example of a ritual of this type is the oracle of Delphi. Here, the Pythia, the priestesses of Apollo, inhaled *Henbane* smoke in order to induce the requisite state of consciousness.

Quintessence—The fifth essence or fifth distillation of alchemy; supposed to be the true essence of the universe and all things; representative of the *Elixir Vitæ* or legendary 'drug of immortality,' *i.e.* the primigenial Entheogen, or the active principle of same. Hence: Quintessential, Quintessentialize, Quintessentiate. See: **Arcanum, Elixir, Philosophers' Stone, Spirit**.

1823 Byron *Juan*, ix. A quintessential laudanum.

1985 Ott *The Cacahuatl Eater*, 30. Distilled alcohol (the quintessence or fifth essence of alchemy in pure form at last?), which had been a precious commodity, became cheap, leading to epidemics of 'alcoholism.'

1986 Luna *Vegetalismo*, 115. All these identifications show us that the **yachay** is the quintessence of the spirit of the various plant-teachers.

1995 Ott *Age of Entheogens*, 33. We... must needs add a fifth, primordial cycle, the *shamanic*... appropriately enough, the shamanic cycle embodies the quintessence of our culture, dealing as it does with what the Vedic priests called *Vac* and the Greek philosophers *Logos*... the Divine Afflatus.

Rapture—Transport of mind, Ecstasy; mystical or prophetic exaltation characteristic of shamanism and visionary states. Hence: Rapt, Raptly, Raptured, Rapturize, Rapturous, Rapturously. See: **Ecstasy, Entheogen, Enthusiasm, Inspiration, Psycholepsy, Psychonaut, Theolepsy, Theopneust**.

[132]

1526 W. de W. *Pilgrim's Perfection*, 272. A rapt, or a rauysshynge of the soule…
1629 Milton *Nativity*, 98. Such musick sweet… As all their souls in blissful rapture took.
1857 Ludlow *The Hasheesh Eater*, 52. The peculiar time of hasheesh… added one more
rapturous element to my enjoyment.

Reformation—The sixteenth century movement to reform the Catholic Church
of Rome; leading to the founding of the Reformed or Protestant churches of central
and northwestern Europe. See: **Counter Reformation, Entheogenic Reformation.**
   1995 Ott *The Age of Entheogens*, 42. Catholic dogma and practice surrounding these 'sacraments' was the main catalyst of the Reformation, which commenced with Martin Luther's
95 theses against indulgences (the sacrament of penance), nailed to the door of the castle
church in Wittenberg, Saxony in October 1517.

Renaissance—The great revival of learning, of the arts and sciences; rescuing classical learning from the oblivion of the millennium-long Dark Ages into which the
Christian theocracy plunged Europe; commencing in the 14th century and lasting
through the 16th. Hence: Entheogenic Renaissance *nov. verb.* See: **Counter Reformation, Dark Ages, Entheogenic Reformation, Reformation.**
   1995 Ott *The Age of Entheogens*, 44. I suggest that, as far as religion goes, we are *still* in
the Dark Ages, and that the Entheogenic Reformation at last heralds the dawning of the
Entheogenic Renaissance, a *spiritual* Renaissance which hopefully will do for religions
what the mediæval Renaissance did for art and science a half-millennium ago.

Sacrament—An entheogenic plant or Potion taken ritually for Communion with
the gods or ancestors resident in the Otherworld; in Christian liturgy, the Placebo
Sacrament of the Host or Eucharist; in Catholic liturgy the Eucharist plus another
six derivative Placebo Sacraments—baptism, confirmation, penance, marriage, ordination and extreme unction. Hence: Sacramental, Sacramentally, Sacramentary,
Sacramentize, Sacramently. See: **Agape, Communion, Element, Eucharist, Host,
Placebo.**
   1959 Wasson *Trans. New York Acad. Sci.* 21: 333. May not the sacred mushroom, or some
other natural hallucinogen, have been the original element in all the Holy Suppers of the
world, being gradually replaced by harmless Elements in a watering down of the original
fearful sacrament?

Santo Daime—Literally: 'Saint Gi'me'; syncretic Brasilian Neo-Christian church
founded in the state of Acre, Brasil by Mestre Raimundo Irineu Serra in the 1930s;
in which the entheogenic Potion Daime or Ayahuasca serves as the Eucharist in Mass.
See: **Daime, Entheogenic Reformation, Eucharist, Hoasca, União do Vegetal.**

[133]

1992 MacRae *Guiado Pela Lua*, 67. Apesar de inicialmente receber chamadas, melodias sem letra que executava assobiando, depois de certo tempo Mestre Irineu começou a receber os hinos que iriam compor seu *Hinário do Cruzeiro*, considerado a formulação básica da doutrina do Santo Daime. [Despite initially receiving *icaros*, melodies without lyrics executed by whistling, after a while Mestre Irineu began to receive the hymns which comprise his *Hinário do Cruzeiro* [*Hymnal of the Crucifer*], regarded to constitute the basic doctrine of Santo Daime.]

Scapegoat—Literally: 'escape goat'; from Mosaic ritual; a goat symbolically imbued with the sins of the people, then banished into the wilderness while another goat was sacrificed; in ancient Greece probably in origin a human sacrifice; derivatively, any being or thing blamed for the sins or problems of others. Hence: Scapegoater, Scapegoating. See: **Panapathogen, Pharmakós.**

1974 [1985] Szasz *Ceremonial Chemistry*, 20. When the ancients saw a scapegoat, they could at least recognize him for what he was: a *pharmakos*, a human sacrifice. When modern man sees one, he does not, or refuses to, recognize him for what he is; instead, he looks for 'scientific' explanations to explain away the obvious. Thus, to the modern mind, the witches were mentally sick women; the Jews in Nazi Germany were the victims of a mass psychosis; involuntary mental patients are sick people unaware of their own need for treatment; and so on.

Schizotoxin—A hypothetical aberrant product[s] of biochemical pathways in the brain; which causes schizophrenia or psychosis in a manner analogous to so-called Psychotomimetic drugs; first suggested by the Osmond and Smythies 'transmethylation hypothesis' in 1952. Synonyms: **Psychotica, Psychotoxin.** See: **Congenihuasca, Endohuasca, Psychotomimetic.**

1994 Callaway *Kuopio Univ. Publ. A. Pharmaceutical Sciences* 15: 25. A major shortcoming of such thinking was in neglecting to consider a useful function for the identified 'schizotoxins,' since they have also been found in laboratory animals and non-psychotic volunteers as well.

Sedative—Of or pertaining to calming, tranquilizing or Soporific drugs or Potions; modern catch-all term to encompass drugs in Lewin's Euphorica, Hypnotica and Inebriantia, plus Hofmann's sixth, modern category, Neuroleptica. Opposite in action to a Stimulant, also known in medical jargon as a *depressant* or *psycholeptic.* See: **Dwale, Euphorica, Hypnotica, Narcotic, Neuroleptica, Somnifera, Stimulant, Tranquilizer.**

Shaman—A medicine-man or priest-doctor of preliterate societies in northern Asia and, by extension, of other areas, particularly the Americas; a specialist in 'archaic techniques of ecstasy,' originally in ecstatic states *naturally* catalyzed by entheogenic plants, later *artificially* induced by secondary techniques like drumming, chanting, fasting, breath control, *etc.* Hence: Shamanian, Shamanic, Shamanism, Shamanist, Shamanistic, Shamanite. See: **Age of Entheogens, Magus, Psychopomp, Shamanize, Thaumaturge, Visionary World.**

1698 Brand *Emb. Muscovy into China*, 50. If five or six of these Tonguese Families happen to live near one another... they maintain betwixt them a Shaman, which signifies as much as Sorcerer or Priest.

1957 Wasson *Mushrooms Russia & History*, 191. Far to the west of the Korjaks and Chukchees, in western Siberia, in the northern lands lying between the Ob and Yenisei rivers, we have fragmentary but reliable reports that the shamanistic use of the inebriating fly amanita has survived into our own times.

1980 Wasson *The Wondrous Mushroom*, 28. María Sabina was The Shaman, the focus for the woes and longings of mankind back, back through the Stone Age to Siberia. She was Religion Incarnate. She was the hierophant, the thaumaturge, the psychopompos, in whom the troubles and aspirations of countless generations of the family of mankind had found, were still finding, their relief.

Shamanize *nov. verb.*—To exercise the profession of a Shaman; acting as intercessor between fellow human beings and the unseen forces of the Otherworld; also to convert to shamanistic belief. See: **Magus, Psychopomp, Shaman, Thaumaturge.**

1901 Anon. *Contemporary Review* Jan., 87. Old Russian settlers in those far-off regions have to a high degree become 'Shamanized.'

1974 María Apolonia in Wasson *María Sabina and her Mazatec Mushroom Velada*, 7. Ti^{4}xai^{13} nti^{1}na^{42}, ti^{4}xai^{13} nti^{1}na^{42}. [*Shamanize, mommy! Shamanize!*]

Smart Drug—A nebulous category of pharmaceuticals, some of them Psychoactive; reputed to enhance serial learning, recall, or other aspects of intelligence, of which the Stimulant Alkaloid arecoline [sometimes misspelled *arecholine*], from the stimulating masticatory palm nut *betel* or *paan* [*Areca catechu* L.], is the prototype. See: **Excitantia, Stimulant.**

1993 Ott *Pharmacotheon*, 149. *Hydergine* has also shown valuable stimulant effects... and has been shown to improve mental processing and performance... making it one of the most sought-after 'smart drugs.'

Soma—Entheogenic plant and Potion prepared from it by the Aryans in the Indus Valley at the dawn of the Vedic Age; *circa* 1500 B.C., and extolled in the *Rg Veda*, especially Mandala IX; also, a god in the Vedic pantheon. Increasing ethnobotanical, linguistic and other evidence is summing up to proof that in origin Soma was some entheogenic mushroom; the strongest case for its identity is Wasson's detailed argument that Soma was *Amanita muscaria* (L. ex Fr.) Pers. ex Gray. See: **Amrta, Elixir, Haoma, Pangk, Tengu, Zoroastrianism.**

> **1932** Huxley *Brave New World* [*Moksha*, 13]. There is always *soma*, delicious *soma*, half a gramme for half-holiday, a gramme for a week-end, two grammes for a trip to the gorgeous East, three for a dark eternity on the moon... The loving cup of strawberry ice-cream *soma* was passed from hand to hand...
>
> **1968** Wasson *Soma*, 3. Unique among these other gods was Soma. Soma was at the same time a god, a plant, and the juice of that plant. So far as we know now, Soma is the only plant that man has ever deified.

Somnifera—An alternate designation within Lewin's scheme of Psychoactive drug subclassification; for what he called Hypnotica, and what we today call *hypnotics*, Soporific Sedatives. See: **Hypnotica, Narcotic, Sedative, Soporific, Tranquilizer.**

> **1970** Jünger *Annäherungen*, 38. Die Drogen können als Exzitantien und Stimulantien, als Somnifera, Narcotica und Phantastica begehrt werden... [Drugs can be craved as excitants and stimulants, as Somnifera, Narcotica and Phantastica...]

Soporific—Of or pertaining to sleep-inducing drugs or Sedatives; or a member of that class, called by Lewin Hypnotica. See: **Hypnotica, Narcotic, Sedative, Somnifera, Tranquilizer.**

Spirit—The vital or animating principle in living beings; a supernatural being, as 'Plant-Spirit'; Quintessence or hidden active principle; distillate, especially distilled Alcohol as *spirit of wine*, often plural. Hence: Spiritous, Spiritual. See: **Alcohol, Færie, Leprechaun, Menehune, Nagual, Numinous, Plant–Teachers, Quintessence, Tengu, Theurgic, Tonal, Visionary World, Wine.**

> **1991** Luna *Integration* 1: 14. In this article I will present seven of Amaringo's visions in which plants and plant spirits are an important element... I will primarily concentrate on plants and plant spirits, and the various roles they play in the shamanism of the area...

Stimulant—A drug or Potion with an exciting or arousing effect; called by Lewin Excitantia [Exzitantia] and known in medical jargon as a *psychoanaleptic*; once used as a catch-all term, like Narcotic, for a mind-altering or Psychoactive drug. The opposite in pharmacological action is Sedative. Sometimes called Stimulantia, after Lewin. See: **Excitantia, Narcotic, Sedative, Smart Drug.**

> **1970** Jünger *Annäherungen*, 39. Dazu kommt, daß Stimulantia und Narcotica oft neben-

einander oder, besser gesagt, gegeneinender gebraucht werden. [Furthermore, Stimulantia and Narcotica are often used together or, more precisely, against each other.]

Strong Drink [Shekar]—An inebriating Potion described in the Old Testament; but distinct from Wine; probably a Soporific or visionary vinous infusion, analogous to ancient Greek Wines, of one or many Psychoactive plants. See: **Deadly Nightshade, Dwale, Metheglin, Nepenthes, Wine.**
1386 Chaucer *Tales of Caunterbury*, Persons Tale. Whan that a man is nat wont to strong drynke.
1914 Wasson *Religion & Drink*, 14. These passages show, too, that 'strong drink' was different from this alcoholic wine, but that it likewise could intoxicate.
1993 Ott *Pharmacotheon*, 157. Was the Biblical *shekar*, 'strong drink,' not an inebriating potion analogous to the ancient Greek wines, some of which were entheogenic potions?

Symposium—Literally: a drinking party in ancient Greece; the title of one of Plato's dialogues involving such; by derivation a [professional] meeting where Inebriation is not the *primary* focus. Hence: Symposiac, Symposiacal, Symposial, Symposiarch, Symposiast, Symposiastic. See: **Dionysus, Kernos, Wine.**
1970 Jünger *Annäherungen*, 462. Das Symposion galt einem der mexikanischen Wahrsagepilze... die in Europa seit langem, allerdings nur theoretisch und esoterisch, bekannt gewesen sind. [The symposion involved the Mexican divinatory mushrooms... which for a long time in Europe were known only theoretically and esoterically.]
1978 Ruck *The Road to Eleusis*, 90. At a symposium or social drinking party, the intensity of the inebriation would be ceremoniously determined by the leader or *symposiarchos*, who decided what ratio of dilution would be used.

Synesthesia—Perceptual phenomenon characteristic of visionary drugs; in which stimulation of one sense organ evokes perception in another; as: 'seeing' sounds or 'hearing' colors. Also: Synæsthesia. Hence: Synæsthetic, Synesthetic. See: **Hyperesthesia.**
1966 Critchley in Klüver *Mescal and Mechanisms of Hallucinations*, 5. Of special interest are the not infrequent occurrence of synæsthesiæ in mescal states, whereby excitation of one sense organ by actual stimuli evokes a train of phenomena pertaining to another sense organ.

Syrian Rue—Common name for the Sedative plant *Peganum harmala* L. or *harmel*; thought to be the primary substitute plant for the Avestan Haoma; source of harmine and allied β-Carboline Alkaloids; today used commonly as substitute for Ayahuasca stem in formulation of Anahuasca or Ayahuasca Analogues. See: **Alkaloid, Anahuasca,**

Ayahuasca, Ayahuasca Analogue, β-Carboline, Haoma, Monoamine-Oxidase.
1994 Ott *Ayahuasca Analogues*, 34. This well-known alkaloid had been isolated from seeds of Syrian rue, *Peganum harmala*, by German chemist J. Fritzsche midway through the nineteenth century.

Tares—See: **Darnel.**

Tecpillatolli—Refined or poetic language of the nobility among the ancient Mexica or Aztecs of Mesoamerica. See: **Afflatus, Logos, Temicxoch, Vac, Word.**
1980 Wasson *The Wondrous Mushroom*, 96. The Nahua of the highest social class spoke their language in an elegant manner known as *tecpillatolli*... for them in *tecpillatolli* the entheogens (or the superior entheogens) were as we have seen *flowers*.
1994 Ott *Ayahuasca Analogues*, 18. For the ancient Aztecs, *in xóchitl in cuícatl*—'in flower in song'—was a metaphor for the entheogenic state *temicxoch*, the 'flowery dream' of the shaman/priest, expressed in *tecpillatolli*, a sacred language of shamans and poets, the divinely-inspired *logos*, oracular speech of the thaumaturge inebriated by entheogenic plants, depicted visually as 'speech scrolls' with appended flowers.

Telesiurgic—Of or pertaining to the performance of Mysteries or magical rites; mystical; pertaining to Hierophants. Hence: Telesiurgics, Telesm [=Talisman], Telesmatic, Telesmatical, Telesmatically, Telestic. See: **Hierophant, Mysteries.**
1678 Cudworth *Intell. Syst.* i., iv., 16: 293. Julian a Chaldean and Theurgist... (who wrote concerning Dæmons and Telesiurgicks)...

Telesterion—The Initiation hall at Eleusis; wherein the annual Initiation to the Greater Eleusinian Mysteries was celebrated. See: **Anaktoron, Dromena, Eleusinian Mysteries, Epopteia, Hiera, Kykeon.**
1978 Ruck *The Road to Eleusis*, 36. Ancient writers unanimously indicate that something was seen in the great *telesterion* or initiation hall within the sanctuary... The experience was a vision whereby the pilgrim became someone who saw, an *epoptes*.

Temicxoch—The ecstatic experience catalyzed by sacramental ingestion of entheogenic Plant–Teachers, in the ancient Mexican Náhuatl language. Literally: the flowery dream; the entheogenic dream, as depicted on the statue of Xochipilli. See: Illustration on page 62; **Plant–Teachers, Tecpillatolli, Xóchitl.**
1980 Wasson *The Wondrous Mushroom*, 58. This being is not with us, is in a far-off world. He is absorbed by *temicxoch*, 'dream flowers' as the Nahua say describing the awesome experience that follows the ingestion of an entheogen. I can think of nothing like it in the long and rich history of European art: Xochipilli absorbed in *temicxoch*.

Tengu—A Japanese mythical race of 'little people'; long-nosed trickster imps said to get 'drunk from eating mushrooms,' particularly the psychoactive *Amanita* species, *tengu-take, A. pantherina* (D.C. ex Fr.) Secr.; *beni-tengu-take, A. muscaria* (L. ex Fr.) Pers. ex Gray; and *ibo-tengu-take, A. strobiliformis* (Paul.) Quél.; testifying to a traditional shamanic use of these mushrooms in ancient Japan. Hence: Ibotenic Acid. See: **Færie, Pangk, Piltzintli, Spirit, Visionary World.**

1973 Imazeki *Transactions of the Asiatic Society of Japan* 11: 46. *Tengu* 'love to have convivial parties among themselves in some forest clearing, and are said to get drunk by eating a certain kind of mushroom.'

1993 Ott *Pharmacotheon,* 341. Ibotenic acid derives its name from the Japanese name for *Amanita strobiliformis... ibo-tengu-take* 'warted Tengu mushroom.'

Teonanácatl—Name in the Náhuatl language of the Mexica or Aztecs of Mesoamerica for a complex of entheogenic mushrooms; now known to represent about a dozen species in several genera, all containing psilocybine and related 4-hydroxy-indoles; literally: wondrous mushroom [erroneously thought to mean 'god's flesh' after Motolinía's mistranslation]. See: **Indocybin,®** **Indole, Magic Mushroom, Ololiuhqui, Péyotl, Xochinanácatl.**

1957 Wasson *Mushrooms Russia & History,* 283. Mictlantecuhtli, Lord of the Underworld, hovers with giant stature over the Indian who is eating his pair of *teo-nanácatl.*

1978 Ott *Teonanácatl* [title]. *Teonanácatl: Hallucinogenic Mushrooms of North America*

1980 Wasson *The Wondrous Mushroom,* 44. The *teo-* of *teonanácatl* means divine or wondrous or awesome, and so *teonanácatl* means the divine or wondrous or awesome mushroom, nothing more and nothing less.

Thaumaturge—Miracle worker, conjurer, Shaman. Hence: Thaumaturgic, Thaumaturgical, Thaumaturgist, Thaumaturgism, Thaumaturgize, Thaumaturgy. See: **Magus, Psychopomp, Shaman, Theurgic.**

1727 Bailey *Univ. Etymological English Dict.,* Vol. II. *Thaumaturgy:* Any art that does, or seems to do Wonders, or... a mathematical Science, which gives a certain Rule for the making of strange Works to be perceiv'd by the Sense, yet to be greatly wonder'd at.

1980 Wasson *The Wondrous Mushroom,* 28. María Sabina was The Shaman, the focus for the woes and longings of mankind back, back through the Stone Age to Siberia. She was Religion Incarnate. She was the hierophant, the thaumaturge, the psychopompos, in whom the troubles and aspirations of countless generations of the family of mankind had found, were still finding, their relief.

Theobotany *nov. verb.*—The scientific study of Entheogens or shamanic inebriants and plant Sacraments. Includes botany, ethnobotany, phytochemistry, pharmacology, archæology and art history. Hence: Theobotanic *nov. verb.*, Theobotanical *nov. verb,* Theobotanist *nov. verb.* Synonyms: **Entheobotany, Hierobotany.** See: **Entheogen.**

1963 Barnard *The Psychedelic Review* 1: 245. If there were such a field as theo-botany, the study of these plants and their cults would be work for a theo-botanist.

Theolepsy—Inspiration or Enthusiasm in the literal sense; divine seizure or possession. Hence: Theoleptic. See: **Ecstasy, Enthusiasm, Inspiration, Psycholepsy, Rapture, Theopneust.**

1886 Maudsley *Natural Causes & Supernatural Seemings,* 222. The incoherent utterances which... the theoleptic... poured out under divine compulsion.

Theomancy—An ancient classical form of Divination. Hence: Theomantic. See: **Chilán, Delphic, Divination, Oracle, Pythia, Vatic.**

1651 Hobbes *Leviathan,* I. xii, 56. These kinds of foretelling events were accounted Theomancy, or Prophecy.

Theopneust—Divinely inspired, enthusiastic. Hence: Theopneustia, Theopneustian, Theopneustic, Theopneusty. See: **Ecstasy, Enthusiasm, Inspiration, Psycholepsy, Rapture, Theolepsy.**

1660 Fisher *Rusticks Alarm* IV. i., 592. Denying any such Theopneustian Divine Inspiration, Revelation, Motion...

Theriac [Theriacle]—An antidote to poison, especially to snake venoms; from a Greek word descriptive of wild beasts and venemous reptiles; in the classical world a sort of universal antidote or Panacea; in ancient Rome Opium was an important ingredient in theriacs, and the root has come to mean Opium in the Near East, while there is modern evidence that opiate drugs are immunostimulants. Hence: Theriacal, Theriacality. See: **Euphorica, Laudanum, Nepenthes, Opium, Panacea.**

1568 Skeyne *The Pest,* 24. One half vnce of guid auld theriac.

1966 Gelpke *Vom Rausch im Orient und Okzident,* 50. Tatsächlich hat das heute in Persien allgemein gebrauchte Wort für Opium, nämlich 'teryâk,' in klassischen Sprachgebrauch die Bedeutung von 'Gegengift.' [Actually, the word commonly used for opium today in Persia, namely 'teryâk,' had the meaning of 'antidote' in classical linguistic usage.]

1989 Escohotado *Historia de las Drogas,* I, 142. A partir del siglo II a.C., la medicina griega y helenística se muestra fascinada por la idea de un compuesto—la *theriaka* o triaca—capaz de inmunizar contra toda suerte de tóxicos. [Starting in the second century B.C., Greek and Hellenistic medicine became fascinated with the idea of a compound—the *theriaka* or theriac—capable of immunizing against all types of toxins.]

Theurgic—Pertaining to the magic of the Egyptian Platonists; for communication with beneficent Spirits. Hence: Theurgical, Theurgically, Theurgist, Theurgy. See: **Magus, Nagual, Numinous, Shaman, Spirit, Thaumaturge, Visionary World.**
> 1678 Cudworth *Intell. Syst.* i., iv., 16: 286. One of those more refined [magicians] who have been called by themselves Theurgists.

Thyrsus [Thyrse]—The symbol of Dionysus and his devotees the Mænads; a sort of staff wreathed with ivy or vine branches. Hence: Thyrsoidal. See: **Deiknymena, Dionysus, Mænad.**
> 1857 Ludlow *The Hasheesh Eater*, 124. Together with troops of Bacchantes I leaped madly among the clusters; I twirled my thyrsus, and cried Evoë Bacche with the loudest.
> 1978 Ruck *The Road to Eleusis*, 88. These mænads also gathered plants on mountainsides as we can know from their emblem, the *thyrsos*, a fennel stalk stuffed with ivy leaves... the ivy that the mænads placed in their *thyrsoi* was recognized in antiquity for its psychotropic properties.

Tonal [Tona]—In Mesoamerican Indian belief: an animal born at the same instant as a person and to whose destiny that individual is ineluctably linked. See: **Nagual, Numinous, Spirit, Theurgic, Visionary World.**
> 1974 Wasson *María Sabina*, xii. Various divining methods were used to arrive at the species of the *tona*, and one was always careful throughout life to avoid injury to animals of the species of one's *tona*. The word *tona* seems... to come ultimately, *via* Zapotec, from Nahuatl *tonalli*.

Tranquilizer [Tranquillizer]—A Sedative drug mainly used in outpatient psychiatry as a relaxing, anti-anxiety or anti-stress agent; also known as an *ataractic* or *ataraxic* drug ['maintaining calm'], or *psycholeptic*. A somewhat nebulous category, the tranquilizers are sometimes subdivided into two subtypes, according to the strength and extent of their actions: the 'minor' tranquilizers, of which *Valium*® is a well-known example; and the 'major' tranquilizers, such as chlorpromazine or *Thorazine*.® Hofmann proposed for such a sixth class of psychoactivity, to accompany the original five of Lewin, which I have dubbed Neuroleptica. See: **Hypnotica, Sedative.**
> 1991 Smith *A Social History of the Minor Tranquilizers*, 132. The Medicalization of Human Problems: The idea that the minor tranquilizers are used as part of a model that medicalizes problems that are essentially social or human is one that has followed these drugs since their early days on the market.

Transubstantiation, Doctrine of—Eleventh century dogma of the Catholic Church;

proclaiming that in Holy Communion, the bread and Wine of the Host are trans-mogrified into the body and blood of Christ; doctrinal basis for the validity of what is obviously a Placebo Sacrament. Hence: Transubstantial, Transubstantiate, Transub-stantiating. See: **Communion, Consubstantiation, Element, Entheogenic Refor-mation, Eucharist, Host, Placebo, Sacrament.**

1959 Wasson *Trans. New York Acad. Sci.* 21: 333. The faithful were not obliged to accept the dogma of Transubstantiation in order to know that they had partaken of the body of Christ.

Tree of Life—A pangæan mythological element; originating in North Asia and rep-resenting chiefly the birch; at whose base there was the 'Food of Life,' the 'Water of Life,' the 'Lake of Milk'; according to R. Gordon Wasson's 'unified field theory' of human culture, these are metaphors for the entheogenic mushroom *Amanita musca-ria* (L. ex Fr.) Pers. ex Gray, which grows in a mycorrhizal or symbiotic relationship with the roots of birch and of other trees. Also, in *Genesis* 2:9, a tree, the eating of which would have conferred immortality on Adam and Eve, whom Jehovah God expelled from the Garden of Eden e're they could sample it. See: **Axis Mundi, Mim-ir's Well, Pangk, Tree of Life, Tree of the Knowledge of Good and Evil.**

1968 Wasson *Soma*, 220. The Tree of Life, the Pillar of the World, the Cosmic Tree, the Axis of the World, the Tree of the Knowledge of Good and Evil—all these were variations stemming back to the birch and the fly-agaric of the northern forests.

1995 Ott *The Age of Entheogens*, 32. Could there ever be a more damning indictment of the spiritual bankruptcy of our vaunted western civilization... than the fact that it has transubstantiated the sacred fruit of the Tree of Life, the veritable well-spring of all cul-ture... into scurvy contraband... made the truth a secret... the *Logos* a dirty word...?

Tree of the Knowledge of Good and Evil—In *Genesis* 2:9: a mythical tree in the Garden of Eden, whose fruit conferred wisdom and of which Adam and Eve ate ag-ainst the orders of Jehovah God; the fruit probably represents the mycorrhizal en-theogenic mushroom *Amanita muscaria* (L. ex Fr.) Pers. ex Gray; thus, a Biblical ver-sion of the Tree of Life. See: **Axis Mundi, Pangk, Tree of Life.**

1968 Wasson *Soma*, 220. The Tree of Life, the Pillar of the World, the Cosmic Tree, the Axis of the World, the Tree of the Knowledge of Good and Evil—all these were variations stemming back to the birch and the fly-agaric of the northern forests.

1986 Wasson *Persephone's Quest*, 75. I hold that the fruit of the Tree of the Knowledge of Good and Evil was Soma, was the *kakuljá*, was *Amanita muscaria*, was the Nameless Mushroom of the English-speaking people.

Tryptamine—A type of organic compound, Indole ethylamine; common in plants and which forms the nucleus of many entheogenic Alkaloids, such as DMT, psilocybine and LSD. See: **Alkaloid, Anahuasca, Ayahuasca, Ayahuasca Analogue, β-Carboline, Delysid,**® **Endohuasca, Indole, Indocybin,**® **Monoamine-Oxidase, Nigerine, Pharmahuasca, Psychotica, Vinho da Jurema.**

1994 Ott *Ayahuasca Analogues*, 24. There is a definite synergy between the tryptamines, ordinarily inactive orally, and the β-carbolines, which by themselves lack interesting effects.

União do Vegetal [UDV]—Literally: 'Herbal Union'; short for 'Centro Espírita Beneficente União do Vegetal,' syncretic Neo-Christian religion founded in the state of Acre, Brasil in 1961 by Mestre José Gabriel da Costa; in which *chá hoasca* ['vine tea'] or Ayahuasca serves as the Eucharist during Mass. See: **Daime, Entheogenic Reformation, Eucharist, Hoasca, Santo Daime.**

1989 Anon. *União do Vegetal: Hoasca*, 11. Só existe uma União do Vegetal—e é a fundada a 22 de julho de 1961, por José Gabriel da Costa. [There is only one União do Vegetal— and that was founded on 22 July 1961 by José Gabriel da Costa.]

Unio Mystica—The mystical experience of totality and oneness with the universe; Ecstasy. See: **Ecstasy, Psycholepsy, Rapture.**

1979 Hofmann *LSD: Mein Sorgenkind*, 219. Dieser Zustand, der unter günstigen Bedingungen durch LSD oder durch ein anderes Halluzinogen aus der gruppe der mexikanischen sakralen Drogen hervorgerufen werden kann, ist verwandt mit der spontanen religiösen Erleuchtung, mit der unio mystica. [This condition of cosmic consciousness, which under favorable conditions can be evoked by LSD or by another hallucinogen from the group of Mexican sacred drugs, is analogous to spontaneous religious enlightenment, with the *unio mystica*.]

1986 Hofmann *Einsichten Ausblicke*, 55. Eine visionäre Erfahrung mit der Intensität des kosmischen Bewußtseins oder *Unio Mystica* ist zeitlich begrenzt. [A visionary experience with the intensity of cosmic consciousness or *Unio Mystica* is temporally bounded.]

Utopiate *nov. verb.*—Entheogen; obscure term derived from conflation of 'opiate,' an Opium-like drug, and 'Utopia,' the eponymous idyllic island of Thomas More's 1516 book. See: **Entheogen, Opium.**

1964 Blum *Utopiates: The Use and Users of LSD 25*, 292. The movement promises much— a return to paradise, a Utopia of the inner life—and so LSD-25 becomes, if one may be allowed a neologism, a 'Utopiate.'

Vac—Sanskrit term for 'the Word'; what the ancient Greek philosophers called Logos. See: **Afflatus, Logos, Tecpillatolli, Word.**

[143]

1972 Wasson *Soma and the Fly-Agaric*, 18. Soma, permeating the *RgVeda*... the potent engine behind the hymns, leads to *mada* (divine possession), generates 'reverential awe,' vibrates with the Word (*vac*), makes for *kavya* (poetic potency)...
1980 Wasson *The Wondrous Mushroom*, 39. We recall the words of Aurelio Carreras: the mushroom *es habla*, 'is the Word'... the *Word* is the thing, just as in Sanskrit it is the *Vac* and in Greek the *Logos*.
1980 Wasson *ibid.*, 225. The mushroom bestows on the *curandero* what the Greeks called *Logos*, the Aryans *Vac*, Vedic *kavya*, 'poetic potency' as Louis Renou put it. The divine afflatus of poetry is the gift of the entheogen.

Vatic—Oracular; of or pertaining to prophecy, Inspiration or Divination. See: **Chilán, Delphic, Divination, Inspiration, Oracle, Pythia, Theomancy.**
   1980 La Barre *Culture in Context*, 50. We need only examine the peculiar vatic personality of the visionary as it is manifested in an 'altered state of consciousness' in order to understand religion psychologically...

Vegetalista—*Shaman* or *curandero*; practicing divinatory healing in Amazonia; especially using Ayahuasca. Hence: União do Vegetal, Vegetalismo. See: **Ayahuasca, Hoasca, Icaro, Shaman, Yachaj, Yachay.**
   1991 Luna & Amaringo *Ayahuasca Visions*, 12. I met Don Emilio and several other *vegetalistas*, which is the name the mestizo shamans use to refer to themselves, to indicate that they derived their knowledge and personal powers from plants.

Vinho da Jurema—Literally: '*jurema* wine'; Portuguese/Tupí name for a traditional Brasilian shamanic entheogenic Potion; prepared from an aqueous extract of the roots of *Mimosa hostilis* (Mart.) Benth.; occasionally with other plant admixtures, such as *Brunfelsia uniflora* (Pohl) Don or *manacá*. Besides *M. hostilis* (*jurema preta*), other species of Leguminosae, such as *M. verrucosa* Benth., *Acacia piauhyensis* Benth. and various *Pithecellobium* species (known collectively as *jurema branca*) might be used in *vinho da jurema*. An Alkaloid, *nigerina* or 'Nigerine,' $C_{13}H_9ON_2$, was isolated from *M. hostilis*, and later shown to have been probably *N,N*-dimethyltryptamine or DMT, active principle of Amazonian Ayahuasca potions. Synonym: Ajucá. See: **Alkaloid, Ayahuasca, Nigerine, Tryptamine.**
   1946 Gonçalves de Lima *Arq. Inst. Pesq. Agronom.* 4: 45. Observações sôbre o 'vinho da Jurema' utilizado pelos índios Pancarú de Tacaratú (Pernambuco) [Observations on 'vinho da Jurema' employed by the Pancarú Indians of Tacaratú (Pernambuco)] [title]
   1980 Schultes & Hofmann *Botany & Chemistry of Hallucinogens*, 154. Although the use of *vinho de jurema*, an intoxicating drink prepared from the root of *Mimosa hostilis*, has apparently become extinct, the drug was once very important in aboriginal cultures in

northeastern Brazil. It was the basis for the ajucá ceremony of the Pankarurú Indians and was employed also amongst the Karirí, Tusha, Fulnio, Guague Acroa, Pimentiera, Atanaya and other tribes...

Visionary World—The Otherworld, or Platonic world of Ideas or Archetypes; into which the Shaman or the Psychopomp voyages under the influence of entheogenic drugs; presumed to be inhabited by the souls of ancestors, Spirits of plants, deities and other 'discarnate entities'; some speculate this corresponds to hyperspace or a higher-dimensional universe. See: **Disembodied Eyes, Færie, Idea, Nagual, Numinous, Psychocosmos, Psychonaut, Psychopomp, Shaman, Spirit, Tengu, Theurgic, Tonal.**

1799 Blake *Letter to Dr. Trusler*, 23 Aug. And I know that This World Is a World of Imagination & Vision... But to the Eyes of the Man of Imagination, Nature is Imagination itself. As a man is, so he sees. As the Eye is formed, such are its Powers.

1960 Huxley *Visionary Experience* [*Moksha*, 276]. The really startling fact about recent pharmacological developments is that a number of chemical substances have been discovered... which permit the opening of the door into the Visionary World without inflicting serious damage upon the body.

Wasson Theory *nov. verb.*—The hypothesis, first elucidated by R. Gordon and Valentina P. Wasson in the 1950s, of the origins of religions and other aspects of human culture, in the primigenial ingestion of entheogenic plants by Shamans in pre- and proto-history. See: **Age of Entheogens, Entheogen, Shaman.**

1990 Ott *The Sacred Mushroom Seeker*, 189. Underlying the theory, which must henceforth be known as The Wasson Theory, is the greatest discovery ever made in the nascent field of ethnopharmacognosy. If, as I believe, The Wasson Theory is true, then the truth will eventually emerge, and Gordon and Valentina Wasson will take their rightful places in the company of the other giants of modern science.

Wicása Wakan—*Shaman*, in the language of the North American Oglala Sioux Indians. See: **Shaman.**

1979 Lame Deer in Halifax *Shamanic Voices*, 70. Being a medicine man, more than anything else, is a state of mind, a way of looking at and understanding this earth, a sense of what it is all about. Am I a *wicásá wakan*? I guess so. What else can or would I be?

Wine—An inebriating beverage made from fermented grape or other fruit juice; in the classical world, a vehicle for infusing herbal Entheogens and other Psychoactive drugs, generally so potent as to require dilution with 3 to 20 parts water, so that the low levels of Alcohol in the beverage as drunk were of scant inebriating significance,

THE AGE OF ENTHEOGENS

and can be seen rather as a preservative than an active principle. See: **Alcohol, Bacchanalia, Dionysus, Intoxication, Kernos, Mead, Metheglin, Nepenthes, Othrörir, Quintessence, Spirit, Strong Drink, Symposium, Vinho da Jurema.**

1978 Ruck *The Road to Eleusis*, 41. We hear of some wines so strong that they could be diluted with twenty parts of water and that required at least eight parts water to be drunk safely... different wines were capable of inducing different physical symptoms, ranging from slumber to insomnia and hallucinations... ancient wine... did not contain alcohol as its sole inebriant but was ordinarily a variable infusion of herbal toxins in a vinous liquid.

Witchcraft—The legal epithet attached to shamanism, herbal medicine, midwifery, conjuring and ecstatic religions in the Middle Ages; whose persecution was the object of the Inquisition; today widely regarded as a brutal episode of scapegoating and of religious intolerance; used figuratively, as 'witch-hunt,' to describe modern instances of scapegoating. Hence: Witch, Witched, Witchery, Witch-finder, Witch-finding, Witching, Witch-monger, Witchy. See: **Auto da Fé, Deadly Nightshade, Dwale, Flying Ointment, Henbane, Mandrake, Pharmacratic Inquisition, Pharmakós, Pogrom, Scapegoat, Witch Doctor.**

1486 Sprenger & Krämer *Malleus Maleficarum*. All witchcraft comes from carnal lust, which is in women insatiable.

1970 Szasz *The Manufacture of Madness*, 10. The word *witch* comes from a Hebrew word that has been rendered *venefica* in Latin, and *witch* in English. Its original meaning was poisoner, dabbler in magical spells, or fortuneteller.

Witch Doctor—Shaman or medicine man; now obsolete and rightly regarded as pejorative. See: **Psychopomp, Shaman, Thaumaturge, Witchcraft.**

1992 Schultes & Raffauf *Vine of the Soul*, 5. The term *witch doctor*, which certainly describes many of the functions of these practitioners, we find unacceptable for its potential pejorative connotations.

1993 Ott *Pharmacotheon*, 266. In any case, the term, in Lamb's usage, is at best equivalent to 'witch-doctor,' evidently the intended meaning, as a pre-publication excerpt in *Fate* was entitled 'Witch Doctor of the Upper Amazon.'

Witches' Ointment—See: **Flying Ointment.**

Witches' Salve—See: **Flying Ointment.**

Word, The—The Logos of the Greek philosophers as primal cause; reason; inspired Divine Word. See: **Afflatus, Logos, Tecpillatolli, Vac.**

1972 Wasson *Soma and the Fly-Agaric*, 18. Soma, permeating the *RgVeda*... the potent engine behind the hymns, leads to *mada* (divine possession), generates 'reverential awe,' vibrates with the Word (*vac*), makes for *kavya* (poetic potency)...

1977 María Sabina in Estrada *La Vida de María Sabina*, 126. *Veo* que el Lenguaje cae, viene de arriba, como si fuesen pequeños objetos luminosos que caen del cielo. El Lenguaje cae sobre la mesa sagrada, cae sobre mi cuerpo. Entonces atrapo con mis manos palabra por palabra. [I *see* the Word fall; it comes from above, as 'though tiny luminous objects were falling from heaven. The Word falls on the holy table, it falls on my body. Then I catch it with my hands, Word by Word.]

1980 Wasson *The Wondrous Mushroom*, 39. We recall the words of Aurelio Carreras: the mushroom *es habla*, 'is the Word'... the *Word* is the thing, just as in Sanskrit it is the *Vac* and in Greek the *Logos*.

1985 Ott *The Cacahuatl Eater*, 42. Among the Aztecs, these entheogenic plants were taken by the *tícitl* or physician as a diagnostic or divinatory aid, to communicate with 'the word' of god and thereby ascertain the cause of the illness and determine the cure.

World Tree—See: **Axis Mundi, Tree of Life, Tree of the Knowledge of Good and Evil.**

Xochinanácatl—A name in the Náhuatl language of the Mexica or Aztecs of Mesoamerica for a complex of entheogenic mushrooms; now known to represent about a dozen species in several genera, all containing psilocybine and related 4-hydroxyindoles; literally: flower mushroom [entheogenic mushroom]. See: **Indocybin,**® **Indole, Magic Mushroom, Teonanácatl, Xochipilli, Xóchitl.**

1980 Wasson *The Wondrous Mushroom*, 80. Fray Alonso de Molina... gives us another word, *xochinanácatl*, '*flower* mushroom' from *xochitl*, 'flower,' precisely the word that the statue of Xochipilli tells us to expect.

Xochipilli—The Prince of Entheogens of the Mexica or Aztecs of Mesoamerica; one of the finest examples of preconquest Mexican sculpture is the statue of Xochipilli unearthed at Tlalmanalco on Popocatépetl—the god's body is adorned with carved flowers including the entheogenic morning glory *Turbina corymbosa* (L.) Raf., source of the Psychoptic Ololiuhqui seeds, the flower of tobacco or *Nicotiana tabacum* L. and other Aztec Entheogens, including rosettes of sectioned caps of the entheogenic mushrooms called Xochinanácatl or 'flower mushrooms' in Náhautl. See: Illustration on page 62; **Ololiuhqui, Piltzintli, Teonanácatl, Xochinanácatl, Xóchitl.**

1980 Wasson *The Wondrous Mushroom*, 58. This being is not with us, is in a far-off world. He is absorbed by *temicxoch*, 'dream flowers' as the Nahua say describing the awesome experience that follows the ingestion of an entheogen. I can think of nothing like it in the long and rich history of European art: Xochipilli absorbed in *temicxoch*.

Xóchitl—Flower, in the Náhuatl language of the Mexica or Aztec Indians of Mesoamerica; metaphorically: entheogenic plant; as in combinations like Xochinanácatl, 'flower [entheogenic] mushroom.' Synonym: Ihuinti. See: **Entheogen, Temicxoch, Xochinanácatl, Xochipilli.**

> **1980** Wasson *The Wondrous Mushroom*, 78. The statue of Xochipilli tells us that *xochitl* could mean in Nahuatl, as a figure of speech, the entheogens and the incomparable wonder-world to which they invite us.

Yachaj—*Shaman*, in the Quechua language of the Upper Amazon. Literally: [s]he who knows. See: **Co-ta-ci-ne, Payé, Shaman, Vegetalista, Yachay.**

> **1992** MacRae *Guiado Pela Lua*, 129. A substância espiritual [*yachay*] também pode ser o conhecimento ritual que dá força espiritual ou até o próprio espírito. Assim, o termo genérico para xamã em quíchua é *yachak*, que significa 'dono de um *yachay*.' [This spiritual substance [*yachay*] may be either the ritual knowledge which imparts spiritual power or even the spirit itself. Thus, the generic term for shaman in Quechua is *yachak* [*yachaj*], which means 'he who possesses *yachay*.']
>
> **1994** Ott *Ayahuasca Analogues*, 18. It is precisely as a result of the divine knowledge conferred on the healer by the plant teacher that such a practitioner is regarded to be a *shaman* [from Tungusian *saman*], *payé, yachaj,* or Mazatec *cho-ta-ci-ne*—'one who knows.'

Yachay—The magical phlegm; an azure essence said to be regurgitated and manipulated by the Ayahuasca Shaman in Amazonia. See: **Ayahuasca, Yachaj.**

> **1986** Luna *Vegetalismo*, 115. All these identifications show us that the **yachay** is the quintessence of the spirit of the various plant-teachers.
>
> **1991** Luna & Amaringo *Ayahuasca Visions*, 13. Only in this way will the neophytes acquire their spiritual helpers, learn *icaros* (power songs), and acquire their *yachay, yausa* or *mariri*—phlegm the novice receives at some point during his initiation…
>
> **1992** MacRae *Guiado Pela Lua*, 129. Os virotes e a baba mágica *yachay*, usada pelos vegetalistas para guardá-los ou retirá-los do corpo dos pacientes, são concebidos como feitos da mesma substância, simultaneamente material e espiritual. [The *virotes* and the magic phlegm *yachay*, used by *vegetalistas* for protecting or extracting from the body of patients, is conceived of as made of the same substance, at once material and spiritual.]

Yajé [Yagé]—See: **Ayahuasca.**

Zoroastrianism—Iranian religion of Zoroaster or Zarathustra; derivative of Aryan religion with Soma/Haoma Sacrament; in modern Parsi sect of which urine is imbibed as in Soma sacrifice. Derivative Manichæism may have involved an entheogenic mushroom Sacrament. Synonym: Mazdaism. See: **Haoma, Manichæans, Soma.**

INDEX

Sacha Runa [Amazonian male plant-spirit]–13
sacrament–11,13,18-19,21,25-7,29,31-2,36-7,
42-4,46-7,52,64,70,79,86-9,96,99,107-9,
112,126,128,**133**,138-9,148
sacred inebriants–17,20,47,64,102,104
Sai-Halász, A., Hungarian chemist–131
salené huby [Slovakian 'crazy' mushroom]– 47
salvanol [thujone, absinthol, tanacetone]–69
Salvia divinorum [Mazatec *ska pastora*]–67
Salvia officinalis [European culinary sage]–69
Samorini, G., Italian psychonaut–24,100
Sandoz Ltd., Swiss pharmaceutical Co–82,101
Santa María Tonantzintla, Puebla–51
Santo Daime / *daime*–13,28-30,50,**80**,**133-4**
Santo Niño de Atocha–32,50-1,127
scapegoat–14,20,119,125,**134**,146
Schenk, G., German psychonaut–46
Schultes, R.E., U.S. botanist–109,116,144-6
Schwammerln, verrückten ['crazy' fungi]–47
scopolamine [Solanaceae alkaloid]–81,97,108
secale cornutum [ergot of rye]–90
Serna, J. de la, Mexican Inquisitor–21
Serra, R.I., Santo Daime founder–50,133-4
Sertürner, F.W., morphine discoverer–71,85
Servetus, M., Swiss scientific heretic– 45
shamanic ecstasy–14,16-18,20,63-4
shamanic inebriants–11-13,21,32,37,40-1,47,
52,65-7,74,76,88,117,119,122,128,130
shaman[ism]–10,13,15-18,20,25-6,30-3,40-1,
45,49-50,52,63,67-8,70,72-6,79,83,85,89,
92,100,109,112-4,116-7,119,121,126-8,
130,132,**134-5**,136,138-9,144-6,148
Shaman's Drum Magazine–31-2
Sharanahua Indians of South America–121
Shuar [Jívaro] Indians of South America–114
Siberia–16-17,40,68,89,95,97,120,130,135,139
Siegel, R.K., American pharmacologist–130
Simons, M., Mennonite founder– 43
sinsemilla [*Cannabis* flower-tops]–94
Sioux Indians of North America–25
Sitting Bull, Dakota Sioux Indian Chief–25
Smythies, J., British physician–96,131,134
Socrates [Athenian philosopher]–82,101

soma–17,38-41,51-2,71-2,88-9,96-7,104,106-
8,111,**135-6**,142,144,147-8
sorceresses [European white witches]–45
Späth, E., German chemist–110
Spenser, E., English poet–114,119
spongia soporifera [dwale]–84
Sprenger, J., German Inquisitor–45,146
Spruce, R., British botanist–65
Stalin, J., Russian tyrant–49
Staples, D., U.S. classicist–37,67,95
Stewart, O.C., U.S. *péyotl* historian–26-7
stimulants– 65-6,87,92,124,129,134-5,**136-7**
supay chacruna [*Psychotria* spp.]–78
Supreme Court, U.S.–21
syncretism–13,23,25-7,29-30,52,77,100
synthetic compounds–12,38,65,113
Syrian Rue [*Peganum harmala*]–72,96-7,**137-8**
Szasz, T., libertarian–45,68,119,123-5,134,146

Tabernaemontana spp.– 48
Tabernanthe iboga [*iboga* plant]–23,77,100
tabernanthine [*iboga* alkaloid]–48
tanacetone [thujone, absinthol, salvanol]–69
Tantric Yoga, Hindu/Buddhist syncretism–52
Taoists of China– 46,106
Tarahumara Indians of México– 49
tares [*Lolium temulentum*, darnel]–80
Taumellolch [*Lolium temulentum*, darnel]–81
Taylor, B., U.S. writer–97
tchai [*Opuntia* sp., *ayahuasca* additive]–121
temicxoch [entheogenic dream]–**138**,147
teonanácatl–11,21,47,**139**,147
Teotihuacan, Valley of México–51
tetrahydrocannabinols [of *Cannabis* spp.]–52
Tetrapterys spp. [*ayahuasca* potion plant]–49
teunamacatlth [*teonanácatl*]–47
theobotany–See: entheobotany
theobromine [*Theobroma cacao* L. alk.]–126
Theodosius I, Roman emperor–42
Theophilus I, Bishop of Alexandria– 42
Thorazine® [chlorpromazine]–141
thujone [absinthol, salvanol, tanacetone]–69
Tibeto-Burman-Chinese tonal languages–16
Titans [Greek giants expelled by Zeus]–94

ACKNOWLEDGEMENTS

I, bird of the entheogenic potion,
drunk in revelry.
I am a song in the broad ring of water,
My heart exists on the shoreline of men,
I am blending my entheogens,
With them the princes become inebriated.
There is adornment.
Acolmiztli Nezahualcóyotl
Deseo de Persistencia [*circa* 1450]

I am beholden to Dr. Robert Montgomery of *Botanical Preservation Corps*, for many invaluable discussions and for encouraging me to publish these idiosyncratic essays in book form. I am grateful to my nullifidian colleagues Dr. Antonio Escohotado of the *Universidad Nacional de Educación a Distancia* in Madrid, Spain, and Dr. Josep M. Fericgla of the *Universitat de Barcelona*, Catalunya, for affording me opportunities in traditionally Catholic countries, to formulate the radical ideas articulated in *The Age of Entheogens*. By turns emotionally-charged epistolary debates over terminology with Dr. James C. Callaway of the *University of Kuopio*, Finland, were an important catalyst to the creation of *The Angels' Dictionary*. I acknowledge my continuing debt to Dr. Steven A. Van Heiden of the *University of Texas* at Austin, for his bibliographic assistance, and I thank attorney Jerry D. Patchen of *Patchen & Mitcham* in Houston, Texas, for his aid in locating and helping me to comprehend legal documentation pertaining to the sacramental use of *péyotl* in the contemporary United States.

It is my pleasure to feature as cover art Donna Torres' superb paintings replete with divers entheogenic motifs of all descriptions, and I thank also her husband, the prominent entheogen specialist Dr. C. Manuel Torres of *Florida International University* in Miami, for painstakingly photographing Donna's paintings for this book.

I am indebted to Tim Girvin of Seattle, Washington, for the line drawings of Xochipilli on page 62, and the Remojadas figurine on page 10. I thank Martín Vinaver of San Andrés Tlanelhuayocan, Veracruz, for the vignettes on the title and colophon pages, from the Mixtec *Lienzo de Zacatepec* and *Codex Vindobonensis*; and Georges Vinaver, for suggesting corrections and improvements to my French translations.

Publication of this book marks the 1600th anniversary of the destruction of the Eleusinian sanctuary, the 40th anniversary of R.G. Wasson's rediscovery of the holy sacrament in México, and the 100th anniversary of Ernst Jünger's birth. May his adventures in the psychocosmos, and the Entheogenic Reformation, long continue!

[159]

This first edition of *The Age of Entheogens*
consists of five thousand copies, printed by Braun–Brumfield
on white 60 pound book recycled, acid-free paper,
with sewn-and-glued bindings for permanence.
Five hundred copies were Smythe-sewn and casebound;
of which 126 boxed copies were signed and numbered
1–100 and A–Z [the lettered copies *hors commerce*].
Printing was finished in August of 1995.